D0987122

The First World War in Fiction

The First World War in Fiction

A Collection of Critical Essays

edited by

HOLGER KLEIN

BARNES & NOBLE

BOOKS

10 East 53d St., New York 10022
(a division of Harper & Row Publishers, Inc.)

© The Macmillan Press Ltd 1976

First published 1976 by
THE MACMILLAN PRESS LTD
London and Basingstoke

Published in the U.S.A. 1977 by
HARPER & ROW PUBLISHERS INC.
BARNES & NOBLE IMPORT DIVISION

Library of Congress Cataloging in Publication Data

Main entry under title:

The First World War in fiction.

Bibliography: p.
Includes index.
1. Fiction—20th century—History and criticism—
Addresses, essays, lectures. 2. European War,
1914–1918—Literature and the war—Addresses, essays,
lectures. 2. European War, 1914–1918—Literature
and the war—Addresses, essays, lectures. I. Klein,
Holger Michael, 1938–
PN3448.W3F5   809.3′9′3   76–28822
ISBN 0–06–493792–5

Printed in Great Britain

Contents

Preface

With the exception of Peter Stern's contribution, for which I am particularly grateful, all these essays have been written expressly for this volume. Ideally, in each case much more space would have been required and everyone is painfully aware of what had to be left out. However, given a certain limited overall length, more advantages seemed to be gained from a wide selection than from fewer studies on an extended scale.

Each essay analyses a particular work or small group of works, considering – with varying emphases – implications both of form and content, and places the works discussed in the context of the author's career and other writings. Beyond these points of common concern the individual essays range freely, and there was no attempt at 'unification', especially none to arrive at a uniform critical treatment. Even if this had been practicable, it would have entailed a loss for the aims of the volume in that the profile of the field would have been levelled and the range of viewpoints and methods with which it can be approached narrowed.

The multiplicity of connections between the works discussed made the arrangement a difficult practical problem. It may appear slightly odd that a collection with a comparative impulse behind it should end up with, on the face of it, a largely national grouping. However, the direct comparisons among the essays made a chronological sequence impracticable, and any attempt to arrange them by prevailing attitudes or by formal characteristics would obviously have created serious difficulties. The order adopted avoids the split into two parts – Anglo-American and Continental-European – which has determined and limited much previous criticism. By and large the sequence moves from the Western Front to the Eastern and Southern Fronts, to return once more to the West, which, as the scene of the most intensive fighting decisively characterised the Great War.

My first and foremost expression of gratitude must be to John Flower. The concept of this collection emerged from our joint teaching of the subject, and the volume owes a very great deal to his insights, advice and active help. I am grateful to all contributors generally for the spirit with which they produced their essays and the patience with which they complied with my efforts to fit them together as far as was possible and desirable. I also wish to thank Paul Kennedy of the University of East Anglia for valuable advice and historical references.

The author and publishers wish to thank the following who have kindly given permission for the use of copyright material: Chatto and Windus Ltd, for an extract from 'The Spanish Farm Trilogy' by F. H. Mottram; Rosica Colin Ltd on behalf of Catherine Guillaume, for extracts from 'Death of a Hero' by Richard Aldington; Faber & Faber Ltd and Chilmark Press Inc., for extracts from 'In Parenthesis' by David Jones.

March 1976   H.M.K.

During the proof-reading stage the sad news arrived of the sudden death of Stanley Cooperman. His contributions to scholarship and criticism speak for themselves; I would like however to record my gratitude that it should have been possible to include an essay by him in the present volume.

July 1976   H. M. K.

Notes on the Contributors

MALCOLM BRADBURY has been Professor of American Studies at the University of East Anglia since 1970. In addition to books and articles on modern fiction and developments in criticism he has published three novels, a collection of parodies and short stories.

STANLEY COOPERMAN was Professor of English at Simon Fraser University, British Columbia. He was the author of *World War I and the American Novel* and many articles as well as several volumes of poetry.

JONATHAN DALE has been a Lecturer in French at St Andrews University since 1964. His special interest is in political and social novels, particularly in France between the wars.

DIANE DeBELL is a graduate of Hollins College, U.S.A., and is now engaged in research at the University of East Anglia on regionalism in the poetry of David Jones and Hugh MacDiarmid.

JOHN FLOWER is Professor of French at the University of Exeter, and author of several books concerned with literature and ideas in France during the past hundred years. He is editor of the *Journal of European Studies*.

MICHAEL GARRETY served as a lieutenant in the Royal Tank Regiment in the Middle East and graduated at Nottingham University. He is now in charge of English Studies at Brunel University.

JONATHAN KING took a Ph.D. at Cambridge and is now a Lecturer at the University of Aberdeen. He has published numerous articles on twentieth-century French literature, history and thought, and is now writing a book on French culture and the Second World War.

HOLGER KLEIN is Lecturer in Comparative Literature at the University of East Anglia. His publications include a book on English Renaissance verse portraits, a German translation of Wycherley's *The Country Wife,* and many articles.

JOHN MORRIS gained a Ph.D. at the University of Nottingham and is now a Lecturer in English at Brunel University. He has published articles on twentieth-century poetry and is himself a poet.

ROBERT PYNSENT took a Ph.D. at Cambridge and is now Lecturer in

Czech and Slovak Language and Literature at London University. His publications include a book on Julius Zeyer and many articles on Czech and modern European literature.

W. D. REDFERN is Reader in the Department of French Studies, Reading University. He has published several books, including one on Giono, and numerous articles.

BRIAN A. ROWLEY has been Professor of European Literature at the University of East Anglia since 1968. His work has concentrated on Goethe, the Romantics, and German literature in the nineteenth century.

W. G. SEBALD was educated at Freiburg, Fribourg and Manchester University and took a Ph.D. at the University of East Anglia, where he is now a Lecturer in European Studies. His special interest is German literature of the last hundred years, particularly Jewish writers.

C. N. SMITH is Senior Lecturer in European Studies at the University of East Anglia, having studied at Cambridge and taught at Aberdeen. His publications include editions of French Renaissance tragedies.

J. P. STERN was born in Prague and served in the Czech army and the Royal Air Force. He has been Professor of German at University College, London, since 1972. He has published several books, including one this year on Nietzsche.

CHRISTOPHER WAGSTAFF was educated at Oxford and at the University of California, Berkeley. He is now a Lecturer in Italian at the University of Reading.

JEFFREY WALSH is Principal Lecturer in English at Manchester Polytechnic. He has done research on Robert Graves and on American war literature, and was editor of *A Tribute to Wilfred Owen*.

1   Introduction

A study of the literature arising from the 1914–18 War needs to be based on a knowledge of the events. In order to gain the necessary perspective, criticism must resort to history.[1] Many factors made this war different from the wars preceding it, made it the First *World* War: the number of countries engaged, the range and extent of the battles that were fought simultaneously on several vast land fronts, as well as at sea and in the air, the duration of continuous fighting, the advanced technology employed, resulting in a mechanisation of killing as unprecedented as the overall number of dead and wounded, the hardships and sufferings inflicted on the non-combatant populations, and above all the 'mobilisation', no longer of relatively small numbers of soldiers, mainly professional, but of entire nations.

The immensity of the fighting and of the national efforts behind it profoundly changed the whole concept of war. Army staffs and political leaders had to adjust to the new reality, and more generally the entire image of war was transformed: it became the central issue of life, demanding a definite stand. Whatever separation may have existed between literature and politics was largely demolished. On the one hand, governments had to justify the sacrifices demanded of whole peoples, and in the age before the arrival of the wireless and of television the printed word was a key factor. What might be termed the 'spontaneous' literary response was thus embedded and often enmeshed in the official propaganda campaigns. On the other hand, socialist and pacifist resistance to the war, which for the most part lamentably, if understandably, folded up in 1914, gained fresh momentum as the slaughter in and near the battle zones and the sufferings and social injustices at home continued. And many governments were as yet either not prepared or unable to control the entire output of print.[2]

Nor did the war of words end when the fighting was over and the true dimensions of the disaster became clearer still. Just as the external consequences of the war overshadowed the years following it, the intense emotions it aroused (which among other things made a conventional arrangement along the lines of the Vienna Congress impossible) were not to be quickly allayed. The war fundamentally affected not only the course of modern history externally, but also man's outlook on the world. This accounts for the permanent interest, indeed fascination it holds.

In August 1914, H. G. Wells expressed with moving eloquence his conviction: 'This, the greatest of all wars, is not just another war – it is the last war.'[3] In fact, nothing less than 'the war to end war' it soon turned out to have been 'not the end, but the prelude to violence' as Ernst Jünger claimed with staggering enthusiasm in 1925.[4] And yet, although it has become the *First* World War, the Second surpassing it in the scope of the fighting, the volume of killings and the scale of destruction, 1914–18 continues to be called the Great War. This name, even more than the numeral 'first', indicates its unique position in the modern consciousness, at any rate in Europe and North America.

To illustrate this position it is useful to turn not to another famous dictum by a famous man, but to chance remarks in quite different contexts. An ordinary thriller of 1965 furnishes a perfect example. Its hero, sixty years of age, holds the conviction 'that Europe, as he understood the word, had committed suicide when he himself had been nine years old. Everything that had followed had been merely the obsequies.[5] Alongside this common image of the war as the demise of a long and rich tradition one must remember the weariness with peace, the verbal militancy and eager welcoming of war emerging from some pre-war and much early war literature,[6] as well as the social and political realities of the so-called 'good old days' and some constructive results of the conflict.[7] These aspects however do not seem to have a firm hold on our memory, they are overlaid by the lasting impression of the mass slaughter and of the disappointments and frustrations which followed.

The First World War is still with us in momentous and mundane ways; many of them have recently been analysed by Paul Fussell.[8] And the literature of this war continues, after relative neglect in the years before and after (though not during) the Second World War, to be read, much of it being reprinted, and to be studied. Indeed, the last fifteen years have witnessed an astonishing revival in critical interest in the subject, especially in Britain, France, and the United States.[9]

The hallmarks of this literature are its vast bulk and its strong commitment; both arose from the unprecedented character of 1914–1918. 'Total' war entailed a massive involvement of intellectuals. It had profound repercussions on those who did not actively partici-pate.[10] Moreover, a link emerged between war and literature unknown before, in that thousands of established and potential writers were directly engaged in the fighting. Thus the literature of the First World War mostly represents the response of civilians – as befits a war that was essentially fought by civilians who had temporarily been turned into soldiers.

On the whole, scholarship and criticism were quick off the mark. The first stocktakings and analytic treatments of this new kind of literature appeared while the war was still going on,[11] to be followed by extended studies,[12] comprehensive bibliographies and guides,[13] fresh anthologies of poems, short pieces and extracts with commentaries, as well as collections of letters.[14] The distinct, though often exaggerated lack of interest in the war on the part of the general public directly after 1918 was strongest in Britain, where it seems to have made publication of war books difficult[15] and also delayed the compiling and analysing activity; it was least evident in France where the publication of war literature was massive in the years immediately following the Armistice[16] and where the veterans' associations were particularly active in the assembling of biographical and bibliographical material.[17] Nevertheless, in general, critical interest on a scale comparable to that evidenced today emerged only as the war books developed into a flood in the later nineteen-twenties.

Most extended criticism, including studies published after the Second World War, operates on a national basis (even when a critic discusses the war literature of a country not his own). Only sporadic glances are cast across the various frontiers, most often at Barbusse's *Under Fire*, Zweig's *The Case of Sergeant Grischa*, Hemingway's *A Farewell to Arms* and especially at Remarque's *All Quiet on the Western Front*.[18] This is in a way not surprising. The war, after all, grew out of intense national feelings which were naturally perpetuated in the consideration of its literary heritage, often regarded as a memorial. On the other hand it *is* surprising: not only because the reading publics were being offered many works in translation, particularly from the later twenties onwards,[19] but principally because of all events the war was an international experience. This is not to deny that there were important national differences, especially as regards America; the point is that there were also so many common factors. On the 'home fronts', similar organisational, economic and social problems faced governments: their solutions affected the individual in similar ways and were accompanied by remarkably similar propaganda.[20] In the front lines the soldier had to contend, on both sides of no man's land, with very much the same enemies besides the 'official' enemy: with the elements; with the living conditions the elements and the methods of fighting imposed; with the emotions all this and the constant proximity of death aroused, with fear, horror, hysteria, anger, exhaustion, boredom, cold, hunger, emptiness; with the rigidity and the shortcomings of the military 'machine'. Notable exceptions in criticism[21] to the national approach, apart from introductions to some anthologies,[22] are Sir Maurice Bowra (1961) and Charles Dédéyan (1971).[23]

The present collection of critical essays aims to give fresh impetus to the comparative approach to war literature by uniting studies of works from six (out of the many) warring nations: Britain, France, Germany, the United States, Italy and Austria-Hungary. Neither the reactions to war, ranging from jubilance to utter rejection (not always in this order) nor the literary forms in which the reactions took shape are confined to any one country. The dividing lines run through all nations, and in order to apprehend the significant developments it is vital to see their international dimension – not as an exclusive alternative to the national context, but as an essential complement to it.

These studies are concerned with war *fiction*. In view of the vastness of the material selection is necessary. And one of the principal non-national categories for comparative work is genre. Fiction offers itself particularly as it continued longest to be used by war writers, no doubt because prose narrative, taking over in part the tradition of the great epics, is especially suited to the full re-creation of historical events and states of society.[24] Moreover, as prose is the most frequently read genre in the modern era, this is the medium in which the war had its widest impact on the reading public.

All works studied here were written and published before 1939. This gives them and discussion of them further common ground and opens a second perspective: the cultural, social and political climate of the war and in particular of the inter-war period. In this connection the contemporary reception of war fiction is significant and instructive.

If war literature was committed, was of necessity political, so was criticism at the time. The cataclysm and its consequences could not be pushed aside.[25] And the political considerations impinged heavily on the aesthetic ones. War literature was in effect mostly treated as separate from other sorts of literature. Rarely does one come across a remark like H. M. Tomlinson's: 'The test for a book about the war is the same as for any other book.'[26]

In the case of war fiction especially this produced complications which again result from the First World War being a war among nations. Fiction here had an immediate, factual correlative of which millions were intensely aware. And the overriding criterion applied to war fiction was truth. The tradition of Realism had created the expectation that fiction would be a convincing mirror, would be true to life. With regard to war novels, however, quite a different demand was made which exacted not verisimilitude, but truth to facts. Thus (besides the extent of personal experience) the proportionateness of selection, the justice of typification, the correctness of detail and accuracy of data were scrutinised assiduously. One must in fairness add that countless writers presented their books as 'truth'. Nevertheless, these are proceedings normally used in assessing works of history, and possibly apposite for the numerous (often apologetic) memoirs and biographies of the great leaders; but they are hardly adequate as the *primary* considerations for works of fiction (though they may have a useful role to play in criticism). This would apply even if the denial or affirmation of truthfulness and 'objectivity' had not depended, as it unquestionably did, on every reader's own personal and partial experience as well as on the image of the war he had himself formed and on his general convictions.

Jean Norton Cru probably carried this approach farthest,[27] but he is only a (sincere) exponent of a universal trend. To take just one example: he dismisses out of hand as a malicious lie Barbusse's story of how a French captain, quite nonchalantly and in cold blood, had a large group of German prisoners murdered.[28] Cru, generally painstaking, did not think he needed any research here – this story simply could not be true. This is an innocuous example, of course, compared to the systematic perversion masquerading as scholarship with which after 1933, guided by party doctrine, German critics simply eliminated as 'un-German' (aiming at writers like Arnold Zweig, who was Jewish) or comprehensively as 'untrue' all war books which did not present the war as the glorious cradle of the new *Volk*, thus fabricating a 'homogeneous' heroic response of German literature to the war.[29] Democracy, the institution which the Entente sought to defend and which the American 'crusaders' came across the Atlantic to rescue and spread, prevented (however badly it may have functioned in other respects) the absolute assertion of one kind of truth, let alone the steps that accompanied it in Germany.

However, even elsewhere the debate was highly charged politically and did not remain entirely theoretical, as is illustrated for instance by the banning of *Švejk* in some countries. In Britain the political dimension was powerfully stressed by Douglas Jerrold who in 1930 warned that the then predominant anti-war tenor of fiction would lead to disaster.[30] The more aesthetic turn which the debate about war books seemed to take in America is, looked at closely, at best a shifting of emphases. For when critics like Archibald Macleish (whom Stanley Cooperman labels 'humanist') demanded 'totality', 'balance' and 'harmony'[31] they were really circumscribing and unfolding what others demanded with the comprehensive term 'truth'.

On both sides of the Atlantic another main issue was debated which runs curiously across the issue of truth: the representativeness of war writers. How far were they in a position to express the experiences of other soldiers? On the one hand the 'common man' could not possibly, it was argued, recreate the conditions, events, and emotions aroused by them; he lacked the literary skill. On the other hand it was asserted that those who had and did use it were not 'common men', in the sense that they were better educated, often separated by their social background, and had generally, because of their artistic disposition, gone through the same experiences as their fellow soldiers or subalterns with profoundly different and therefore atypical reactions.[32] Interesting errors on the part of critics are on record,[33] The problem is a real one, however, as is shown by genuine examples of privates' accounts such as Frank Richards' or Hans Zöberlein's.[34] Their war seems very flat and 'unreal' by comparison, not even two-dimensional but one-dimensional. The other side is illustrated by authors like Barbusse or Pierre Bouvier who make the situation of the writer explicitly part of their books. And although they want to stick to the truth, or in Bouvier's words do *not* want to 'make literature' out of the war,[35] they do exactly that. However, in contemporary criticism neither the universality of this problem (which after all arises in all fiction taking the masses, taking history for its subject) nor possible theoretical answers[38] were energetically considered, because the central interest did not lie in the aesthetic-philosophical question as such but in the political implications.

For the representativeness of war novelists was usually challenged in the case of anti-war literature, although the characteristics attacked are also prominent elsewhere.[36] The blood and guts, the morbidity and sadism seem to have been resented much less where the war was put across as making sense of a sort, be it ever so gruesome. It was the writers like Remarque who were branded as 'a morbid and hysterical section in all countries.'[37]

The political heat has now gone. The fundamental problem remains, and it is not everywhere accepted that it presents an impasse which is largely beside the point as far as the lasting effects of war fiction are concerned. With greater calm, but still insistently the demand for truth is being repeated, for instance by Maurice Genevoix, himself a war writer. Assuming the role of speaker for the survivors he depicts how they often 'felt as though dispossessed reading certain accounts, hearing certain words', and how their thoughts return 'to what they know to be, beyond *their* truth, *the* truth'.[38] Against this notion one must raise the doubt whether *the* truth about the war experience ever existed or can, if it did, be recalled. The often violent disagreements among veterans about particular books illustrate that what a war novel conveys is an *image* of the war. And it is important to realise that the purposefully non-fictional accounts in collections made at the time[39] or fifty years after the war in George Panichas' *Promise of Greatness* are also, in their way, images.

.   .   .

In criticism generally, however, the passage of time and perhaps also the intervention of a second world catastrophe have produced great changes. As the First World War receded from actuality into history the literary aspects of war fiction assumed growing importance. The historical dimension has not been (and should not be) forgotten; but whereas in retrospect one can say that in the inter-war period all war books were primarily considered on the level of documents, criticism can now concentrate more on aspects which it is specifically equipped to discuss. One of these is to go beyond noting political bias to analysing the ways in which it is woven into the literary artefact (sometimes indeed revealing 'sunk' bias) by employing criteria and methods which are also applied to other kinds of literature. Indeed the distinction has been progressively dismantled, possibly – as Michael Hamburger suggests for poetry – because war in all forms has become a feature of modern life, and a permanent concern of literature[40] and consequently of criticism. A more important aspect is the quality of these works. This implies replacing the question 'is this true?' (which has been shown to rest on problematical foundations) by the question 'is this a good novel?' – which often includes the question 'is it true to life?', but in an aesthetic and general rather than a factual, specific sense. This approach rests on problematical foundations too (as witness, for instance, the disagreements about quality in the present collection of essays). Evaluation is however one of the central concerns of criticism. And it is not an impasse, because the criteria and methods of assessment can be reasoned and the results argued about.

A further important aspect is the interrelation between these novels and other works of a different kind, the integration of the fiction of the Great War into the wider framework of overall developments in modern literature. On an author-specific level this has been furthered increasingly in monographs. On a national level it has been furthered in major studies by John Aldridge, Bernard Bergonzi, Frederick Hoffman, Micheline Tison-Braun, Stanley Cooperman, Mario Isenghi, Maurice Rieuneau and Paul Fussell,[41] though the attempt at synthesis often enforced abstraction and surface summaries. Certainly as far as the international dimension is concerned, one doubts, because of the magnitude of the subject and the complexity of interactions whether, as Genevoix confidently asserts, 'the propitious time as finally come for the vast syntheses'.[42] Or rather, one might agree that the time for them has come but seriously doubt whether enough work has as yet been done which would allow them to be made. Existing examples, however brilliant in many respects, rather increase than allay these doubts.[43]

The concept underlying this volume is that at present a useful alternative to the synthesising survey is a collection of detailed analyses, by different hands, of major works from several countries. It can more sharply throw into relief the enormous range of fictional re-creations of the war, highlighting distinct, often surprising similarities and affinities as well as contrasts. This format also makes it possible to support value judgements by specific illustration. Moreover the problems posed by war fiction in itself and in its relations to other literature can be brought out more clearly through the co-presence, indeed at times the clashes, of various critical approaches brought to bear independently on concrete and significant examples.

In order to achieve these objectives and with them new perspectives for the further study of the subject in some directions, limitations in the choice of war fiction before 1939 had to be introduced. To secure a reasonable measure of comparability, the accounts studied here are confined to the war on land and to the European scene. Furthermore, fiction restricted to the home experience during the war[44] was not included. On the other hand it would have been wrong only to consider works showing exclusively the front. The interaction, for the soldiers, of experiences in the trenches and experiences in the hinterlands is an essential feature of war fiction.

Even within the field thus delimited many more authors would have deserved attention – to mention just a few: Blunden, Carossa, Céline, Duhamel, Montague, Montherlant, Read, Sassoon, Unruh, Werfel. However, within the scope attained there is considerable range in many major respects. With regard to the transformation of personal experience, it reaches from Graves describing 'what I was, not what I am' (the past self becoming in part a fictional character as the autobiography orders and stylises experience)[45] and Jünger to very far-reaching transmutations in Giono, Mottram and Zweig, with Marinetti's *roman vécu*, Cummings, Drieu la Rochelle, Aldington and Dorgelès presenting intermediate steps on a rising scale of fictionalisation.

As far as prevailing moods and attitudes can be encompassed in such complex works, disillusionment and alienation are manifested in Dorgelès, Dos Passos, Ford and Graves; despair comes to the fore in Hemingway and Remarque, accusation in Williamson and Aldington, with Kraus adding the dud explosive of satire; simple endurance in Mottram and Manning, clothed in humorous, all-embracing methodical madness by Hašek; renewal, defeating the war internally through a counterforce which in Cummings is humanitarian and socially progressive, in Wiechert traditional and Christian, in Giono animistic; the heroic response, triumphant in Franconi, nostalgic in Drieu, threnodial in David Jones; the will to fight for a better world in Barbusse and, overlaid by a note of embittered warning, in Zweig; finally, there is the detached and at the same time exultant embracing of a new age of automated violence in Marinetti and at least incipiently in the early Jünger of the *Storm of Steel.*

Structurally, episodic works like Drieu's *Comedy of Charleroi* and Franconi's *Untel* are opposed to *Three Soldiers* by Dos Passos and later, carefully and effectively structured books such as *All Quiet on the Western Front, The Patriot's Progress, Her Privates We.*[46] The scope of the action is richly varied, from a few months in the war in *L'alcova* to the lives of two generations in Aldington's *Death of a Hero.*

The solutions to the basic problem of composition in war fiction – how to link the general fate to the fate of particular characters illuminating it – are widely spread: the majority of works achieve it by the demonstration of the impact of war on essentially anonymous, private but representative individuals or small groups; and the concentration on impact rather than event enables them to make the common soldier or subaltern, a figure occupying an accidental and peripheral position in the war as history, a figure occupying an essential and central position in the war as fiction. On one side of this large group are the accounts of individuals not overtly claiming representativeness – Graves and Jünger. On the other side are the 'reconstitutions of history':[47] conceptually, though not in narrative technique traditional, Tolstoyan – Ford's tetralogy, which has much in common with Jules Romains' *Les Hommes de bonne volonté,*[48] and Alexander Solzhenitsyn's *August 1914,*[49] where the inspiration of *War and Peace* (often evoked in criticism as either an imperative or, on account of the vastness and diffuseness of this war, an impossible model) has been fully realised; and radically different, modernistic both in concept *and* in method, blending of heterogeneous and not uniformly assimilated material into kaleidoscopic tableaux – Dos Passos' *U.S.A.* and Kraus' *The Last Days of Mankind.* The latter also transcends the sphere of fiction itself in the direction of epic drama, just as Jones' *In Parenthesis* transcends it in the direction of epic poetry.

Further resemblances, variations and differences among the works treated, as well as in others only evoked and still others behind them, arise under such aspects as symbols, style, time-shift, directness or indirectness of commitment, recurrent situations, themes and motifs. They emerge from these essays, which collectively, through the analysis of some of war's 'myriad faces',[50] as reflected in the sensibilities of twenty-two writers, aim to contribute to the study of this important area of modern fiction and of society from the turn of the century to the eve of the Second World War.

2 Love and War: R. H. Mottram, *The Spanish Farm Trilogy* and Ernest Hemingway *A Farewell to Arms*

Michael Garrety

> For here the lover and killer are mingled
> who had one body and one heart.
> And death who had the soldier singled
> has done the lover mortal hurt.
>
> Keith Douglas

R. H. Mottram's *The Spanish Farm Trilogy* and Ernest Hemingway's *A Farewell to Arms* have some similarity in that they both deal with love-relationships during the First World War which are casual or incidental, but vital to the action in each book. Although *The Spanish Farm*, the first novel in Mottram's trilogy, and more particularly Hemingway's book can be described as novels of love and are often read as such, they are both war novels, because the relationship described could only exist in, and be modified by, the context of war, and serve both as a reflection and a criticism of it. Love and war, the creative and destructive urges, may appear superficially antithetical and mutually exclusive but yet are mingled in the human being, and the experience of each is intensified by confrontation with its opposite. The creative artist has the task of demonstrating this duality.

The unjustly neglected *Spanish Farm Trilogy* consists of *The Spanish Farm* (1924); *Sixty-Four, Ninety-Four!* (1925) and *The Crime at Vanderlynden's* (1926): the three were first published together in 1927.[1] The first novel was one of the first English 'war-books' to evaluate critically the experience of 1914–18, appearing only two years after C. E. Montague's *Disenchantment*, whose tone of sober disillusionment it echoes, and well in advance of the spate of books published from 1928 to 1932. It received immediate acclaim, winning a literary prize;[2] no doubt its quiet persuasiveness made it acceptable, in contrast to the more strident and rebellious tone of the later writers considered today more representative of anti-war feeling. Although Mottram has recently been written off as a 'remarkably competent story-teller'[3] and not rated as highly as, say, Ford Madox Ford, there are good reasons for agreeing with more favourable contemporary opinion.

Ferme l'Espagnole in French Flanders, the 'Spanish Farm' of the title, is the focal point of the whole work, reminding us that the area occupied by British armies in the war had been fought over for centuries by many others since the days of the Duke of Alva. Mottram places the war in the historical context, as David Jones' *In Parenthesis* places it in the mythological. Throughout the war the farm is in the immediate rear of the battle-zone and all but engulfed by the German advance in March 1918, becoming once more a blockhouse as in the Spanish Wars. It is constantly subject to the depredations of billeted English troops, the demands of space needed by the organisation of supply and, later, the attentions of German artillery.

As the farm endures, so does its personification in Madeleine, younger daughter of the farmer Jerome Vanderlynden. She tries to manipulate the accidents of war to preserve the farm and to seek news of her departed lover, the patriotic aviator Georges. She comes into contact with the English infantryman Lieutenant Skene, initially over the business of billeting troops at the farm, and later in the mutual comfort of a short-lived love in Paris. The weaving of chance and design in the fortunes of Skene and Madeleine makes compelling reading and serves to complement rather than hide the symbolism Mottram uses: Madeleine is identified with the Spanish Farm and both represent the endurance of nature in the face of war:

> ... a land of unexampled fertility, of that satisfying beauty which exists only where form and colour are the clothing for home and plenty. And clean across it lay the chain of those old Spanish farms, from the Artois to West Flanders, memorials of the time not four centuries ago when men had fought for that rich land. Generation after generation, fighting and grabbing and snatching – Romans and Franks, Spanish and French and Huns, and nature covered it up, and went on producing more than ever war destroyed. 'Yes,' thought Skene, 'but we die of the process – we others.' (p. 300)

Madeleine is the product of the tradition of centuries:

> Large boned, ... her figure, kept in check by hard work and frugal feeding, promised to grow thick only with middle age. Anyone looking at her face would have said, 'What a handsome woman,' not 'What a pretty girl.' ... That internal quality that made her simple shapeliness so much more arresting ... was ... the gradual distillation of the hard-lived generations gone before. How much of it came from the cultivators who had hung on to that low ridge ... and how much from the Spanish blood of Alva's colonists who had held the

old block-house-farm amid all the unfriendliness of climate, native inhabitants, and chance, none can now say. (p. 28)

Mottram agreed that she was a composite portrait, as John Galsworthy supposed in his preface to *The Spanish Farm*, but she is also certainly what Galsworthy added: 'the only full, solid, intimate piece of French characterisation which has resulted from that long and varied contact. Madeleine is amazingly lifelike.'

Mottram has a sympathy for and understanding of the French character which contrasts greatly with the contempt, or at least misunderstanding, that is found in many other English war-books. Robert Graves, for instance, in *Goodbye To All That* prefers the Germans to the French. Such an attitude is probably one with the front-line man's general condemnation of the inhabitants of back areas, be they civilians or Sassoon's 'base details': Mottram is in contrast better equipped to sympathise with Flanders peasants whose land is ravaged by war. His experience embraced front-line service and a more thorough involvement than usual with administration and supply in areas just behind the line, occasioned by his temporary staff-attachment as a French-speaking officer dealing with civilian complaints. He found in Flanders a countryside and population not unlike his native Norfolk where tradition and a settled way of life endured: the people who contributed to the characterisation of Madeleine and Jerome Vanderlynden no doubt reminded him of home and the kinds of people mentioned in his *Autobiography with a Difference*.[4] This understanding of the French is not confined to the major characters of the trilogy; it is to be seen in the more complete study of D'Archeville inserted after *The Spanish Farm*, and in the studies of 'Virginia' and 'The Common Secretary' in *Ten Years Ago*.[5] But in any case there are no individual villains in Mottram's writing – he does not for instance blame members of the staff for his own discomfort: he may be wary of the 'headless man' in *The Crime at Vanderlynden's*, but he does not hate the man whose identity is recognisable.

The peasant virtues of Madeleine and her truth to herself are not to be contemned: her single-mindedness, tenacity, determination, simple cunning, business acumen and lack of great imagination are her strength. She is as feminine and apolitical as the land itself; the war is for her a *bêtise*, a stupid thing that men do: it is her enemy as much as bad weather which ruins the crops. Yet she is not over-careful, grasping or ungenerous: when she freely makes a decision she gives freely, as in her relations with Georges and Skene. In addition to Madeleine as symbol, Mottram has created a highly individual and complex character, for myself the most memorable and striking in war literature, and one of the great characters of fiction.

The love of Skene and Madeleine is treated with a sensitivity and delicacy which makes it completely believable. It differs greatly in kind from other examples of sexual relationships in wartime, such as the squalid brothel scene in Henry Williamson's *The Patriot's Progress*; Robert Graves' 'young Welsh boys' in *Goodbye To All That* who 'did not want to die virginal'; or the hopeless affair of the young officer and a deceitful Parisienne in Richard Aldington's short story 'Love for Love'. Skene is not seeking mere sexual relief, neither has he illusions of permanency:

> Promiscuous women did not tempt him. Madeleine did. To be cared for – to be wanted – to have someone looking for his letters – arranging to meet him – that staid, demure, yet physical responsiveness – that was the thing. (p. 429)

Although the relationship may be termed irregular, and evidence of the way conventional behaviour is questioned and undermined by war, the overriding impression here is of two perfectly respectable people behaving quite naturally, finding relief from the stresses of war. Mottram shows how they lack other mutual interests, but have a great deal of mutual understanding; their love is a 'sober companionship', rather than an impassioned affair. Both are seeking a pre-war domesticity in an unpropitious time. By its very nature it cannot last, once the circumstances which created it are gone:

> Then, as he swung his leg, in its soiled army clothes, over his horse's back, she knew. She did not want him, had never wanted him, nor any Englishman, nor anything English. He was just one of the things the War, the cursed War, had brought upon her, and now it, and they, were going. Good riddance. Nor was her feeling unreasonable. The only thing she and Skene had in common, was the War. The War removed, they had absolutely no means of contact. Their case was not isolated. (p. 233)

The character of Skene is more fully realised in *Sixty-Four, Ninety-Four!* where the relationship is seen through his eyes, as a complement to Madeleine's view. The hero of the second novel in the trilogy is not a schoolboy with no pre-war experience of life with which to compare the war, nor an intellectual with over-emotional reactions, but 'an average Englishman of the professional classes', 'neither exceptionally handsome, brave nor rich', a diocesan architect in his thirties, hardworking, rather prim, and astonished at the way he can get through the business of war with an almost professional pride. Believing in the justice and necessity of the conflict (he had volunteered in 1914 in the 'New Army' spirit) he suffers the trauma of trench warfare, which is described laconically but accurately:

... Nothing to be seen but vapour – freshly torn earth – broken pickets – shredded wire – bodies and water – and all visible surface whipped with vicious bullets. No message could reach him, no ammunition, no medical aid. ... By two o'clock the enemy were enfilading the little trench. Skene crawled along, literally over his men, some sleeping the sleep of exhaustion, some grim and pale, shivering as they clutched their rifles. The wounded were quiet, very white, either dead or collapsed. At the end of the line, Skene found his Sergeant lying on his back, his cap over his face. Skene pulled him by the arm, but the arm came away in his hands. (p. 320)

He soon learns the nature of a war of stalemate: 'So ended the Brigade affair. Skene had lost half his men, had not seen a German, and had come back to his starting-point.' (p. 321)

Through Skene's English middle-class eyes, Mottram emphasises how the war changed settled ideas, destroying restraints and established habits, particularly in the middle-aged. Discussing the various forms of misappropriation – 'wangling', 'scrounging' and 'winning', he sees Skene, the 'law-abiding, decent professional man from a county town', as unashamed. But not only has the war become a way of life; it has also changed in nature. After the Somme any individual character of units enlisted on a local basis, and the spirit of the 1914 volunteers, disappeared in the enormous dimensions of that battle. We see through Skene's experience that the war has now become a business, where the old-fashioned regular officer is replaced on the staff by a new type of 'highly placed civilian organiser', better equipped to deal with what has become a matter of administration and technological application; in short, but for one essential difference, war is now an industry, as Mottram reflects in his autobiographical account of his war experience in *A Personal Record* (1929):

There, stretched across the world, lay two gigantic factories, equipped with an inconceivable plant of all sorts and manned by whole nations who were simply so many operatives, controlled by officers whose functions were those of foremen, or accountants. Yet even so, the simile will not hold, for the majority of those operatives were the material on which the vast organisation worked, and the finished article made out of them was death. The whole industry had a likeness to mining ventures, in which work becomes more diffi-cult as it progresses.[6]

The realisation of this truth about the war came later to the English than to the continental countries; England (or at least middle-class England) could retain her illusions longer. Towards the end, Skene reflects that 'her children ... entered [the war] with an ingrained romanticism possible only to those who live in comfortable leisure, with enough to eat and drink, no frontiers, and plenty of novels.' (p. 467)

The lucky Englishman could fight his battles on other nations' territory – and Skene, realising here that he too is lucky in a way because he is not dying of Madeleine's absence, combines the personal and national themes. Skene is also Mottram's observer here, almost an outsider, in contrast to the impulsive and fanatic Frenchman D'Archeville, who nevertheless '*meant* his war' (p. 250). As the careful, middleclass professional man Skene is appalled at the waste of material, such as wood and bullets, as well as the waste of men in inconclusive attrition warfare, and he is a persuasive witness to the author's theme of the 'Nightmare of Waste'.

Once the individual has been overtaken by the machine, victory is also an illusion; it is not even an anticlimax but rather the ending of a way of life, and quite hollow, as Skene reflects in the deserted battle zone:

> Was this what they had fought for, this draggled scrap-heap; bereft now even of the comradeship that had once made it bearable – robbed now even of its importance as the frontier where Justice and Fairplay stood at issue with Oppression and Greed? (p. 530)

Skene returns to England for demobilisation disenchanted, feeling that 'home' is really with his dead comrades in some Flanders graveyard, but also that he has worked out some personal destiny. But there has been no victory; the only winner is 'Uncle', the uncomplaining English-Canadian veteran who dies of Spanish influenza at the end of the war, and thus has the wit to miss an ignoble peace where 'careful meanness' will replace 'lunatic waste'.

In the near-perfect construction of *The Spanish Farm* unity is imposed by Madeleine and the farm where she starts and finishes, where she suffers but can dominate both earth and transient armies. In the central section, away from the farm in pursuit of Georges or in brief respite with Skene, she is out of her natural environment and less able to master her suffering. The experience of Skene throughout the war provides a different and looser unity in *Sixty-Four, Ninety-Four!* although the matter of the love story dovetails exactly with its counterpart in the first novel of the trilogy. The last novel, *The Crime at Vanderlynden's*, is in some ways a pendant to the others; although it has its genesis in the farm, it is more discursive and reflective about the war, gaining its unity from the use of motifs.

The tone here is lighter in places. The story concerns the efforts of Captain Dormer, a similarly middle-class but less imaginative version of Skene, to discover the perpetrator of the 'crime' – the destruction of a family shrine by an anonymous, battle-weary English soldier in search of shelter for a pair of mules. Dormer, after service in the front line, is temporarily attached to the staff because of his knowledge of French; his search for evidence of the offence takes him all over the British sector. Although his search may resemble a kind of detective story, and there is some humour in the misunderstandings and incongruities in relations between French and English (though never at the expense of the French) the overall tone is ironic and sombre. The trivial incident grows alarmingly and disproportionately, endangering Allied relations and becoming a matter concerning 'the dignity of France'; it also becomes an obsession with Dormer: the documents pursue him in and out of battle, contributing ultimately to his neurosis. But the story is not, I think, intended merely as an illustration of official 'red tape'; the humour is grimmer than that.

The only evidence Dormer can find is that the soldier's number is 6494 – the number used in words sung to sick parade bugle call; and his name may be 'Smith' – a similarly anonymous description. He becomes associated in Dormer's mind with a recurring nightmare of a headless corpse once seen in battle: neither has any identity – both are Everyman. Dormer also day-dreams of an army as a 'giant without a head'; slowly the crime and the nameless soldier become the Army, the war itself, pursuing him. The 'Headless Man' stands in his mind for '. . . all that mass whose minds were as drab as their uniform, so inarticulate, so decent and likeable in their humility and good temper' (p. 784).

But without cohesion and direction, without the pre-war order, the Headless Man let loose symbolises the Russian revolution. Dormer typically reacts against any threat of domination and he, or Mottram, reflect on possible counter-action we should now call fascism. The Headless Man is a powerful image; a passage from the second novel is also comparable prophetically to Wilfred Owen's 'None will break ranks, though nations trek from progress'.[7] or Yeats' strange beast in 'The Second Coming'. In a transit camp for prisoners and refugees of many nations, a disillusioned French corporal speaks to Skene:

> . . . This pot-pourri of races and tongues is the remnant escaped – and has had the good luck to preserve life, without home or family, existing like beasts for years. What have they learned? Nothing, my lieutenant, give them rifles and rum, a flag to follow and a master to drive, and they would start another war to-morrow! (pp. 551–2)

Henry Williamson found Mottram's battle scenes 'deficient and unsatisfying'.[8] Leaving aside the question of what type of 'satisfaction' is desired from a war novel (the understatement of the descriptions seems effective enough) and whether words alone can ever adequately describe such things, it is ironic that Mottram should have been so criticised when so many books about the war were censured at the time for imbalance, for dwelling too much on the horrors of assault and not enough on the boredom and waiting in between. The panorama of the trilogy is large enough to include the fact that 'the great art of war lay not in killing Germans, but in killing time' (p. 626): the theme of waste takes in not only the spectacular waste of hopeless mass attacks, but also the continuous nibbling away of lives and courage in 'routine' trench warfare. Mottram's work provides the kind of detail needed for an overall picture of war if we are to understand how such a thing is possible – troops may suffer huge losses but the survivors do recover with remarkable speed; most men are greatly adaptable and continue to do their jobs with unimaginative endurance. In no other writer are we made aware of the detail of that complex and hierarchical autonomous society created by the English in Flanders, and how it was possible to keep the whole thing going, day after day. Where else but in Mottram's ironic but sympathetic view of the staff do we learn, say, of the difference between the 'Q' side of Divisional Staff which kept the soldier supplied and fed, and the 'G' side which made the plans to get him killed? *The Spanish Farm Trilogy* might well be called a primer of the Western Front.

Other contemporary criticism found the work indispensable to the social historian of the future, whereas a modern critic considers Mottram . . . 'a superficial writer, who is most at home in rendering the characteristics of the social surface, rather than plunging to moral or psychological depths',[9] having affinities with John Galsworthy. These views call into question the nature of the novel as a form, and remind us that it needs a very wide definition. Mottram's contribution to social history is found not so much in the documentary content of the trilogy, although that is valuable enough, but in that he puts on record 'Not what we did, or what was done to us, but what we thought of it all . . . what is being gradually forgotten', as another contemporary put it.[10] This inner truth of the feelings of men is one of the particular contributions to truth that only imaginative literature can provide: in the trilogy we have the indispensable thoughts and feelings of an intelligent but not exceptional man of the time, the 'representative Englishman' of Skene/Dormer.

On the question of superficiality, we must again ask what is wanted from a novel. The moral and psychological depths of Skene and Madeleine in particular are, I should have thought, deep enough: we are certainly left in no doubt about what they feel, why they act as they do and what they represent. Mottram's thoroughness and lack of obscurity leaves no room for critical detective-work: clarity should not be mistaken for superficiality. His strength lies in his ability to particularise the universal, and to give his symbols of the eternal woman or the headless man clear, human, practical and realistic grounds. There is also a grandeur and nobility in his writing which should gain the attention of future readers, as the cathartic ending of *The Spanish Farm* instances:

> So Madeleine remained in the Spanish Farm, and saw no more English, for the Labour Corps broke up and went, and she did not care. She was engrossed in one thing only: to get back, sou by sou, everything that had been lost or destroyed, plundered or shattered, by friend or foe, and pay herself for everything she had suffered and dared. And as there was a Madeleine more or less widowed and childless, bereaved and soured, in every farm in north-eastern France, she became a portent. Statesmen feared or wondered at her, schemers and new business men served her and themselves through her, while philosophers shuddered. For she was the Spanish Farm, the implacable spirit of that borderland so often fought over, never really conquered. She was that spirit that forgets nothing and forgives nothing, but maintains itself, amid all disasters, and necessarily. For she was perhaps the most concrete expression of humanity's instinctive survival in spite of its own perversity and ignorance. There must she stand, slow-burning revenge incarnate, until a better, gentler time. (p. 234)

Ernest Hemingway's *A Farewell to Arms* (1929)[11] is of far less complex construction than R. M. Mottram's trilogy, and offers no such panorama of the war. Although at first received badly by some on moral grounds, it has long achieved a singular fame in the literature of both love and war. The relatively simple and well-known story of Lieutenant Henry and the English nurse Catherine Barkley is a successful extension of two previous sketches from *In Our Time* (1925): the passage where Nick Adams is wounded and makes his 'separate peace', and 'A Very Short Story' where a soldier and a nurse have an impermanent affair.[12]

The novel is conceived in personal and individual terms: Hemingway's lovers are not representative of national characteristics. Henry is an expatriate American serving (for no clearly stated reasons) with the Italian Ambulance Corps against the Austrians; he is an observer, far less involved than Skene in the meaning of the conflict. It has been argued that he is representative of America leaving involvement for post-war isolation,[13] but the struggle portrayed here is rather one of the individual against a society which will dehumanise him and seek his extinction in its ultimate manifestation of a nation at war. This theme is common to other American literature of the First World War; for example, in Dos Passos' *Three Soldiers* there is no escape from the

machine. In this situation, man is faced with the only fact he has
– the certainty of death. Hemingway is not writing social history,
despite the fame of the Caporetto section described by Walter Allen as
'probably the finest piece of writing on war in the English language',[14]
but asking 'What can a man be sure of; how should he act in these
circumstances?' His answers are fiercely honest and tragically devoid
of hope.

Hemingway's hard, clear style, his 'rhetoric of understatement' is a
most suitable means of examining the basis of experience of war and
love. Certain physical things we can be sure of: abstract concepts are
corruptible and untrustworthy:

> . . . I had seen nothing sacred, and the things that were glorious had
> no glory and the sacrifices were like the stockyards at Chicago if
> nothing was done with the meat except to bury it. There were many
> words that you could not stand to hear and finally only the names of
> places had dignity. Certain numbers were the same way and certain
> dates and these with the names of the places were all you could say
> and have them mean anything. Abstract words such as glory, honour,
> courage or hallow were obscene beside the concrete names of villages,
> the numbers of roads, the names of rivers, the numbers of regiments
> and the dates. (p. 185)

This is a final judgement on the ephemeral idealism of war, far more
concise and uncompromising than, say, that found later in George
Orwell's *Homage to Catalonia*. In his paring away of layers of customary abstract learned responses to arrive at a bare reality, Hemingway could be said to have created a new toughness of response which
is as unreal as the preceding romanticism, because it does not face the
whole picture of man, which includes sentiments as well as physical
appearance and sensation. This is actually the strength of his later
satiric and Swiftian essay 'A Natural History of the Dead'.[15] Such
things needed to be said at the time. But in the novel the significance of
verifiable exteriors reinforces the themes of the work; Hemingway is at
his best in the kind of setpiece description which opens *A Farewell to
Arms*, with its images of pregnancy, rain and death. He achieves in
prose what the Imagists sought in poetry: a hard, clear image, the
language of common speech, the exact word and an end to vague
generalities.

Similarly, Hemingway's use of reticence and 'oblique dialogue' make
the love story objectively convincing. The conversations of the lovers
are like the dialogue of a Howard Hawks film, with its 'imaginative
omissions' which make understood the emotion underlying the commonplace but real language of men and women:

[Catharine said] '. . . Listen to it rain.'
'It's raining hard.'
'And you'll always love me, won't you?'
'Yes.'
'And the rain won't make any difference?'
'No.'
'That's good. Because I'm afraid of the rain.'
'Why?' I was sleepy. Outside the rain was falling steadily.
'I don't know, darling. I've always been afraid of the rain.'
'I like it.' (p. 128)

– and again the forboding image appears significantly.

The two themes of love and war covered by the ambiguous title are so inseparably welded together that they appear as aspects of one existence, rather than in opposition, or complementary. Although classed as a 'war novel' it might be better described as a novel of love set against a background of war, which by its violence enhances the transience of human life and hope. In any case, once the hero leaves desultory participation in the war for the shock of wounding and defeat, or desultory whoring for a permanent love-relationship, the actions connected with both are equally strenuous or harrowing. Henry's escape from the firing squad after Caporetto is even surpassed by the epic row to freedom in Switzerland – a daunting feat which is however possible, as at least one enthusiastic American has proved. Henry's wounding is described in bone-jarring detail but Catherine's death in childbirth is perhaps more painful to read, the laconic 'It did not take her very long to die' only emphasising this. Sometimes a man can and must act, showing that 'grace under pressure' of Hemingway's heroes; sometimes he must endure and accept with dignity the nothingness which will inevitably be his lot, and for which there is no compensation in abstract speculation.

Out of the experience of violence in war, Hemingway develops a fatalistic, almost nihilistic philosophy. The blind chance of war, which saves Mottram's hero from inevitable death in the trenches, has Hemingway's hero very nearly shot by his own side despite all his efforts to do his job efficiently. If there is any providence, it cares no more for men's affairs than Henry cares for the ants burnt in the camp fire (p. 230). The attempt of Catherine and Henry to make a saner life away from the war is also doomed: they are trapped by society, but their escape into love is no escape from life, for death is always waiting, in or out of war. Man is trapped socially and biologically; life is an unfair game, and the only inescapable fact he has is death:

Now Catherine would die. That was what you did. You died. You

did not know what it was about. You never had time to learn.
They threw you in and told you the rules and the first time they
caught you off base they killed you. Or they killed you gratuitously
like Aymo. Or gave you syphilis like Rinaldi. But they killed you in
the end. You could count on that. Stay around and they would kill
you. (pp. 329–30)

This philosophy is reminiscent of Fulke Greville's 'wearisome condition
of humanity', but in the century before the watershed of European
experience in the First World War it had been in abeyance, hidden
by the false hopes of progress, democracy and applied science.

What does Hemingway find of positive value to place against this?
There is the professional code of conduct: Henry makes a clear distinction between the brave and competent people he has met:

I was not against them. I was through. I wished them all the luck.
There were the good ones, and the brave ones, and the calm ones
and the sensible ones, and they deserved it. (p. 237)

and the cowardly and indiscriminate carabinieri:

So far they had shot everyone they had questioned. The questioners
had that beautiful detachment and devotion to stern justice of men
dealing in death without being in any danger of it. (p. 229)

There is also the power of love

We could feel alone when we were together, alone against the others.
I have been alone while I was with many girls and that is the way
that you can be most lonely. But we were never lonely and never
afraid when we were together. (p. 252)

But this is not enough to avoid the overall impression of hopelessness.
In contrast to Skene and Madeleine, whose love is possible because the
limitations imposed on it are accepted, Henry and Catherine stake
everything, and are therefore tragically bound to fail in a world of
social and natural violence. The world of Hemingway's novels may
seem inadequate, but we should have difficulty in arguing that it is not
the world we live in:

If people bring so much courage to this world the world has to kill
them to break them, so of course it kills them. The world breaks
everyone and afterwards many are strong at the broken places.
But those that it will not break it kills. It kills the very good and the
very gentle and the very brave impartially. If you are none of these
you can be sure it will kill you too but there will be no special
hurry. (p. 252)

Mottram's characters have a (somewhat battered) society they can return to, but Hemingway's have already become the aimless wanderers of *Fiesta* (1926), where the hero Jake has been literally as well as symbolically emasculated by the war, but still follows the code of conduct. The hero in later novels does reluctantly accept involvement in society again, as in *To Have and Have Not* (1937) and *For Whom the Bell Tolls* (1949), although the latter novel is less satisfying than *A Farewell to Arms*, the hero being less well-defined and the love more romanticised. In Hemingway's ultimate masterpiece, *The Old Man and the Sea* (1952) the struggle is again of a man tragically alone against nature, suffering with dignity.

Hemingway's description of the Caporetto retreat[16] did not endear the book to fascist Italy, but unlike the reactionary Douglas Jerrold, who attacked the book quite unreasonably in his notorious *The Lie About the War* (1930), he was not fooled by Mussolini, as can be seen from his first-rate journalism for the *Toronto Daily Star*.[17] In his picture of the battle police on the Tagliamento, 'all young men ... saving their country', we can see the genesis of fascism! Hemingway had more political acumen than he is often credited with. His warnings for the future proved more accurate than those of Mottram, who in the preface to *Sixty-Four, Ninety-Four!* and in *Ten Years Ago* wished to avoid the return of the 'Nightmare of Waste' and the destruction of European civilisation in future war which would happen if the truth about 1914–18 were forgotten. Europe just survived in the Second World War, although Mottram's warning still applies to the possibility of a Third.

It is true that no war literature of the period succeeded in avoiding a future war, but to class this as 'failure' is to give to literature a function out of keeping with its nature, for although no writer prevented the Second World War, *neither did anyone else*, in any walk of life. A similar modern confusion of cause and effect would blame that war on the writers for inculcating a pacifist temper on the Europe of the Thirties. Creative literature reflects society; it makes manifest the spirit of the age, but as Auden said, it 'makes nothing happen'.[18] Rather, in the work of these two writers as in others, it sets the record straight.

3 John Dos Passos' *Three Soldiers*: Aesthetics and the Doom of Individualism

Stanley Cooperman

Readers who know the work of John Dos Passos[1] only through his mature writing – particularly the *U.S.A.* trilogy, with its cross-sectional narrative, anarchistic pessimism, and successfully developed unamistic architecture – are likely to be disappointed by *Three Soldiers*, which antedates *U.S.A.* by a decade. Published in 1921, *Three Soldiers* is the work of a young writer who, despite his use of modern warfare (mass, technologcial conflict) has for his primary response aesthetic rather than ideological indignation.

The John Dos Passos who wrote *Three Soldiers was still*, as Malcolm Cowley has remarked, 'a late romantic . . . an aesthete moving about the world in a portable ivory tower'.[2] Less interested in the physical realities of machine warfare than its psychological effects on young North Americans who were unprepared for it no matter what their backgrounds, Dos Passos in *Three Soldiers* is concerned both with cultural naiveté, and the essential mindlessness of mass organisation itself. The war, in his novel, is essentially a catalyst rather than a subject: unlike writers like William March or Thomas Boyd,[3] for whom the horrors of machine warfare were the basic materials for narrative, Dos Passos uses the military situation provided by the Great Crusade as a metaphor for twentieth-century civilisation, and in this respect the book is cultural diagnosis rather than realism: one does not read *Three Soldiers* for data on the specifics of combat (the novel is almost completely without battle scenes), but rather to understand how the mobilisation of an entire civilisation meant the supremacy of what Henry Adams termed 'The Dynamo' over all individual action or reaction.[4]

It is the machine of living rather than the machine of killing which in *Three Soldiers* emerges as the ultimate destructive force; and what it destroys are precisely those traditional values of individual pride, individual aesthetic action, individual success which – for Americans – the Great Crusade was undertaken to protect and enhance. The military environment becomes, in *Three Soldiers*, the microcosm of twentieth-century technological culture: that is, a world in which ambition combined with moral compunction is comic, aesthetic action is a *non sequitur*, and pride is an archaic form of sentiment. The 'Buzz-saw' of *U.S.A.* makes its first appearance in *Three Soldiers*; and makes its appearance not in any Hemingway-like situation of existential combat, but in the rear-echelon camps, the offices, the strategies the absurdities, the sordid and ignoble realities of organisation *as* organisation. And it is this fear of, and outright hatred for, the proliferation of bureaucratic power, which was to shape much of Dos Passos' future work – and which, indeed, accounts for the increasing 'conservatism' which, in his last years, made his very name anathema to liberal critics and academics in the United States.

The tripartite division of *Three Soldiers* rests on alternating narrative segments focused on Fuselli, a young city-dweller from San Francisco, himself the son of immigrants and a small clerk from a semi-slum background; on Chrisfield, a farm-boy from Indiana, whose knowledge of Europe is so vague as to be almost mythological ('Is the stars the same over there, overseas, as they is here?'),[5] and whose concept of violence is intensely personal rather than abstract; and on Andrews, a music student-cum-poet from Virginia, who enlists in the army for aesthetic and metaphysical rather than political reasons, and who abstracts all experience into intellectual formalism. The intent, of course, in the choice of such protagonists is obvious enough: a cross-section of America, or Americans, and in this respect *Three Soldiers* foreshadows the vastly more sophisticated structure of *U.S.A.*, in which a variety of techniques (stream-of-consciousness, external biographies, 'newsreels' and montage) combine with a complex series of interrelated narratives to form a composite cultural portrait.

Of his three protagonists, however, Dos Passos can utilise only two as centres of consciousness; one can therefore seriously question whether the novel is truly based on a tripartite structure at all. Chrisfield is very much subordinate to Fuselli and Andrews, and indeed is represented primarily in those narrtive segments devoted to his companions. One cannot escape the conclusion that at least in the beginning of his career, Dos Passos was unable to make the aesthetic leap beyond an autobiographical protagonist (Andrews), or an urban protagonist (Fuselli). Chrisfield himself, in short, and the mind – the reality – he represents, is no less foreign to Dos Passos than is Eisenstein the New York Jew, and – like the latter – a mere cultural stereotype. Chrisfield is a creature of pulp magazines and cinema ('The Westerner'), and remains alien both to Fuselli and to Andrews; he is defined largely by action (that is, violence), by stage-dialect, and by nostalgic reminiscences that seem at times a coagulation of 'My Old Kentucky Home' and Mark Twain:

Then he thought of the spring on the plains of Indiana and the mocking-bird singing in the moonlight among the flowering locust trees behind the house. He could almost smell the heavy sweetness of the locust blooms, as he used to smell them sitting on the steps after supper, tired from a day's heavy plowing, while the clatter of his mother's housework came from the kitchen. He didn't wish he was back there, but it was pleasant to think of it now and then, and how the yellow farmhouse looked and the red barn where his father never had been able to find time to paint the door, and the tumble-down cowshed where the shingles were always coming off. He wondered dully what it would be like at the front. It couldn't be green and pleasant, the way the country was here. Well, he didn't give a damn. He went to sleep. (pp. 129–30)

At any hint of complexity, indeed, Christfield simply 'goes to sleep' – or occupies himself with thoughts of personal violence and sexual lust. The most orthodoxly naturalistic of the characters in *Three Soldiers*, Chrisfield is the least aesthetically satisfying: except in terms of external action, which alone gives him – like the traditional protagonist of naturalist fiction – significance, or as a stage-mechanism within the consciousness of Andrews (whose major response to Chrisfield is that he does not 'understand' the latter's violence), Chrisfield, as an independent protagonist, hardly exists at all. There is a great distance separating the young novelist attempting to create his primitivistic Indiana farm-boy in *Three Soldiers*, and the mature artist who so vividly sets up a vast cast of protagonists in *U.S.A.*

Quite aside from his lack of individual development, however, Chrisfield serves as an important element in the mosaic that Dos Passos does achieve in *Three Soldiers*: his indictment of military organisation as the proliferation of bureaucratic anachronism. For Chrisfield is potentially the best soldier among the three major protagonists: unafraid of physical violence, courageous in the face of danger, anxious to get on with his personal encounter with the enemy, Chrisfield finds himself stymied, at every turn, by a military machine which in all respects but technology is a Circumlocution Office where the frontier virtues of courage and pride and direct action are no longer relevant. Chrisfield, indeed, ends as a deserter not because of any stern 'military necessity', but because of its antithesis: the deliberate and sordid reduction of the individual according to military codes appropriate to nineteenth-century definitions of who and what the peacetime 'sodjer' was, but grotesque for an army composed essentially of civilians primed with heavy doses of propaganda to Save the World.

'This ain't no sort o' life', mutters Chrisfield in his own sullen rebellion, 'for a man to be treated lahk he was a nigger' (p. 139).

'Ah didn't git in this here army to be ordered around by a goddamn wop' (p. 23). As an enlisted man, Chrisfield discovers a perpetual denial of everything which his own rural background had defined as the nature of manhood: clear and immediate response to personal insult; egalitarianism between employer and 'hired hand'; avoidance of any public humiliation except at the risk of personal retaliation; and – above all – the assumption of certain inviolable areas of virility itself: individual and independent responsibilty to do the job agreed upon; a scorn for mendacity and fawning; and freedom of movement when the task assigned had either been accomplished or was no longer necessary.

It is the violation of these codes which, finally, drives Chrisfield to murder and desertion – the latter, significantly enough, occurring after the actual fighting had long since been over. Throughout his 'training', however, Chrisfield had been exposed to continual violation of every code in which he had been taught to believe, and the result is the growth of slow, irresistible anger, unfocused violence, and a need for assertion, through violence, of manhood itself:

> Chrisfield marched with his fists clenched; he wanted to fight somebody, to run his bayonet into a man as he ran it into the dummy in that everlasting bayonet drill, he wanted to strip himself naked, to squeeze the wrists of a girl until she screamed. (p. 152)

Chrisfield's murder of Lieutenant (formerly Sergeant) Anderson, then, must be understood as something more than gratuitous narrative sensationalism: the action, and the monomania which produces it, has for its origins a cultural complex of which Americans had always boasted, and which the American army at the time of World War I did its best to eliminate – but at terrible cost.[6]

From the standpoint of the aesthetics of fiction, a serious problem with the Chrisfield segments – as there is with those sections of *Three Soldiers* presented through the consciousness of Fuselli and Andrews – is the ubiquitous intrusion of Dos Passos into the mind which ostensibly bears the weight of narrative: the novelist is repeatedly given to pausing, in the very midst of his action, for scenic observations, colour-metaphors, and elaborate, subjective literary allusions which could not possibly relate to the mind experiencing them:

> The whip-like sound of rifles had chimed in with the stuttering of the machine guns. Little white clouds sailed above him in a blue sky, and in front of him was a group of houses that had the same color, white with lavender-grey shadows, as the clouds. (p. 185)

This sort of thing is less damaging in the case of Andrews, where the protagonist is a young aesthete, than it is in the narratives of Chrisfield and Fuselli – although even with Andrews, as we shall see, there are moments when the novel virtually ceases, while Dos Passos indulges in cultural name-dropping or literary tourism.

There are scenes, however, when Dos Passos does permit action and dialogue to create their own effects, and at these times we see flashes of the writer who was to produce, in *U.S.A.*, a major work of the decade. When Chrisfield, for example, together with a companion, 'invade' a French farm (p. 171), the result is authentic comedy, subtle character-response, and – through controlled implication – a counterpoint of the casual brutality of the war itself. Such scenes, at the time *Three Soldiers* was published, shocked American public opinion, which had for so long been fed a diet of propaganda pastels relating to clean-cut American 'boys' sent to save La Belle France, virtuously carrying the banners of Christian faith against a simian foe.

If Chrisfield is crushed by a military organisation that represents the end of the Winchester-on-the-wall frontier tradition of individual pride and virility, Fuselli is absorbed by an apparatus less military than socio-economic: attempting to escape his non-status as a clerk in civilian life by embarking on his Great Adventure, Fuselli discovers an army which resembles nothing so much as a large corporation – precisely the environment from which he had hoped to escape by donning the uniform. In the beginning, however, the opportunities seem endless: 'Gee . . . this war's a lucky thing for me. I might have been in the R C Vicker Company's store for five years and never got a raise. An' here in the army I got a chance to do almost anything' (p. 43). As a soldier, Fuselli suddenly – albeit briefly – enjoys a status beyond all his experience. He was a hapless spectator of, rather than partici-pant in, power all his life, and the uniform is a magic cloak endowing him with an importance he had never known:

A few moments later he stood stiffly at attention. . . . Somehow it made him think of the man behind the desk in the office of the draft board who had said, handing him the papers sending him to camp, 'I wish I was going with you,' and held out a white bony hand that Fuselli, after a moment's hesitation, had taken in his own stubby brown hand. The man had added fervently, 'It must be grand, just grand, to feel the danger, the chance of being potted any minute. Good luck, young feller. . . . Good luck.' Fuselli remembered un-pleasantly his paper-white face and the greenish look of his bald head; but the words had made him stride out of the office sticking out his chest, brushing truculently past a group of men at the door. Even now the memory of it, mixing with the strains of the national anthem, made him feel important, truculent. (p. 11)

Fuselli's background, of course, shapes his reaction to the military

organisation no less than does Chrisfield's, but with this vital difference: where Chrisfield expects immediate combat in terms of personal
encounter, and is virtually destroyed not by the fighting but by its
absence, Fuselli – the small-time urban clerk – sees the army, indeed
war itself, as a means for social and economic self-aggrandisement. In
this respect Fuselli's subsequent career is a parody not of war, but of
the Great American Dream: truculent and brusque with his equals,
always cautious about 'getting in wrong' with his superiors, inevitably
translating every military necessity into careerist terms, Fuselli is
interested neither in ideology nor in violence, but in 'getting ahead'.
That he ends his career as a shuffling panhandler in the back-alleys of
the military machine, is one of the more successful ironic progres-
sions of the novel.

Ironic reversal, indeed, shapes Fuselli's entire career. At the very
first we are introduced to the unfocused dreams, the meaningless
leisure, the vague yearning of the city clerk and his friends, surrounded
by the signs of power in which they can never hope to share. San
Francisco – the ships in the harbour, the Golden Gate Bridge, the rich
avenues and beautiful women – are, Fuselli reflects, 'like the front of
a high-class theater' (p. 12): a spectacle for him to witness rather than
a reality for him to enjoy. And Fuselli's image of military life is no
less theatrical: his very interior monologues relating to combat are
drawn from the popular cinema – especially the propaganda pieces
which were being produced at the time[7] – together with heavy doses
of sexual sentimentality (his Girl Back Home) and chances for personal
promotion through the ranks. Europe itself simply does not exist,
except in terms of picture-postcard sentimentality:

> It's swell over there . . . everything's awful pretty-like. Picturesque,
> they call it. And the people wears peasant costumes . . . I had an
> uncle who used to tell me about it. (p. 27).

Fuselli's own father had come from Italy in steerage, close to, but
enormously set apart from all the glamour of an 'ocean voyage';
reflecting on this, Fuselli remarks – with the truculence characteristic
of his early appearances in the novel – 'I'd stay home if I had to do
that' (p. 13). It is, of course, precisely as a 'steerage' passenger that
Fuselli is to make his voyage overseas; only on board the stinking,
overcrowded troop ship does Fuselli come to understand that the
'military necessity' involves a continuation rather than departure from
his urban clerkdom. At this point the metamorphosis begins: the young,
sturdy soldier – not without potential for courage and independent
manhood – whines and fawns his way toward the one ideal he
manages to hold: his corporalship. Tail-wagging geniality replaces
truculence; personal effacement and enforced humility replace cour-

age. Only in his dream does Fuselli enjoy episodes of proud insubordination (e.g. p. 62), and by the time he does receive his temporary promotion, he has become an emotional clerk once again.

Essentially, however, it is the moral reversal represented by sexual sentimentality that completes Fuselli's personal destruction – or rather, absorption – into the garbage-dump of military service. His involvement with Yvonne is the final reductive element in Fuselli's process of reversal. Yvonne herself is a French girl who demonstrates all the signs of being 'nice': she knits, and she has a mother; she cooks, and she has a sister and brother; she runs a neat little shop, talks pleasantly, and has never bobbed her hair. The result is inevitable: Fuselli (much to Yvonne's amusement) proposes marriage after their brief affair, is cuckolded-before-the-fact by his own sergeant, assents to this for fear of endangering his promotion, but discovers that his military 'career' has been ruined by venereal infection.

The punishment is court-martial. After the intervening years, it is perhaps difficult for new generations of readers to understand how thoroughly the American Army at the time of World War I was imbued with Christian ideals – especially as these ideals related to the sexual purity of American boys. Fuselli, at any rate, finds that just as his expectations of military status had led only to self-effacement, fear, and humiliation, so his insistence on moral 'right' and romantic sentiment leads only to court-martial and a permanent labour assignment. And it is at this point that Fuselli finally surrenders: 'I don't give a damn' are virtually his last words in the novel. The fly-speck, the 'insect' of individuality has found the dung-heap at last, and is content. With 'good eats' and regular opportunities for drunken sex, Fuselli is not destroyed by the military corporation: he simply vanishes beneath its weight, surviving as a subterranean parody of Horatio Alger.

It is John Andrews, however, very much the focus of sensibility in *Three Soldiers* despite the novel's unanimist pretensions, who perceives the military environment as a comic juggernaut, 'the damndest fool business ever'. But Andrews takes this juggernaut far more seriously than does e. e. cummings (character in his own novel); nor can Andrews simply retreat into idyllic love, as does Hemingway's protagonist in *A Farewell to Arms*. Neither art nor love is a final solution for Andrews, who searches almost desperately, with puritan monomania, for the assertion of some noble act. Viewing love as a sign of self-indulgence rather than strength, he must give up love to prove his own will; viewing art as the ultimate value, he must give up art in order to achieve the supreme gesture unmotivated by self-interest.

Like many other young men who had been bored by their humanistic, essentially nineteenth-century studies at university, Andrews had volunteered for the Crusade in order to achieve meaning through willed sacrifice; he objects to the 'slavery' of army life largely because it exists quite independently of his own consent. There can be no self-abnegation, after all, without freedom to choose, and for this reason Andrews' actions at the end of the novel are entirely in character. Refusing to clear up his legal difficulties (the charge of desertion) which, as Genevieve tells him, are far from insurmountable, and deliberately destroying his work on the 'Queen of Sheba' symphony, he succeeds in playing his almost biblical role to the hilt.

'I have made a gesture,' he announces to the nonplussed Genevieve, 'feeble as it is, toward human freedom' (p. 423). Imbued with the vision of John Brown, haloed by the drifting pages of his music, scorning the milk and honey of that very school assignment he had intrigued to secure, returning to the wilderness of the prison stockade comforted only by his sense of righteousness and purity of will, Andrews becomes what he had desired from the very beginning: the central protagonist in a modest crucifixion – a major motivation, in actual fact, for many of the World War I volunteers from Eastern universities in the United States.

Critics have been impatient, even harsh with Andrews; if his method of renunciatory action does appear somewhat too precious, however, too 'arty' and melodramatic, this may well be a comment upon our own moral environment rather than his. Contemporary readers, after all, are likely to lose patience with any protagonist who is overly self-dramatic (in this respect the Hemingway hip-hardboiledom still rules the roost), while the wilful destruction of his own music may seem inept rather than morally willed. For Andrews himself, however, and for the literary audience of the twenties, such a gesture of renunciation could be both deeply courageous and moving precisely because of the aesthetic sacrifice involved.

Andrews, at any rate, who enlists because of a need for sacrificial gesture, and who does so without political or ideological illusion, discovers in the military environment a situation which apparently makes any such gesture impossible. Out of this reversal comes his role as anti-hero: what I have elsewhere termed the hero of negative action.[8] Just as Fuselli, hoping to escape from the office, finds himself sentenced to perpetual clerkhood, so Andrews finds himself without any chance to carry through the motives for his enlistment. Having renounced civilian life as both vulgar and mechanical, he discovers vulgarity and mechanism to be the very basis of the Crusade itself. From the moment he enters the recruiting office, with its aura of imbecile routine and sterility, he must continue his search – a search for meaningful sacrifice – that cannot be realised while he is retrieving cigarette butts or begging an indifferent officer for permission to attend school.

But neither can this search be realised through any simple escape from humiliation and bestiality: Henslowe's advice to dismiss the entire machinery from his mind and 'have a good time' is simply not Andrews' way. Nor, finally, is it enough to flee into aesthetics as a composer in khaki. It is not 'freedom' that Andrews wants, nor the chance to escape from being a 'slave among slaves', but rather the opportunity to perform an act of nobility. 'Half by accident he had managed to free himself from the treadmill,' he reflects, and then makes the ultimate self-indictment: that he had not 'made a gesture, however feeble, however forlorn, for the sake of other people's freedom' (p. 431). And this failure is, indeed, more terrible to him than all the 'slavery' he so rhetorically observes throughout the novel. Refusing to humble himself to achieve a 'freedom' he will not claim, Andrews destroys his music, awaits the military police, and submits to degradation once again, but this time with full knowledge of what is in store. The terms of his original gesture toward individuality and renunciation (his enlistment) have been met at last: Andrews defeats the machine by an act of negative will – a sentimental act, perhaps, but an act nevertheless.

This negative act, however, is diluted in terms of aesthetic impact because Andrews' protest and emotion alike come framed in a filigree of baroque verbiage. It is not Andrews' insistence upon gesture, his indignation, or his fierce pride in individuality that seem gratuitous, but rather the fact that the prose surrounding Andrews is so completely over-ripe, so undigested within the narrative itself. The difficulty is simply that Andrews all but vanishes beneath literary and musical allusions, adjectives, colour poems, chiaroscuro 'moments', and enamelled surfaces: Dos Passos the young artist flexes his vocabulary, but the resulting prose too often has little relationship to the experience which must be rendered, moving almost without warning from rhetorical protests to subdued, tone-poem appreciations of landscapes, old churches, young girls, paintings, and whatever is sufficiently picturesque to offer the novelist himself a chance for linguistic bravura.

Dos Passos' problem, of course, was resolved in *U.S.A.*, where the various elements are separated into 'Camera Eye' (aesthetic rebellion), 'Newsreel' (social landscape), 'Biography' (political comment), and the straightforward narrative progression of his protagonists. Only in his later work could Dos Passos translate his own duality – young poet and social realist – into a narrative system where the various parts remain separate but offer thematic support to the work as a whole. The difference, however, is largely one of technique: the philosophical and moral orientation of *Three Soldiers*, with its insistence upon the ultimate validity of individuation, and its distrust of all socio-political-military structures, remains constant throughout Dos Passos' subsequent career.

4   The Painful Process of Unthinking: E. E. Cummings' Social Vision in *The Enormous Room*

Jeffrey Walsh

There is more than a tinge of absurdity and grim irony in what happened to the American writer, Edward Estlin Cummings (1894–1966), during his brief involvement in the First World War. Having crossed over from the United States to join the Norton-Harjes American volunteers in France, he found himself, after only three months driving ambulances, ignominiously arrested by the French authorities whom he was helping to defend. Cummings, the most ardent of francophiles, was suspected of being an enemy of France. The experience was traumatic; it forced home to him the irrationality of war, and it served also to radicalise his social conscience. Cummings was imprisoned in a detention camp for over three months, where he played an active part in the struggle of his fellow detainees against their gaolers. This experience of resistance taught him the strength of solidarity in the face of oppression, and more importantly he learned to value the friendship of his socially ostracised fellow prisoners.

The immediate cause of Cumming's arrest was some letters written by a pacifist friend, William Slater Brown, which discussed the insurrection of local French troops earlier in 1917. Any mention of French mutinies, later the subject of two novels by American writers, Humphrey Cobb's *Paths of Glory* (1935) and William Faulkner's *A Fable* (1955), was regarded as a serious breach of military security. It is hard to conceive of Cummings as a subversive writer in view of his later conservatism, but at this point in the war he seemed a dangerous hothead to the French authorities. His letters home to his parents, written at the time, are full of extreme, often anarchistic, views; and he and Brown with their fondness for the Paris of the Communes, their contempt for the military hierarchy, and their questionable contacts (Brown knew the anarchist Emma Goldman) thoroughly antagonised their superiors. Cummings's subsequent incarceration in La Ferté Macé internment camp acted as a catalyst in his artistic development, and this essay seeks to explore some of the ways in which *The Enormous Room* illustrates this change.

In *The Enormous Room*,[1] which takes its title from a church-like hall where the prisoners are housed, Cummings's narrator describes his journey to La Ferté Macé, Orne, France, as a pilgrimage, drawing freely and ironically upon the symbolism of Bunyan's *The Pilgrim's Progress*. He finds himself in a predicament analogous to Christian's because, like Bunyan's hero, he too is a *nouveau* whose difficult path culminates in self-awareness. His encounters in La Ferté with thieves and prostitutes, as well as his friendships with the noble human beings whom he portrays as the Delectable Mountains, are stages on the way to enlightenment. Like Christian also he passes from the Slough of Despond (his section of the Ambulance Corps) and undergoes tribulations which prove ultimately to be beneficial. The narrator's hardships included filthy living conditions which caused him to suffer from infected fingers, but these infirmities contribute to his growing social vision. Even filth has its purpose, to complete his moral separation from well-scrubbed America. Cummings, the son of a Unitarian minister, as David E. Smith has shown,[2] made successful metaphorical use of *The Pilgrim's Progress* as a structural underpinning for *The Enormous Room*.

The organisation of Cummings's novel enacts its narrator's rebellion against the values of those who have imprisoned him, and traces the parallel evolution of his artistic consciousness. He rejects the herd-instinct of society and, through trial, is reunited with his pre-social or primitive self, a process which leads to moral understanding. Initially he appears to withdraw from social obligations as he turns his back on 'patriotism', 'honour', and all the spurious values he enlisted to uphold, but the end product of his defiance is an affirmation of belief in the integrity of individual men and women. The journey undertaken by the narrator of the novel, a prototype of Cummings the emergent artist, is one of moral regeneration, which is why it is appropriate for the novelist to utilise religious language and symbolism ironically related to Bunyan's famous allegory. The narrator of *The Enormous Room* makes two journeys, one a specific geographical one to La Ferté in the early part of the novel, and a more significant quest, involving the book as a whole, which symbolises a spiritual and artistic awakening.

Dependent upon the motifs of pilgrimage and progress are other related underlying patterns. The book is founded upon a paradox, that freedom in the modern world is gained only through imprisonment, when it is uniquely possible to see things in true perspective. The consequence of this paradox is that in prison one is likely to meet the finest people, the gentle nonconformists who are most easily oppressed by the functionaries of the State. The story-teller of *The*

Enormous Room, therefore, illustrates through his experience a central reality of the modern world. The communication of this truth is best understood if it is related to a historical facet of the American war writer's cultural situation. The person who narrates the novel is a familiar figure in American literature, the intellectual who makes a pilgrimage to Europe, the matrix of Western civilisation, and witnesses its moral decay. He is at the same time the novitiate in war, one of a line of innocent young men who learn for themselves of its horrors (one recalls the celebrated initiation of Henry Fleming in *The Red Badge of Courage* or of Walt Whitman in *Specimen Days*).

There is in *The Enormous Room*, as in these earlier examples of classic American war literature, an overall suggestion of the power of experience to transform and illuminate. This is symbolised as the reader is conducted imaginatively from the mundane world of the ambulance barracks to the transcendental one of the prison cell which takes on an aura of holiness despite its filth and the frequently obscene language of its inhabitants. The change of scene dramatises the potential for growth in the human psyche, when the vulgar and brutalised officials, both American and French, are supplanted by the 'divine' innocents, the Delectable Mountains. At first reading *The Enormous Room* may appear to be random, eclectic and diffuse, but on closer acquaintance one finds that it is unified by its metaphors of quest, change and development. Its loose unity is also reflected in the novel's experimental word-play, as fairly straightforward narrative prose is superseded by more poetically-heightened rhetoric and syntax. The novel moves interconnectedly from a disavowal of society to a renewed acceptance of it, from a rejection of corrupt officialdom to a recognition that society means simply a galaxy of individuals. From the disenchantment of the book's opening chapter one is carried onwards to the transfigured vision of New York in the final pages, a city seen anew and with deeper understanding. The narrator has now arrived at authentic social awareness through his solidarity with his fellow-prisoners; he has defended their cause, fought their battles, and is finally able to articulate on their behalf the insights so gained through the medium of art.

If Cummings's novel has any traceable conceptual framework it is this poetic exploration of the meaning of community. The word 'poetic' is used advisedly because the narrator's intuitions do, on occasions, as in the incantatory farewells to Surplice and Jean le Nègre, approximate to the poet's states of inspiration, when lyricism is the dominant mood of the writing. This growth towards understanding is conveyed in the contours of the narrative as it moves from chronology to stasis, from a recording of physical events to what seemingly amounts to meditation. These psychological and artistic transformations are interfused with the narrator's adoption of co-operative ventures in the prison as alternatives to the bourgeois way of life that he has left behind. The reader accompanies him from personal vision to social vision, from atrophied tradition to the experimental functions of art, from abstractions such as *La Patrie* to the actuality of human beings, such as the Zulu or the Wanderer. Cummings's dynamic use of artistic form here places him in the mainstream of Modernism, the foremost intellectual movement of his time.

The Enormous Room differs in a variety of ways from other American war novels of its period, a major difference being the degree of overt authorial involvement. Most of Cummings's contemporaries sought to relate unobtrusively to their fiction, and to fictionalise as fully as possible their war experience. In *The Enormous Room* the converse is true: on every page of the novel we encounter what is transparently Cummings himself, strategically ordering the action, panegyrising, striking at governments in the role of agitator or satirist, and never the invisible author. The book, because of this, seems to lie outside the genre of the novel since it draws so heavily on a fusion of diary, memoir and autobiography; and its texture is more personal and idiosyncratic than we normally expect to find in fiction. The novel's point of view is retrospective and critical, as the artist-hero looks back at his former unenlightened self. Cummings's own problematic encounters with new modes of experience are witnessed in letters to his parents written during the time of his imprisonment,[3] and also in his *six non-lectures* (1953) when he outlines interestingly the personal synthesis reached after La Ferté, '. . . I was myself: a temporal citizen of eternity; one with all human beings born and unborn.'[4] The ideology here manifested is utopian and transcendentalist, indicative of the deep social commitment found in *The Enormous Room* itself.

An informal use of fictional devices contributes to the air of playfulness that permeates the novel in sharp contrast to its grim subject matter. Narrative organisation, for example, appears to be relatively unsophisticated: there are no bemusing shifts of perspective or complex structural ironies; and yet the structure of the novel is flexible enough to allow Cummings's comic vision ample scope. The narrator, who addresses the reader directly, has the freedom to digress and elaborate, and so Cummings's own distinctive voice is incorporated into the fiction. The narrator is a version of Cummings himself, and his stance is usually one of nonchalant irony which is appropriate to a victimised but defiant intelligence. Overall the address of the narrator tends towards garrulousness.

This is often irritating when the reader feels he is being buttonholed, but it has its positive side when Cummings breaks with literary convention. An example is his declared intention of escaping from the tyranny of fictional time. People within *The Enormous Room* are enslaved by routine, and it is against this false social mechanism that Cummings, the artist, rebels. His fiction embodies his protest in that he chooses to dispense with the chronological method of narration. *The Enormous Room*, after its first four chapters, substitutes instead an internal and rhythmical principle of organisation which is more appropriate than the 'diary method' because Cummings feels in retrospect that the captivity he has undergone is best articulated impressionistically. He rejects the chronological in favour of the symbolic, wishing to evade the constrictions of 'temporal dimension' because his power of imaginative recall contrariwise is associative and teleological. The effect of Cummings's abandonment of chronological time is that his narrator creates the illusion of a suspension of time in which he is better able to profile the evolving structure of his consciousness and his parallel disenchantment with tradition. 'Fixed' change, implied by what one critic of Cummings's work has referred to as 'novelistic' time,[5] embodies the idea that man is the incarnation of time, a product of the formal standardisation imposed by the State's institutions. Cummings's transfigured men, the heroes of his novel, are liberated by their imprisonment from this systematisation. The barely perceptible plot of *The Enormous Room* and its unorthodox break from the sequential both contribute to our understanding of this process of liberation, the form of the novel thereby felicitously embodying its meaning.

In a valuable article Marilyn Gaull has linked Cummings through his uses of language in *The Enormous Room* with semanticists such as Korzybski, Sapir and Hayakawa.[6] In order to overcome the discrepancy between existent forms of language and the new reality that he encountered Cummings pioneered new language practices, creating improvised linguistic correspondences, different verbal contexts and strange symbolisations. This functional approach to language necessitated a break with discredited linguistic forms such as propaganda, official rhetoric and dead literary language. Marilyn Gaull concludes from her discussion of Cummings's experiments that he differed from the semanticists because his aims, unlike theirs were not social, and ultimately he rejected the 'claims of society'.[7] While accepting the broad lines of her thesis, I believe that she is incorrect in this conclusion. Although he deplored in art the stereotyped 'social conscience', Cummings demonstrates in *The Enormous Room* through his innovatory uses of language the artistic potentialities of a radicalised social conscience, which an examination of his linguistic experiments clearly demonstrates.

Although lacking the sustained inventiveness of Cummings's later works such as *Eimi* (1933), *The Enormous Room*, as Malcolm Cowley has correctly stated,[8] probably had a 'lasting effect' upon American prose. It language derives its spontaneity and colloquial energy from what linguisticians refer to as 'code-making'. Cummings succeeds in renovating language by his experiments in syntax, grammar and spelling and by such strategies as coining new words and manipulating language registers. His intention of creating a new style appropriate to his radical perceptions is indicated by his satiric attacks upon deadened language which for him signifies moral stultification. The narrator, for example, frequently through his own speech parodies the stilted rhetoric of bureaucrats. One sentence is particularly remarkable for its cumulative effect. Lifeless expressions such as *per se, vice versa* or 'respective', abbreviations such as C.O. or g. and g., and clauses drawn out by punctuation and the inevitable parenthesis, all combine to suggest the blindness of officialdom. Cummings informs his reader, in an off-hand way, that 'during the warlike moments recently passed' governments confused greatness with goodness and thought with belief:

> After all, it is highly improbable that this poor socialist suffered more at the hands of the great and good French Government than did many a C.O. at the hands of the great and good American government; or – since all great governments are *per se* good and *vice versa* – than did many a man in general who was cursed with a talent for thinking during the warlike moments recently passed; during that is to say an epoch when the g. and g. nations demanded of their respective peoples the exact antithesis to thinking; said antithesis being vulgarly called Belief. (p. 154)

The antidote to debased official language of moral obfuscation is the idiosyncratic and exploratory language of the narrator when he pays tribute to his friends. Often the element of improvisation in these passages recalls the intricate phrasing of jazz where deep feeling is similarly conveyed through experimental lyrics. An example is the narrator's farewell to Jean le Nègre, a magnificent savage in the tradition of Queequeg in *Moby Dick*. Here the image-laden prose tentatively seeks out meanings in its celebration of human resilience,

> – Boy, Kid, Nigger with the strutting muscles – take me up into your mind once or twice before I die (you know why: just because the eyes of me and you will be full of dirt some day). Quickly take me up into the bright child of your mind, before we both go suddenly all loose and silly (you know how it will feel). Take me up (carefully; as if I were a toy) and play carefully with me, once or twice, before I and you go suddenly all limp and foolish. Once or twice before you go into great Jack roses and ivory – (once or twice Boy before we together go wonderfully down into the Big Dirt laughing, bumped with the last darkness). (p. 296)

Cummings's use of language in *The Enormous Room* bears a uniquely personal stamp. Inevitably verbal comedy draws upon the traditional rhetorical devices employed by the satirist, irony, periphrasis, and hyperbole, but in addition Cummings creatively uses modern slang making an idiom both highly individualistic and yet distinctively American (a gendarme, for example, is graphically described as a 'rube movie-cop personage' or as a member of the 'gum-shoe fraternity' whose victim insultingly looks 'several blocks through him').

In a book where transitions are rapid the narrator may easily catch the reader off guard by capturing instead of this comic voice the tone of the political dissenter or anarchist. The language then becomes formal and coolly rational with more than a hint of menace. Examples of this occur when the narrator sounds a note of warning to the French authorities for their inhumane treatment of his friends, the Machine-Fixer and Bill the Hollander.[9]

It is possible to detect the influence of Cummings's fusion of the sacramental and the scatological, his blend of high seriousness and hudibrastic comedy in the work of recent American novelists who have written of war. Joseph Heller's satiric exposure of bureaucracy in *Catch 22* (1966) is akin to that of *The Enormous Room*, and William Eastlake's colloquial yet embellished style in *Castle Keep* (1966) or *The Bamboo Bed* (1970) has affinities with that of Cummings. Like these writers, Cummings conceived of war as a manic incoherence, a state of madness whose illogicality demanded from the novelist a commensurately 'different' language and form. It may therefore be no coincidence that the principal character in Kurt Vonnegut's *Slaughterhouse-Five* (1970) is named Billy Pilgrim, obliquely complementing the manner in which *The Enormous Room* ironically relates to Bunyan's famous allegory. Cummings's fictional response to his war imprisonment is retrospectively seen to be a sophisticated one which anticipated the movement away from naturalism in American war writing during the sixties and seventies.

In the later chapters of the novel, which are devoted to panegyrics of the Wanderer, the Zulu, Surplice and Jean le Nègre, Cummings introduces the reader to autonomous human beings in whom selfhood remains intact despite all attempts to subjugate it. Whereas many war artists such as Nash and Nevinson and novelists such as Dos Passos and Barbusse emphasised the way individuality was obliterated by war, Cummings chose to stress the opposite. *The Enormous Room* is essentially about the intractability of the individual when caught up within depersonalising forces. Portraits of richly individualised men pack the novel (there are scores of them) who appear to be larger than life and who exist in living defiance of the dehumanisation that threatens to engulf them. An example is the Zulu to whom Cummings refers in the following manner as though affirming the endurance of the human personality and its resistance to stereotypes:

> There are certain things in which one is unable to believe for the simple reason that one never ceases to believe them. Things of this sort – things which are always inside of us and in fact are us and which consequently will not be pushed off or away where we can begin thinking about them – are no longer things; they, and the us which they are, equals A Verb; an IS. The Zulu, then, I must perforce call an IS. (p. 239)

Cummings's reverence for the perfection of the inner man, as displayed in his portrait of the Zulu, recalls the transcendentalism of Emerson and Thoreau, and Cummings echoes these New England writers, his regional literary ancestors, in his stress upon the inviolability of the soul. Like them also, he praises natural man, who is unshackled by prejudice, education or habit, and whose dignity is derived from self-reliance. The Zulu is such a man, who has the power to communicate without the aid of language, such is the magnetism of his presence. The force of such men countervails the depredation of war, as they have command over 'the unwritten and the unspoken' as well as over 'the unspeakable and the unwritable'. Because of this they are beyond the reach of the gaolers who seek to degrade them.

Zulu, Surplice, the Wanderer and Jean le Nègre, the Delectable Mountains of Cummings's novel, have an inviolable identity similar to that which the artist himself must cultivate. In the prison of La Ferté, which is analogous to the world outside its walls, only art has the potential to create a new order of relations and of understanding. The novelist indicates the affirmative value of this potential new order by pointing to its opposite when he castigates 'the Great American Public' for its 'defunct ideals and ideas' which are a consequence of misplaced education. Authentic art cannot flourish until the

>   *... bon trucs*
> (whereby we are taught to see and imitate on canvas and in stone and by words this so-called world) are entirely and thoroughly and perfectly annihilated by that vast and painful process of Unthinking which may result in a minute bit of purely personal Feeling. Which minute bit is Art. (p. 309)

The true artist must submit himself to a creative annihilation which leads to a process of rebuilding and consolidation. By insisting on this 'amputation' of the past Cummings rejects existing cultural values. Art is, by implication, a part of the process that leads to the formation of a more democratic social order. This is clearly illustrated in the person of the painter Count Bragard, an inhabitant of the camp who claims to have known Cézanne and Vanderbilt and who turns out to be a confidence trickster. Art is shown to be not the prerogative of such as Bragard, who represents the decadence of high culture; it belongs equally to the prisoners who joyfully collect for Cummings leaves and other objects when he wishes to study colour in abstract art. Bragard's values are elitist and stultified, the expression of a rarefied high culture; authentic art resists reification and involves a revolution of the intelligent who share a vision of common human sympathy.

The unorthodox form of Cummings's novel, its early abandonment of the chronological method of narration and its subjective framework, which stresses the wholeness of the individual man or woman, should not detract from a recognition of what Cummings has in common with other Lost Generation writers. Like Dos Passos and Stallings, Boyd and Hemingway, he came to regard his contact with the human debris of war as a deepening of his education: as an aesthetician and creative artist he disowned the traditional art forms that he associated with the older intelligentsia who had supported the War; and, as did his contemporaries, he felt a profound sense of cultural disaffiliation from his father's generation. Cummings's novel goes beyond these shared attitudes however in its unique apprehension of the psychology of the prisoner of war camp. This is outwardly shown in *The Enormous Room* by the great number of people who are socially deracinated from their local environment. In this situation where, for example, the Wanderer, an archetypal refugee and one of Cummings's noble characters, is unfeelingly separated from his wife and children, people are constantly on the move. Significantly La Ferté is a *Porte de Triage*, a halfway house and receiving-station from which prisoners are shunted on to other destinations, and some of the most moving scenes of the novel involve partings, perhaps the most memorable being when Cummings and Brown bid farewell to Surplice.

The case of Surplice, an uneducated Pole who is defined by his association with filth and who is frequently spotted from head to toe with excrement, illustrates almost clinically how persecution originates. While Cummings recognises the inward radiance of Surplice, which shines through the superficial dirt, the other prisoners exploit his inadequacy and add to his suffering. They attempt to torment him by calling him 'Syph-lis' and 'Chaude-Pisse the Pole' and by giving him menial tasks such as emptying the urine pails, but in so doing they degrade themselves by imitating the actions of their own oppressors. When shown courtesy by Cummings and Brown, Surplice becomes a reconstituted man, proud, erect, appreciative and modest, and yet to the other inhabitants of the camp he is merely 'a symbol of all that is evil'. Ironically Surplice enjoys his humiliation which entails wearing the 'cap and bells' because this constitutes a recognition of his existence.

La Ferté offers many opportunities for this kind of exploitation and, as a by-product, heroism also flourishes.

Despite the verminous aspects of behaviour displayed in their treatment of Surplice the prisoners, including the criminals and vagrants, are capable of facing up to their common humanity, the more sensitive of them realising that they are dependent upon each other and that property is valuable only in so far as it is shared among others. Cummings and Brown, also acknowledging this, escape the privileges of their class and reject its competitive ethic by sharing their private possessions with their outcast companions. It is in these circumstances of common deprivation, when men have time to reflect upon their own adversity and the misery of others, that genuine social vision is possible. Insights gained from this disavowal of privatisation may also be applied to the State's ideological justification for war when it is necessary to drill beneath propaganda and investigate what the novelist refers to as the 'careful and ornate structures of *"La Gloire"* ' Cummings has a chance to do this when one of the women, Lena, is tortured by the *Directeur* in punishment for a trivial misdemeanour. Her fate exemplifies how the security services of a democracy at war operate at ground level. Lena is barbarously confined to her filthy *cabinot* for sixteen days, and Cummings has the chance to witness her martyrdom. He notes 'the indestructible bravado of her gait and carriage, the unchanging timbre of her terrible laughter in response to the salutation of an inhabitant of The Enormous Room'. Lena was seriously ill and probably dying, and the novelist 'watched the skin gradually assume a distinct greenish tint (a greenishness which . . . suggested putrefaction); heard the coughing to which she had always been subject grow thicker and deeper. . . .' Cummings is both intellectually and emotionally affected by witnessing Lena's fate, and the atrocity contributes to the growth of his moral humanism,

> . . . I realised fully and irrevocably and for perhaps the first time the meaning of civilisation. And I realised that it was true – as I had previously only suspected it to be true – that in finding us unworthy of helping to carry forward the banner of progress, alias the tricolour, the inimitable and excellent French Government was conferring upon B. and myself – albeit with other intent – the ultimate compliment. (p. 181)

In passages such as this, where Cummings synthesises analysis and observation, he manages successfully to capitalise on his privileged insider's position. I know of no American writer of either the First or Second World War who was able to depict so effectively the corrosive effects of incarceration: we have to go back to an unacknowledged American Civil War classic, *John Ransom's Diary*, originally entitled

Andersonville, for an American account of war imprisonment that is in any way comparable. The tone of Cummings's account of Lena's torture is that of a super-articulate prisoner empowered to speak on behalf of the helpless casualties of war, the social flotsam wrongly and easily picked out as likely to give trouble, above all, the inarticulate, the dirty and the hungry.

The overriding impression of *The Enormous Room* derives from incidents such as these when Cummings anarchically strikes at the apparatus of the State in defence of his belief in political freedom. This is the basis of his social vision.

5   Henri Barbusse: *Le Feu* and the Crisis of Social Realism

Jonathan King

Henri Barbusse was born in 1873. Before the war he worked as a civil servant and journalist; he published poems, prose-poems and one novel, *L'Enfer* (1908), all of which are heavily marked by Symbolism. He volunteered for the army in 1914 and served in the front line from December of that year until early 1916, when he was hospitalised. He was active in founding, with Romain Rolland, the Amsterdam-Pleyel movement and joined the Communist Party in 1921. He became a member of the Party's Central Committee and his work after the war became increasingly ideological, including studies of Lenin and Stalin. He died in Moscow in 1935.

Le Feu, the novel which made him famous, was written in the trenches and completed in hospital. It first appeared in instalments in *L'Oeuvre* from August 1916, and in book form later the same year, when it was awarded the Prix Goncourt.[1] By 1918 it had sold a quarter of a million copies and had been translated into several languages. Strangely, it was left untouched by the censor, but, being the first really unvarnished account of life in the trenches to appear in France, it created an enormous stir and gave rise to some violent political and literary controversy.[2]

All critics have since agreed that *Le Feu* is in some sense a 'realist' work. Few, however, have attempted to develop this assumption stylistically or historically. Most discussions of Barbusse's realism have treated 'realistic' as a synonym for 'true', and have involved rather sterile discussions of the accuracy of Barbusse's picture of trench warfare.[3] This is a pity, since a deeper treatment of this aspect not only illuminates *Le Feu* but also casts some light on the nature and development of realism, particularly social realism, itself.

The development of realism in literature was intimately connected with developments in science. The inference of general laws from the empirical observation of reality, the construction of rational hypotheses regarding the behaviour of matter or of humans passed, as a broad working method, from the hands of natural or behavioural scientists into the hands of writers. Nineteenth-century science combined minute attention to the particular with an inbuilt urge to reach out and grasp the universal, the secret principles of matter and of society. It involved the gifts of the observer, working towards an ever more detailed picture of reality, and the gifts of the prophet or visionary, working towards an ever wider perspective, an ever more inclusive pattern, or set of images. This if of course most obviously true of the social science of Marx and the biological science of Darwin, the two figures who exerted the most profound influence on the realism and naturalism of late nineteenth-century literature. Darwin's painstaking observations of the natural world culminate in the assertion of an evolutionary biological time scale, as Marx and Engels, through sociological and economic research, seek to establish a dialectical pattern on the whole of human social history.

Balzac, writing before Marxist and Darwinian thought had penetrated the literary consciousness of Europe, could present the individual and the social, the human and the historical, as a whole. There is little sense, in Balzac, of the individual being involved in a process which transcends him or is separate from him. The transcendent force in a Balzac novel is the passion which emanates from the individual himself. There is no cosmic *background* to the action of a work by Balzac, no sense of time flowing in an historical or evolutionary rhythm, behind and beyond his characters, no film behind the stage. On the contrary, what background there is is presented as an organic part of the characters, and what history there is seems to be an inextricable part of the life of the individual.

This type of realism, which, in the work of Balzac, Stendhal or Flaubert, is most satisfying in a literary, aesthetic sense because it lends wholeness of concept and unity of tone to the novels of these writers, is not easily compatible with the developments in natural and social science which dominated the latter part of the nineteenth century. For Marx, although man makes his own history, this history is also something which transcends him as an individual; it is much more than the aggregate of individual actions. For Darwin, not only man as an individual, but man as a species is transcended in a broader current of biological evolution and conflict. A chasm begins to appear between the foreground and the background of human existence, between what men are and what they are a part of. This had profound consequences for literature, particularly as this literature was showing an ever greater receptiveness to and respect for scientific thought.

These consequences are particularly evident in a writer like Zola. Zola believed in the scientific method which formulates general laws and predictions on the basis of careful observation. In other words, he

believed that the novelist, like the scientist, had to be at the same time
objective and prophetic, had to do justice to the foreground and background of human existence, the action on the stage and the back-
projection of social and biological evolution. Transferred to the realm
of literature, the achievement of such aims involves the combination
of two literary modes – the documentary and the visionary, a combination which involves a potentially awkward mixing of styles. To convey
the evolutionary sweep of history in *Germinal* Zola has recourse to a
sometimes heavy symbolism involving the transformation of the setting
of the novel. He sensed that the key to history no longer lay with the
individual bankers and aristocrats of the *Comédie Humaine*, but with
the masses. But the masses had little conscious grasp of their role: they
were a part of social and genetic evolution in spite of themselves.
Their individual actions, the minutiae of their lives, their expressed
and unexpressed thoughts, could not easily carry the message of their
historical role. This could only be done by a transformation of the
setting of their drama into a symbolic terrain, pregnant with hope and
fear, violence and creativity.

Such, in brief, was Zola's method of combining the documentary
and prophetic modes implicit in his variety of social realism. It was a
method which, to a degree, sacrificed aesthetic unity to the demands of
an acute sensitivity to historical evolution and the role of the masses in
this evolution. But the problems Zola faced – whether or not he himself
saw them as problems – remained for the novelist working within the
traditions of social realism. From the Naturalists onward, through the
work of the Unanimists of the early twentieth century, the populist
and proletarian schools of the nineteen-twenties and nineteen-thirties,
powerful documentary had an irresistible tendency to culminate in
clumsy prophecy, observation to be abandoned in favour of vision.
Critics were unanimous – and still are – in seeing these clashes of style
as aesthetic errors, clumsy gaffes, motivated by the desire to propagate
a political or spiritual message. This, as I hope we can now see, is only
part of the truth. Clumsy propaganda and banal prophecy did become
almost an integral part of social realism. The desire to grab people and
rub their noses in the squalor all around them obviously goes hand in
hand with the desire to change, to improve, to preach. But the awkward lapses into the language of prophecy are not always wilful. They
are symptomatic of a crisis within the history of realism itself, of a
problem not easy to overcome. Realism had at some stage to bring
within its orbit the masses as well as the individual, just as it had to
take account of suggestions emanating from the world of science that
some kind of blind, but not necessarily malevolent, force was at work
in human history. Realism was forced to be increasingly close to documentary journalism at the same time as being forced in the direction

of prophecy and vision, allegory and symbol. It acquired the subject matter associated with Naturalism together with the methods of Symbolism. This is one way, I believe, of seeing the development of social realist fiction from Zola to its sad apotheosis in the seven brave tractor drivers.

Barbusse's *Le Feu* marks a key moment in this development. The writer who wished to provide some kind of realist treatment of the First World War was confronted with the above problems in a peculiarly concentrated form. The masses were now present in vast numbers as protagonists in the outcome of history. The worker, the peasant, the bureaucrat was lifted out of his normal environment and made the lynchpin of the various armies. Not so much tactical brilliance or technological superiority, but the sheer weight of numbers would largely determine the outcome of this war. On the other hand, this most plebeian and democratic of wars was also the most obviously apocalyptic, representing, in both its material and spiritual aspects, a genuine crisis of civilisation, not just another shifting of pieces in the diplomatic chess game of Europe. The 'sense of an ending', prefigured in so much *fin de siècle* art and literature, was written into every action of the war, every new episode of mass slaughter, every new scar on the landscape of the Western Front. Furthermore, the writer – novelist or poet – found himself, due to the sociological promiscuity implicit in a mass conscript army, at very close quarters with representatives of those strata of society which previously may have formed the object of rather more detached 'research'. His record of the war would tend simultaneously toward documentary and toward epic, his style oscillate between the demotic and the matter-of-fact required by documentary, and the symbolic and visionary required by his sense of proximity to the apocalypse. If the surface reality of life in the trenches could be captured by recording objectively the ordinary soldier's habits of speech and behaviour, the significance of the war could most obviously be perceived by turning one's eyes away from the trenches themselves, on to the landscape separating the two armies.

Trench warfare created on the one hand extreme intimacy and on the other the sense of being marooned in an alien and desolated landscape; two lines of underground, smelly slums separated by a scarred, lunar terrain. Barbusse's novel contains what can almost be thought of as two separate pieces of literature: a documentary about men at war and a poem about the landscape of war, much as *Germinal* is both a documentary about the life of miners and a poem about destruction and fecundity. But Barbusse was less able than Zola to maintain an organic connection between the two, because the dualism of his material was more extreme.

The terrain in part created by the battles of the Western Front was obviously something new in warfare. Previous to the First World War, armed conflict had left little imprint on the natural landscape. But on the Somme and the Marne, as the artillery grew more powerful and more sophisticated, new rivers could appear overnight, hillocks disappear, craters be carved out of level ground, trees be scythed down and sucked into the mud; barbed wire, pickets and corpses could rust and freeze into prematurely aged forests of steel and flesh, wood and bone. Whole villages would vanish, river-beds dry up, strange new plants grow where they shouldn't. All this – which the soldiers could gaze at day in and day out – was somehow visible evidence that the war, that history itself, had gone beyond man's control, that not just the fate of nations, but the fate of the material world itself was at stake here. The reality of this war was a grotesque mixture of the apocalyptic and the banal, the small-scale and the large-scale, noise and silence, ever-changing landscape only temporarily populated and never-changing, over-populated trenches. One or two random remarks in Barbusse's war notebook show how deeply he was aware of such contrasts. 'The war goes on only because of the hidden labours of these tiny, ant-like creatures. Because of the vast numbers, each soldier is as if invisible and silent. ... The Truth. The battlefield. The vast night. The men like so many worms.'[4] What artist would be capable of conveying the wholeness of the experience, of encompassing within a single style what the soldiers did individually and the consequences of their actions as a mass? Where was the connection between the mundane humanity of the ordinary soldier's response to war and the destruction the war was bringing to life and to nature? The stylistic duality of *Le Feu* reflects the difficulty of expressing the connection, if indeed the connection exists.

To convey the horrific landscape of trench warfare Barbusse employs an imagery and a vocabulary which are highly figurative, tending always away from description towards symbolism; while to convey the way of life of the soldiers he uses a style which is objective and colloquial. Landscape and men – the tableaux which make up *Le Feu* alternate regularly between the two. Descriptions of actual combat are comparatively rare.

And yet the landscape is formed in part from the flesh and bone of the soldiers themselves. As, on the morning after an engagement, the dawn casts some light on the battlefield, the sentries glimpse the petrified remains of their fellow soldiers. Through the rain and mist they can see 'strange heaps of clothing, slimy and sticky with reddish-brown mud ... the dead are slowly emerging from the darkness' (pp. 126–7). In fact, so great are the numbers of dead that the battlefield has itself turned into a conglomeration of buried and half-buried corpses:

'The ground is so full of dead bodies that where the earth caves in limbs stick out of the ground like rows of spikes ... the soil here is made up of several layers of corpses ... the earth is itself corpse-like ... German corpses lie mangled and broken, like debris in the wake of a hellish flood' (p. 223). The vocabulary becomes increasingly figurative and employs more and more conventionally 'literary' images: 'This stream of filth and flesh ... these plague-ridden shores, this valley of destruction (p. 223).

Pestilence and flood – the archetypal images of disaster and punishment – lend to the descriptions their intensely apocalyptic tone. Sometimes, under ceaseless torrential rain, trenches turn into rivers and shell craters into lakes:

> Everything is inundated. The battlefield is not asleep, it is dead. ... Row upon row of still, silent shapes, watery, muddy bundles. These are the sentries. They didn't have time to extricate themselves from the mud. (pp. 266–7)

The ground between the trenches is an 'unearthly resting-place', a naked arm protrudes from the mud, the arm of a soldier drowned before he could move out of his shell-hole. 'Hell is water' (p. 269), Barbusse concludes.

A war where the soldier may as easily die from drowning as from gunfire obviously has an unprecedented and unnatural quality. In trying to destroy each other, two vast armies are destroying the world itself, laying the ground bare like a skeleton, inundating it with floods, setting it on fire, changing its shape, corrupting its subsoil with putrefying flesh. This observed reality can most readily be conveyed with imagery which is apocalyptic and visionary: 'everything has the odour of a great cataclysm', 'the scene looked like the half-dried up bed of a river, shattered and expanded, abandoned both by the waters and by men', 'petrified ocean', 'the field like a necropolis, riddled with holes', 'a world mangled in a cataclysm ... huge rocks scattered like the ruins of ancient monuments'.[5]

In his other war novel, *Clarté*, published three years later, Barbusse allows this apocalyptic tone to get quite out of hand, merging it with a grandiose imagery and a religiosity which are no longer controlled by a firm documentary purpose. The soldiers of *Le Feu*, up to the closing chapter of the book at least, by their very ordinariness throw the landscape of war into horrifying relief. But in *Clarté* the commitment to realism surrenders almost totally to prophetic pretensions. The hero of *Clarté* has a vocabulary and a sensibility all too easily in tune with his surroundings. The tension between humanity and historical crisis is destroyed, as the cataclysm is no longer perceived as alien, but accepted and almost revelled in.

In *Le Feu*, however, the divorce between the soldier and the war, between the men crouching in the opposing trenches and the lunar wasteland confronting them, is absolute and daunting. One chapter in particular in Barbusse's novel expresses powerfully this divorce. This chapter is entitled simply 'Le Barda', or 'The Pack'. Set between two apocalyptic battle-scenes, it shows Barbusse's documentary gifts at their best. It is a good example of one of mimetic realism's most valuable qualities: humane attention to the concrete details of existence. The contents of the soldier's pack, the painstaking inventory of the paraphernalia he carries around with him, tells us more about the realities of life in the trenches, its squalor and its superstitions, than pages of dialogue or narrative.

Barbusse's squad is spending the night in a barn, prior to going into the front line the next day. Private Volpatte is inspecting with care the contents of his pack, haversack, and pockets. Here everything is on a small scale, tiny tokens of the man's practicality and his affections. First come the 'essentials': handkerchief, pipe, tobacco pouch, cigarette papers, knife, wallet, cigarette lighter. (At this point one is reminded of another, comparable memorable chapter in *Le Feu*, called simply 'Matches', which conveys, again obliquely and powerfully, the exigencies of life in the trenches. Here the squad finds itself without matches, therefore unable to smoke, keep warm, eat or see, and is finally driven to kill a stray German soldier in order to get a box.) After the bare essentials come the more idiosyncratic objects which experience has taught Volpatte to value: two leather bootlaces wrapped round a pocket watch, a square mirror and a round mirror, the latter broken, a small bottle of turps, another of mineral essence, another empty, the buckle from a German soldier's belt, a German epaulette wrapped in paper, a dart, scissors, canteen, a stub of pencil and a stub of candle, a tube of aspirin and opium tablets, several empty tins. Other objects are not easy to identify and their purpose somewhat unclear. Volpatte explains to the narrator: the fingers can be cut out of the German officer's glove and used to cover the end of his rifle barrel; the telephone wire is best for sewing on buttons; the white thread is much superior to the regulation issue ... The list is virtually endless and could be duplicated, with myriad variations, for every infantryman's pack. What strikes the narrator most among Volpatte's belongings is an enormous bundle of miscellaneous papers: writing paper, a notebook stuffed with bits of paper, letters and photos, the most prized being of his wife and children. A map, an old newspaper, a pack of cards, an impromptu chess set made of pieces of paper.

Another soldier, Barque, is anxious to show the superiority of his belongings, which include a German soldier's pay-book, iodine, a Browning revolver, two knives. An argument develops around the relative merits of the various prize possessions: string, nails, buttons. Research shows that each soldier has a total of eighteen pockets about his person, pockets which, like the pack, are used to contain valued and sometimes eccentric items of equipment: compass, tinderbox, a tin whistle (this last given to the owner by his wife, who suggested he could use it to summon help if wounded on the battlefield). Subsidiary questions arise, such as where is the best place to carry your water bottle. Finally, discussion turns to the contents of the wallet, which rarely holds any money and is used for carrying letters from home. Barbusse sums up:

> A melancholy array indeed. Everything made for the soldier is coarse, ugly and of poor quality, from their cardboard-like footwear to the tattered badges held together with frayed cotton, to their ill-fitting clothes, badly-made, badly sewn, of threadbare harsh cloth – like blotting paper – which keeps out neither sun nor rain, their webbing, which is as brittle and torn as wood shavings and their flannel linen which is thinner than cotton, their tobacco which is like straw. (p. 149)

But if the equipment issued to the soldiers is bad to the point of being useless, the private belongings, some of them of sentimental value, few of them of practical value, serve mainly to weigh the soldier down. All this paraphernalia is a mere supplement to the load carried on the back, the heavy gear – tent canvas, iron rations, blankets, spare boots.

The conversation dies away in stray recollections of home, job and family, in disconnected anecdote and half-hearted protest. Some sleep is snatched before dawn and the march back to the front line. The narrator looks round at his fellow soldiers: 'these creatures huddled here together, brought by events from every part of the country. I look at them all, sunk in inertia and forgetfulness, some of them clinging desperately to their pitiful preoccupations, with their slave-like instincts and ignorance' (p. 156). And the chapter concludes on a note which in some ways is the key to the novel: 'faced with this profound vision of the wretched human darkness which fills this shrouded cave, I begin to dream of some great indefinable light' (p. 156). This dream of a 'great light', the dream which will become explicit in the visionary conversations which conclude the book, and which has already been stated in a kind of prelude called 'The Vision', follows from the tension between the apocalyptic setting and the intensely human and limited actors, with their banal concerns, between on the one hand the 'pitiful preoccupations' and 'slave-like ignorance' and on the other the 'unearthly resting place', the 'world mangled in a cataclysm'.

In a note, Barbusse refers to one of his aims as being to 'deepen the tragic aspect of the banality of war' (p. 294). This he achieves effortlessly by juxtaposing chapters like 'The Pack' or 'Matches' with settings of epic violence and destruction. These chapters are masterpieces of documentary realism.[6] But we can already see, from the remarks of Barbusse at the end, that he is deeply bothered by the tensions implicit in the contrasting aspects of war. He can be faithful to the reality of the soldier's life, he can succeed in puncturing the absurd romanticising of the *poilu* which goes on in civilian circles. He can keep his promise to reproduce his comrades' conversation without censoring the *gros mots* with which it is liberally sprinkled.[7] He reproduces dialect, the fractured syntax of popular speech; an attempt is even made to represent phonetically the sounds and rhythms of colloquial French. By being a scrupulous observer of material reality, faithful recorder of the demotic, Barbusse is writing within the traditions of social realism. But he is also within its traditions in his sense of the epic, his grasp of evolutionary forces, his awareness of a society collapsing, of a civilisation on the brink of apocalypse, in his sense of a 'great light'. And all this he expresses through his evocation of the setting of war, through the highly symbolic vocabulary and prophetic tone of the descriptions of the deathly landscape of no-man's land. Not until the very end of the novel, in the chapter called 'The Dawn', does Barbusse attempt to fuse within a single style both events and actors, and he does so in a way which is obviously fraught with danger. He abruptly endows the soldiers of the squad with a visionary sense equal to his own,[8] with an improbable articulateness and sense of history, with a vocabulary commensurate with the magnitude of the events they are involved in. This eloquence is clearly incongruous: a representative piece of conversation goes as follows: 'In reality the soldier's sacrifice is a veiled form of suppression. Those drawn from the masses to storm the enemy trenches have no reward. They launch themselves into the terrifying void of everlasting glory' (p. 285).

That ingredient of social realism which requires scrupulous verisimilitude is sacrificed to its visionary proclivities, its sociological sensitivity to its historical sensitivity. It is not so much that the ending of *Le Feu* represents an abandonment of social realism; rather it represents the surrender of one of its elements to the other, as Barbusse's novel as a whole reveals the mixture of styles implicit in the genre. The chapter 'The Pack' and the chapter 'The Dawn' are equally representative of that genre. In the same way as *Germinal*, though of course far more blatantly, *Le Feu* ends with a statement of faith which, in manner as well as substance, is somewhat at odds with what has gone before. Furthermore, to clinch his belief in the possibility of historical and evolutionary progress, Barbusse, like Zola, is forced away from people towards an image drawn from nature, from reality to abstraction, from observation to prophecy:

And as we prepare to join the others, to go back to war, the dark sky, heavy with cloud, slowly lightens above our heads. From between two masses of cloud, a shaft of light emerges, and this light, small, melancholy, vulnerable as it is, nevertheless proves that the sun exists. (p. 286)

One way of seeing *Le Feu*, then, is as a work which marks a critical point in the history of social realism. Indeed, one might almost see it as a terminal work.[9] The 'proletarian' and 'populist' schools of fiction which proliferated in France and elsewhere in the nineteen-twenties and nineteen-thirties produced little of value. If the writer within these groups was politically committed, the prophetic and epic sweep of the genre degenerated into the mouthing of Communist orthodoxy.[10] Otherwise, history was banished altogether and the writer concentrated on the apotheosis of the 'common man'.[11] In other words, social realism became a decadent genre, and both these forms of decadence are, in a sense, prefigured in *Le Feu*, but there rendered almost imperceptible by the novel's astonishing documentary force. But neither the strengths nor the weaknesses of Barbusse's novel can be appreciated, still less explained, unless one stops seeing it purely as a 'war novel' and attempts to place it in the history of realist fiction.

6 The Soldier's Stage: Roland Dorgelès, *Les Croix de Bois*

John Flower

> Ah, si tout cela pouvait
> n'être que du théâtre
> Louis Aragon

Few French writers in the twentieth century have owed their reputation to a single work to quite the same extent as has Roland Dorgelès
to his second novel, *Les Croix de Bois* (1919). Dorgelès (real name
Roland Lécavelé) was born in Amiens in 1886 and educated in Paris,
where his parents hoped he would eventually follow a career as an
architect. He soon tired of the academic discipline at the Ecole des
Arts décoratifs, however, and became involved with the bohemian
world of the Lapin Agile café in Montmartre, striking up a close friendship with Francis Carco and Pierre Mac-Orlan. Like many of his contemporaries he tried his hand at journalism, writing in *Paris-Journal*,
Fantasio and *Sourire*, and at play-writing, two short pieces *Merci d'être
venue* (1913) and *Pour faire son chemin* (1914) appearing shortly
before the outbreak of war.[1] Dorgelès's recollections of these early years
in *Quand j'étais Montmartrois* (1936) suggest he was a rather irres-
ponsible, rootless young man with a taste for practical jokes.[2] At the
same time a feeling that the older generation had abandoned its duties
towards the young was beginning to develop in him, becoming particularly strong as the threat of war increased. Dorgelès sided with the
pacifists and although he was not an outspoken critic of rampant
nationalism like Romain Rolland he was arrested outside the Gare de
l'Est for participating in an anti-militarist demonstration. But this
attitude was short-lived. As he admitted subsequently, for him as for
so many others, the prospect of being left in a minority was too daunting: 'Those who stayed behind were ashamed and the next morning
there were going to be thousands of us laying siege to the recruiting
offices in order to join up, only afraid that we might arrive too
late.'[3] In August 1914 therefore he joined the army on the wave of
enthusiasm and patriotism[4] which was to carry so many of his fellow-

countrymen to their death, hoping to be reunited with his friend Mac-Orlan in the 269th Regiment. Instead Dorgelès was sent first to Rouen with the the 39th and subsequently to Champagne and Artois, where from September throughout the winter of 1914–15 he experienced military action as a member of a machine gun team. In July 1915 he was made a corporal and was twice mentioned in despatches. After being wounded he was posted in 1916 to the aviation section of the armed forces but only succeeded in crashing a training plane and was fortunate to escape with his life. During his convalescence in Paris Dorgelès was asked by Maurice Sorton, the editor of *L'Heure*, to write a novel and together with his friend Régis Gignoux produced in fifteen days a piece of satirical make-believe, *La Machine à finir la guerre*. Although this first novel appears to have passed virtually unnoticed[5] the experience was sufficiently encouraging for him to consider working at the material he had already begun collecting in note form in a copy of *Le pasteur Jarousseau au désert* given to him by one of his lieutenants. After his convalescence he was sent to Longvic near Dijon as an instructor. Here he at last found the opportunity to write at leisure and the idea of *Les Croix de Bois* rapidly materialised:

> Everything that I had stored up burst in an instant as if pierced by a scalpel. My head, my heart and even my flesh were so swollen with war that without the outlet of a pen in which blood flowed in the place of ink I would have died stifled.
>
> I worked relentlessly, evening, morning, in all my free moments and on the coldest days in winter I often got up before daybreak, swathed in blankets to go on with the page which I had stopped the previous evening. One fear spurred me on: that of dying without leaving any work.[6]

In spite of its having been conceived and written during the war years *Les Croix de Bois* was not published until 1 April 1919 – the very day Dorgelès himself was demobilised – by which time a number of other novels deploring the devastation and dehumanising effect of war had already appeared – Montherlant's *L'Exil* (1915), the early volumes of Genevoix's *Ceux de Verdun* (1915–22), Duhamel's *Vie des Martyrs* (1917) and *Civilisation* (1918), for example. With the exception of Barbusse's *Le Feu* (1916), however, none could pre-empt the claim of *Les Croix de Bois* to be the most influential anti-war novel of its time. Yet ironically the success of the earlier novel can be seen to be in part responsible for the enthusiastic reception given to *Les Croix de Bois* even though Dorgelès, unlike Barbusse, was denied the accolade of the Prix Goncourt which went narrowly instead to Proust for his *A l'ombre des jeunes filles en fleur*. By way of compensation Dorgelès had to be content with the Prix Vie Heureuse awarded by a jury of lady writers and critics; as he remarked not without a trace of bitterness in 1920: 'The old men had wounded me; the gentle hands of women now tended me; what more could I ask for?'[7] In fact Dorgelès had little to worry about. *Les Croix de Bois*, widely translated and made into a film in 1932 continued to be a best-seller, and Dorgelès was able to devote the rest of his life to writing. Much of his later work, especially his novels, is of a more popular kind and he never recaptured the atmosphere of *Les Croix de Bois* on such a large scale again. Thereafter until his death in 1973 and especially during the occupation he continued to criticise intolerance and oppression in any form.

In order to arrive at a publishable version of his material Dorgelès had to overcome two main obstacles. The first was one of sheer bulk. When he came to 'write up' his notes he found he had a surfeit of material – 'a pyramid of episodes where I chopped about at random'.[8] The second was the censor. As a result of his objections three entire chapters were removed ('La Boule de gui', 'Permissionnaires', 'La Rouquine') though they were eventually published in *Le Cabaret de la Belle Femme* (1928). But Dorgelès decided at the last minute to defy the censor and to retain what in many ways is his most bitter comment on war, 'Mourir pour la patrie', a chapter which deserves to be compared with Barbusse's account of the execution of a deserter in 'Argoval' (*Le Feu*, Chapter x). Yet Dorgelès did not intend his novel to be simply a random selection of disparate episodes in the lives of one or several soldiers; nor a thinly disguised account of his own wartime experience. His ambitions were much grander:

> Not for one moment did I think of keeping the diary of my regiment. My ambition was greater: not to tell the story of *my* war, but of *the* war.[9]

And in an interview with Frédéric Lefevre and again in his own *Souvenirs sur 'Les Croix de Bois'*, he insists on his role as a witness: 'If I write it is in order to be of service [. . .] my ambition is to be the lyrical witness of my generation',[10] and 'I learned to suffer in order that I could act as a witness for those who have suffered so much.'[11] Underlying this was a moral stance, a feeling that society lacked 'a higher form of morality',[12] and a belief that literature if not openly didactic should at least be purposeful. In the words of the curious Christ-like figure Magloire in *Saint Magloire* (1922): 'All words are useless which do not attempt to make life better.' Yet if it is compared to *Le Réveil des Morts* (1923), in which Dorgelès – not unlike Barbusse in *Clarté* (1919) – allows his personal feelings to distort the psychological authenticity of his characters and his narrative technique, *Les Croix de Bois* is free from any extensive, overt moralising. Indeed as contemporary reviewers noted, whatever similarities existed between

various episodes in the two novels, this was the principal difference
between it and *Le Feu*.[13] Inevitably, however, some is present even if
Les Croix de Bois rarely has the heavy socio-political implications of
Barbusse's novel. It is arguable for example that the pairing of Gilbert
Demachy and Sulphart, the young middle-class intellectual with the
older member of the working class, has a social if not a political significance; similarly the passing reference to German and French soldiers
being buried in the same field and sharing the same crosses (p. 184)[14]
is an obvious pointer to Dorgelès's attitude to the war. Other examples
of this kind are not difficult to find (e.g. p. 110 and p. 257) and Dorgelès also occasionally succumbs to the temptation to allow his own
thoughts to interrupt and colour his narrative. When he does so the
results are usually unhappy, the implied bitterness and anger of much
of the novel evaporating into reluctant resignation and even sentimental piety:[15] 'Come, come! there will always be wars, always, always . . .'
(p. 202); 'and yet the rain could not surely be hoping to wash all that
mud, to wash those rags, to wash those dead bodies? Though it were
to rain all the tears of heaven, rain a whole deluge, it would blot
nothing out. No, an age of rain would never avail to wash all that
away' (p. 257); and the whole of the closing chapter 'Et c'est fini',
for example. In the main, however, Dorgelès has his attitude to the
war, and in particular his criticisms of it emerge though his descriptive
and narrative techniques.

One of the principal contributory factors to the generally limited
stature of war literature is its repetitiveness: themes, problems and
above all targets for authors' bitterness reappear, albeit with differing
emphases from book to book. Yet this is one area where the earlier
books have a distinct advantage. *Le Feu*, *Vie des Martyrs* and *Les Croix
de Bois*, for example, were all confirmations of a suspicion about the
real nature of war, which had been developing since the middle of
1915, and were, in 1919, still relatively fresh.

Apart from Sulphart's return to civilian life in the final two chapters
of the novel the entire action of *Les Croix de Bois*, like that of most of
these early works, takes place at the front. While civilian life may, on
occasions, be nostalgically recalled with pleasure and envy (e.g. p. 2
and p. 6) it is more generally, especially for the *poilus*, a subject for
scorn seen to be peopled by profiteers and cowards ('the shirkers in the
rear' as Vieublé calls them on p. 252) whose wilful refusal to see the
war for what it is is encouraged by the romantic and totally misleading accounts provided by the popular press (e.g. p. 12 and p. 279).
Furthermore the attitude of the government representative who
'laughed, discreetly, behind his neat gloved hand' (p. 151) at the court
martial, and Sulphart's treatment and fate once he has left hospital,
illustrate the absence of real concern for the plight of those who risk

their lives for their country. But Dorgelès's anger and contempt is not reserved for non-military matters alone. As Demachy soon discovers, his training has been ill-conceived and his equipment inadequate; medical facilities are nauseatingly primitive (p. 269); gunners are often incompetent, firing on their own advance troops (pp. 40, 41). But above all it is is the commissioned officer class which is a target for his criticism: Barbaroux the major on horseback who bullies the lagging foot-soldier (p. 28); Demachy's cousin in his staff car (p. 239); the general who salutes the returning soldiers with 'a great dramatic gesture of his naked sword' (p. 201); Cruchet who sentences Sulphart to four days' imprisonment for long hair (p. 56); Morache who is a coward: 'We hadn't set eyes on him for ten days, since the morning of the attack' (p. 196). Finally the most biting illustration of the division between the two classes of men occurs in Chapter xv when a group of wounded soldiers, one of whom has a smashed jaw, arrives at a farmhouse serving as an officers' camp:

> They hesitated at going in, for the over-bright light made their eyes blink. For all that they crowded in close by the door with the noise of dragging, shuffling boots, and passing the cups from one to another they drank eagerly. At every mouthful the chasseur took, the wine passing through his holed chin fell down on to his coat in a thin stream.
> 'I say, let's both drink to one another's health,' the commandant said to him (p. 268).

Here as in the large majority of these incidents there is no commentary, the mixture of physical repulsiveness and the officer's utter insensitivity conveys Dorgelès's indignation perfectly.

To illustrate such divisions, however, is only a minor aspect of Dorgelès's intention, which is to show war to be an experience that shapes and limits an individual's behaviour and activities in a manner hitherto unknown to him. Like Barbusse, though to a lesser degree, Dorgelès suggests that the world of war is an elemental one; we are constantly aware of the presence of earth – frequently the cold mud of the battlefield and trenches – and of water, 'this water which seeps in in spite of everything' (p. 234). The soldiers too, aggressors and victims in turn, are reduced, their sensitivity dulled, their lives little more than a fight for survival and a series of primitive functions, eating, sleeping, excreting. Dorgelès emphasises this idea of war as a self-contained experience by the manner in which he works an image of the theatre into his text. Soldiers are like actors who have been thrust on to a new stage and into a new play with little rehearsal. Their sets are a warscape in which real nature has been either stripped away altogether ('there was now in front of the moon only a filmy

curtain; the wind pulled it aside and the fields appeared quite bare'
(p. 47)) or replaced by an artificial one in which the dead and wounded
form an essential part: 'a cloud of shelling hid the horrible scene.
But still the firing could be heard behind the moving curtain.
The smoke dissipated. Nothing was moving now...yes...an arm
moved still, barely moved' (pp. 41–2). Like an actor waiting in the
wings Demachy watches the lights of distant fighting as if they were
made by a silent firework display (p 31). Inevitably, however, having
certain roles imposed on them, by being asked to play mere parts in a
world in which light and darkness, chaos and silence alternate with
dramatic abruptness, Dorgelès's characters are threatened by anonymity. This, of course, was a real danger for soldiers and Dorgelès further
acknowledges it by an equally extensive use of what has become perhaps
the most common image in war literature, that of the animal herd.
Sometimes this is quite explicit – 'their weary flock' (p. 2); 'everybody
went to his place with the docility of horses that knew their corner'
(p. 13); 'a great flock of emaciated men' (p. 193); sometimes it is only
implied – 'lying close to keep themselves warm' (p. 14); '[Sulphart]
was uttering cry upon cry, now shrill, now hoarse, now terrifying and
now plaintive, thrusting one back and jostling others over' (p. 21).
Aware of the dangers the men resist, dressing or decorating their
uniforms in peculiarly individual ways (p. 3); Dorgelès also attempts
to preserve distinctive manners of speech throughout the book. Yet
given the generally artificial nature of the situation such attempts can
run the risk of caricature. It is possible that with the description of
Lucie, the grocer's daughter (pp. 93–4) Dorgelès consciously allows
this to occur in order to illustrate how indiscriminate soldiers could
eventually become about women. Elsewhere, in the case of Bouffioux
for example, it is less successful if only because he has a more substantial role to play in the novel. As it is he is portrayed as the archetypal coward, fat and always volunteering for jobs for which he has
no experience but which will keep him away from the action.[16] Ultimately he is obliged to join the squad and by refusing to take a watch
can be said to be responsible for Broucke's death. But there is no indignation expressed; just as when he is (justly) killed himself (p. 262)
Dorgelès refrains from drawing a moral. Once again description
is allowed to carry his attitude – and the one he wishes to prompt in us
– for him. The principal centre of interest of *Les Croix de Bois*
therefore is not what Dorgelès has to say so much as how he chooses
to say it.

In spite of the various cuts which he was obliged to make in his
original text its basic episodic, anecdotal style remains unharmed.
As such *Les Croix de Bois* is not unusual. Many of the novels written
during or shortly after the war shared this feature,[17] their authors not

yet possessing that necessary perspective which would enable them to give a total view of the events of 1914–18. Dorgelès later recognised this himself: 'It's curious, the deepest impressions only came clear to me later with hindsight. At the time I concentrated on little details and these often prevented me from being able to judge the whole.'[18] We do not find in this early war literature for example the kind of careful interweaving of themes and images which Giono achieves in *Le Grand Troupeau* (1931) nor the sustained, highly personalised, even fantasied, reaction to war which Drieu offers us in *La Comédie de Charleroi* (1934). It is tempting of course to argue that such proximity to the events could be a disadvantage and even to suggest that early war novels could not be as successful as those written ten or fifteen years later. Yet again we should beware. In spite of Cru's accusations[19] of factual and historical inaccuracy many of these novels have an immediacy and vigour about them which convey the sense of the fragmented life of the front-line soldier in a strikingly authentic manner. *Les Croix de Bois* is no exception. Dorgelès presents us with a series of self-contained episodes (rather than seeing them as scenes, some contemporary reviewers likened them to *nouvelles*),[20] experiences in the life of a squad of men and in particular of a new recruit. In so far as there is a chronological sequence of events in the war the pattern of the book may be said to be linear, but he makes little attempt to link one episode sequentially with the next. The effect is a cumulative one. Consequently in terms of overall structure *Les Croix de Bois* does not readily conform to what can legitimately be considered the 'normal' structural pattern of war novels which emerges over the years: introduction, development, climax (frequently the only sustained account of direct action) and aftermath, sometimes of a reflective, philosophical nature. There is, to be sure, a basic framework: Chapter I, in which Demachy arrives, is clearly introductory; Chapter XVII, the aftermath. But even while the only full account of action occurs in what is roughly the third quarter of the novel there is sufficient elsewhere – in Chapters III or VII for example – for this not to emerge as the natural climax except by virtue of the fact that it culminates in Demachy's death. Indeed the only conscious effort Dorgelès might be said to have made concerning the structure of *Les Croix de Bois* is the positioning of the short Chapter IX 'Mourir pour la Patrie' as the central episode. Here his account of an execution, of the soldier's fear, of his summary trial and imprisonment, not only illustrates his ability to make a strong emotional impression by a few words – 'Is that a soldier, that blue heap? He must still be warm.' (p. 150) – but also that the brutality and inhuman nature of war does not necessarily demand descriptions of epic scale. Indeed it is this sense of proportion and telling detail which

Dorgelès displays in *Les Croix de Bois* which adequately compensates for the absence of any carefully developed structure in the novel as a whole.

As we have already seen there is, throughout the novel, the idea that war is something akin to a theatrical experience. It is hardly surprising therefore that many of the individual episodes should have the characteristics of a dramatic scene: Dorgelès provides a setting, introduces his players and allows dialogue or reported dialogue to sustain the action.[21] Furthermore Dorgelès has the ability to create an appropriate atmosphere and convey it to the reader. In addition to 'Mourir pour la Patrie' three episodes in particular should be mentioned. In Chapter vi 'Le Moulin sans ailes', the peculiar behaviour of the farmer Monpoix suggests that he might be acting as an informer; Dorgelès allows the mystery to remain, providing clues for his reader but no positive evidence, so that he too like the narrator is overcome by 'an inexplicable anxiety'. Chapter viii, 'Le Mont Calvaire', is notable for its tension and for Dorgelès's exploration of the soldiers' psychological reaction to the knowledge that the Germans are tunnelling beneath their shelter in order to mine it. Again their feelings of fear and uncertainty are transmitted to the reader who, when the mines do eventually explode, finds his own sense of outrage tempered by one of relief that the soldiers have escaped in time. But of all the episodes in the novel the one which possesses these qualities most fully is Chapter xiii, 'La Maison du bouquet blanc'. Here the humorous if boorish behaviour of the soldiers prompted by the rumour that a house with a bunch of white flowers on its door contains prostitutes is violently deflated at the end in a manner which if a comparison with the *nouvelle* is made is worthy of Maupassant himself: 'It is the custom in this part of the country to place a bouquet at the door of a house where a child has died' (p. 228).

In addition to such examples of the manner in which Dorgelès attempts to control the general pace and temper of his novel we should note his role as omniscient narrator-character and his attempt (not unlike Williamson's in *The Patriot's Progress*) to present Demachy's experiences as a kind of odyssey. Already we have noted that Dorgelès for the most part refuses or fails to accept the privileges which omniscience can grant him to interject or to moralise at will. Yet he does both participate in the action as Jacques Larcher and, Balzac-like, record the private thoughts and conversations of his companions, particularly for example in Chapter xv when Demachy dies, having been wounded and abandoned in a wood, or in Chapter xvi during Sulphart's convalescence and return to civilian life. With his manipulation of Demachy Dorgelès might be said to have aimed at some kind of unifying feature. War for him is an educative process. He arrives full of naive optimism listening eagerly to the sound of gunfire beyond the hills (p. 6). When he first experiences trench life at the front he enjoys the wasplike sound of passing bullets (p. 32) or the acrid smell of shells: 'The wind, dissolving the thick eddying whirls, brought a breath of sulphur to us, a strong smell of powder. Gilbert breathed it in until it made him drunk' (p. 37). But especially under the tutelage of Sulphart he changes. From the young man who on his first night places his handkerchief soaked in eau de cologne over his face, so strong is the smell in the shed where they are sleeping (pp. 14, 15), he becomes the hardened soldier who tramples through rotting corpses (p. 189) and builds walls with the bodies of his one-time friends. While it is arguable that this change is no more than that which any new recruit will undergo, Demachy carries none of the Every-soldier qualities of John Bullock. In general Dorgelès is less intent on exploring his reactions to the experiences he is forced to endure than on the experiences themselves. Arguably therefore the scattered nature of Dorgelès's arrangement of his material is effective: it is the immediate – 'only the actual present, only today itself' (p. 92) – rather than the long term which emerges most strongly as his main concern in *Les Croix de Bois*.

One final observation concerning the style of the novel and Dorgelès's detailed use of language should be added. In most cases there is little that is particularly unusual about it. He is, for example, conscious of the value of resorting to the present tense in order to convey a sense of urgency and immediacy. Similarly his syntax can reflect a change in the temper and pace of an episode, particularly one of action, when it becomes disjointed and brittle (e.g. pp. 35; 192–3; 217):

> Les coups précipités nous cognent sur la nuque./Cela tombe si près qu'on chavire,/aveuglé d'"éclatements./Nos obus et les leurs se joignent en hurlant./On ne voit plus,/on ne sait plus./Du rouge,/ de la fumée,/des fracas . . . (p. 326)
>
> [The hurried slamming blows hammer us on the nape of the neck. It is falling so close that you go all anyhow, blinded with the bursts. Our shells and their shells join and do yelling battle together. You can no longer see, can know nothing now. It is red, and smoke, and uproar . . .] (p. 217)

More characteristic, however, is his ability – perhaps due to his experience in journalism – to capture the striking and the unusual: a dog licking up warm blood (p. 113) or rabbits whose fur is on fire running through the ranks of marching soldiers (p. 29). He also regularly uses images which mix features of life at the front with those of a normal existence: sudden light is 'a spadeful of daylight' (p. 212); shelling an 'infernal game of bowls' (p. 162); German bodies in barbed wire 'the beads of a funeral rosary' (p. 192); soldiers' hats in a flooded field are 'strange waterlilies' (p. 122); the freshness of spring 'fell on your shoulders like a damp cloak' (p. 148). Unfortunately as though he is unsure of the virtue of simplicity Dorgelès occasionally strives for effect and his writing appears mannered: a smile is 'forgotten, still on my lips like a banner of the fourteenth of July that no one has remembered to take down' (p. 67), for example. Elsewhere we find learned allusions like those to *Hamlet* (pp. 63, 168) which are simply out of place, though only twice does Dorgelès resort to the kind of heavy symbolism which flaws so many subsequent war novels. The shadow of a cross upon the body of the sleeping Lambert (p. 171) is a premonition of his death (pp. 179 and 195), while the fighting insects – 'a big red-brown beetle with a thick cuirass, and a blue insect with slender fine antennae' (p. 175) – which Demachy watches before the attack clearly represent the two armies, and the victory of the smaller one the outcome of battle, if not of the war as a whole.

Like Dorgelès's momentary lapses into moralistic comment, however, these are relatively minor blemishes in a book which attempts to give, and for the most part succeeds in giving, an honest, authentic account of the war experiences of an ordinary soldier. If Dorgelès appears to lack the politically motivated anger of Barbusse or the intense compassion of Duhamel, it is only because he offers us a wider range of emotional response than his fellow novelists. Indeed it is this rounded quality, conveyed as we have seen through the accumulation of incident, which is the outstanding feature of the novel. This is not to say that Dorgelès understates or allows us to forget the essential horror and inhumanity of war, rather that he allows a realist appraisal of the situation to take precedence over a distorted or incomplete one. Events which would appear outrageous in normal life are accepted without fuss or comment. War creates an insulated, self-contained world with its own values and rules, and, as Sulphart discovers, one which is unknowable for those who have no direct experience of it. It is a problem which Dorgelès acknowledged: the fact that his novel continues to be a best-seller suggests that he had found a solution.

7   Drieu La Rochelle : The War as 'Comedy'

Jonathan Dale

The war came to Drieu[1] as a golden opportunity to prove his worth and overcome his sense of failure and social inferiority. It initiated him into the adult world. The infantry charge which he had led at Charleroi on his first day in action provided him with a mystical revelation of his true nature which remained a point of reference throughout his life. Despite its subjective importance, however, his war experience was in reality surprisingly limited. His time at the front amounted to little more than ten weeks and none of the five spells exceeded a month or so. Moreover, Drieu saw virtually nothing of the grimmest phases of the war, between February 1916 and October 1918.

His attitude to the war did not become fixed once and for all during the fighting. *La Comédie de Charleroi* (1934)[2] expresses a later view when reflection has reinforced the element of disenchantment which had been in the war years little more than an intermittent dissonance in an otherwise harmonious exaltation of the warrior spirit. This reading of his collection of war poems, *Interrogations* (1917), is confirmed by a letter written that same year in which, whilst conceding that the war had belied his hopes, he could still affirm: 'And yet I had desired the war and I still accept it.'[3] His later claim that his disillusionment dated from 1915 is, at the least, misleading;[4] the *Comédie's* largely negative view of the war is a post-war development.

It was not, indeed, until the early twenties[5] that a definite change of heart emerged. In the following decade Drieu's commitment to peace through a federation of European states was unbroken; he exposed the evils of modern war and attempted to prove that it is bred by nationalism, not capitalism.[6] From 1931 he began to add to his theme of peace through institutional change, an expression of his personal determination to refuse military service in any future war. Not that Drieu was a pacifist in the full sense; he continued to accept the necessity of violence in many situations. Yet, in the early thirties, he did even come to admire those humanist pacifists who lived out their beliefs without regard to personal danger.[7] It is in this frame of mind that

Drieu wrote the *Comédie* in 1933, significantly first publishing one of the stories in *Europe*, a periodical founded by Romain Rolland and devoted to the cause of peace.[8] There are as yet few traces of Drieu's imminent evolution which, through the mounting danger of war and the increasing urgency of a revolutionary alternative to the crisis-ridden French economic and political system, was to lead him back via revolution to an acceptance of war. By the end of the thirties his commitment to peace has vanished, yielding to a resurgence of his underlying political pragmatism with its all too ready acceptance of violence.

La Comédie de Charleroi comprises six stories which critics have tended to treat as independent entities. The few general interpretations have identified its unity with the continuity of the narrative viewpoint and have equated the first person narrator with Drieu himself.[9] In this way the *Comédie* can be interpreted, aided by the legend of Drieu's egocentricity, as an inward-looking work of self-analysis.

Such an equation of first-person narrative with autobiography is particularly widespread in the case of war fiction, though often misleading. If, in the *Comédie*, Drieu does base his stories on his wartime experience, his account of it is not wholly accurate, still less complete. He omits, for example, all reference to a second infantry charge, in Champagne,[10] and to a later heroic exploit for which he was awarded the *Croix de Guerre*. The discrepancy between Drieu's attitudes during the war and the narrator's in these stories is also, as has been suggested above, very wide.[11] An analysis of the total change in Drieu's treatment of France confirms this. He had never been a narrow-minded nationalist; one would not expect him to present the war as a national crusade or war of justice, or to depict the Germans as objects of hatred. None the less a vibrant patriotism sounds in many of the poems of *Fond de Cantine*, which were written between 1915 and 1919, and is still present in 1922 in *Mesure de la France*. Not only did Drieu banish this note completely from the *Comédie* but in it he singled France out as an object of derision. He was clearly projecting on to the war his current preoccupations which included a conviction that France, in its mediocrity and indecisiveness, was the sick man of Europe *par excellence*.[12]

If the essence of the *Comédie* is not autobiography, still less is it a portrayal of the war in its everyday reality. Drieu makes no attempt to rival the many powerful evocations of the war, in its horror or monotony, of his predecessors. This is no work of faithful record. It is rather a description of the world through the self and the self through the world. The static opposition of objectivity and introspection[13] is transcended in the consciousness of a universal decadence, a disease manifested equally in self, war and modern society. The theme of the *Comédie* is that same comedy of decadence of Drieu's novels of sexual analysis.

Drieu, then, through the war is attacking contemporary civilisation as a whole, which has debased the ideal of war as all other ideals. The most categorical expression of this enlargement of the theme is the Infantry Officer's: 'All that's the modern world' (p. 239). The disease afflicting war has likewise mutilated love and architecture (p. 246). When he describes the war as a huge metropolis (p. 163) the nature of the parallel becomes clear: both are manifestations of mass society,[14] where the anonymous individual is caught up in an impersonal structure. Such explicit statements and comparisons are strongly reinforced by symbolic elements in Drieu's descriptions, which have been largely disregarded. A battlefield becomes the battlefield of modern life in its anonymity (p. 149), its drab featureless uniformity (p. 249); in the description of Verdun (p. 249) it represents the void at the heart of modern life. There, the human form is buried out of sight and nature's forms destroyed by the bombardment. Later the narrator encounters a soldier with his face shot away (p. 315), the sight of which drives him from the battlefield never to return. The destruction of human and natural forms represents the death of Man and of human creativity in the decadence of the modern world.

A lapse of time may be expected to favour wider perspectives. That the wider perspective in Drieu's case should be that of universal decadence is hardly surprising. The current of cultural pessimism had run strong in Europe in the first quarter of this century and Drieu had bathed in it from the outset. Decadence had become a powerful myth in all his writing. During the mid and late twenties, however, it had been tempered by his belief in the feasibility of a federal Europe under the leadership of a reformed capitalism – a late spasm of creative energy in a dying civilisation. By 1933 this dream had become irrelevant; it was confronted on the one hand by a deteriorating international situation following Hitler's accession to power and on the other by the world slump, which had exposed the inability of capitalism to overcome its contradictions and had led to a severe political and social crisis destructive of reformist positions. Drieu's horror of modern war remained, but was now divorced from a convincing strategy for the preservation of peace. Politically he was in a no-man's land between his past reformism and his future fascism, turning perhaps towards the latter but paralysed by his strong reservations about its German and Italian forms, particularly about their militarism. In France itself, in any case, he saw no prospect of radical change. With the internal and international outlook so bleak, Drieu naturally painted his *Comédie* in his palette's darkest shades, expressing more powerfully than ever his mortification at the rottenness of the modern world.

A structural analysis confirms the existence of a concern for the unity of the work as a whole. Firstly, Drieu has multiplied cross references between the stories to bind them together.[15] More important, his order-ing of the episodes is not chronological. 'La Comédie de Charleroi' treats August 1914 from a perspective in 1919; 'Le Chien de l'Ecriture' moves from February 1916 to some time in the twenties; 'Le Voyage des Dardanelles' is set in May 1915 and has no later fictionalised perspective; 'Le Lieutenant des Tirailleurs' looks back at February 1916 from a vantage point in 1917; 'Le Déserteur', set in 1932, only cursorily glances back to August 1914; and 'La Fin d'une Guerre' again has no later fictionalised perspective in its account of an event of October 1918.

He deliberately groups those which share common features: for example the first two stories have in common a narrative viewpoint which is doubly retrospective, and the two more theoretical episodes in dialogue form are placed together near the end. More fundamentally, these alterations to historical sequence are made in the interests of a progressive deepening of the mood of demoralisation. In this light 'La Fin d'une Guerre' clearly forms a conclusion to the work as a whole rather than an independent episode, for its effect depends on a weakened resurgence of the zeal shown by the narrator in the opening story followed by its – this time – final extinction.

This structurally unifying movement between an initial exaltation and a growing disillusionment is only an aspect of the wider unity of the work which stems from its antithetical nature. This governs almost every aspect of the work, thematic and stylistic, and issues in a series of oppositions – between the *élan* of the charge and its negative counterpart of flight, between heroism and malingering, pride and cynicism, lyricism and its deflation. These oppositions, however, though vital, are contained within the yet more fundamental antithesis between both *élan* and flight on the one hand and the unheroic acceptance of a passive role in a dehumanising war on the other. In a world where choice is reduced to the passive acceptance of an inhuman event or its refusal, heroism, paradoxically, resides in flight. Yet, in relation to the initial dream of exaltation, the loss is immense.

The narrator's immediate response to the war is through a myth derived from childhood dreams and his reading of Nietzsche.[16] He views it as an opportunity to break out of the mediocrity of his daily existence and to realise himself more completely, body and soul (p. 66), in the intensity of action at the risk of death (p. 73). In the energy generated and released he discovers a truer freedom and a creativity which arise in the refusal of the given, of the inert masses, of all that is a death-in-life (p. 70). The hero raises himself up above the prostrate around him in a movement in which his own self too is transcended (pp. 69–70).

The individualism of the myth is patent. Political perspectives are excluded; patriotism and justice are irrelevancies. In this Nietzschean world history marches on without rhyme or reason and war is but a noble occasion for the clash of conflicting energies (pp. 71–2).[17] The individual's action is not justified by any contribution it makes to meaningful historical development but by the mere fact of the mark it makes on the world. The essential image for such action is, as for Malraux's Adventurers, aesthetic or formal: the narrator describes himself as 'sculpting the shapeless mass of the charge' (p. 74).

Sexuality provides an alternative image. The *élan* of the infantry charge at Charleroi, the principal embodiment of this myth of war, is masculine creativity or spirit wresting itself from its state of givenness and imposing its mark on formless matter just as, in Drieu's mythology, the male dominates and forms the female. If the *élan* is so short-lived it is not merely the effect of the German guns but because it is an ejaculation (p. 70).

Drieu demonstrates progressively the anachronistic nature of this myth in a world war with its scientifically organised mass slaughter at the hands of an unseen enemy. Such warfare is destructive of man's freedom and creative initiative; rigid hierarchies and organised masses of men leave little room for spontaneity: the test is of industrial power rather than human courage (p. 241). Men bury themselves deeper in the earth and wait inertly instead of raising themselves above it (p. 249). The war is an anti-war in every respect, a corruption of the dream. Its anti-human nature is epitomised by the ruined face of the wounded man.

This same duality emerges in the transformation of the narrator's relationship with his comrades.[18] He presents himself as a self-conscious bourgeois intellectual. He is an outsider (p. 199), distrusted by the soldiers and N.C.O.s around him. He longs, however, for contact with the people (p. 35), is attracted to manual work – if only briefly (p. 305) – and envies the physical strength of the labourer (p. 29). This desire for contact is rarely consummated. The *Comédie* contains almost nothing of that off-duty *camaraderie* which is so characteristic of the First World War novel. The narrator's one positive experience of a type of fraternity is of a quite different kind, occurring as it does in the intensity of action, during the charge (p. 64). A collection of individuals in dynamic action together fuses into an organic unity; shaping the world, the group itself is vouchsafed its form. Such a fraternity is distinctively hierarchical: the group recognises and adheres to a leader who has emerged spontaneously from it by virtue of his inner worth.

This mystical union of self and group in attack, this sense of wholeness never returns after the abortive charge at Charleroi. Its failure leads to the disintegration of the group and a consequential development of imagery of fragmentation. Each member turns back into a self-centred, isolated unit; the narrator himself tears away from the battle on his own. Binding love is replaced by divisive hatred, directed both at others and at the self: 'Now I was beginning to feel disgusted with all those blokes around me. Or disgusted with myself' (p. 81).

There is one – inadequate – form of escape from the isolation of defeat. The individual, aware of his meaningless situation, may attempt to lose his consciousness of it by plunging into the frenzied tumult of the crowd, which is without form because it is devoid of purpose. This is a debased fraternity, that of the urban crowd in all its anonymity and atomisation. The 'Voyage des Dardanelles' provides many illustrations of this. The narrator exclaims during one such scene: 'And I was there, lost in the middle of it all, exulting in my anonymity' (p. 174). As the possibility of creative action vanishes the directional image of the charge is replaced by the whirling movements of a drunken crowd (p. 195), and of its symbolic counterpart, the spinning top (p. 231).

The antithetical structure of the world of the *Comédie* seems to suggest that modern life, in war as elsewhere, is destructive of the possibility of creative action without which there can be no organic community. Man is progressively reduced to the wretched alternative of frenzied immersion in the anonymous mass or the demoralising cynicism of the outsider isolated in an absurd world. In the *Comédie*, it is true, demoralisation is the only source of hope.

What can be the significance of the 'comédie' of Drieu's title in this dark context? Most critics have interpreted it as 'role-playing' and confined their analysis of it to the 'Comédie de Charleroi' episode where the comedy of inauthentic roles is most in evidence.[19] There the narrator's experience of the war is framed in the social comedy of Mme Pragen's exploitation of her son's death at Charleroi to nourish her own prestige. Her view of the war is wholly mythical, seen as it is through the role of heroic mother which she has since assumed and which blinds her to the reality of the decadence within herself and the war alike. The narrator is able to expose her self-deception but even his position is ambiguous since he is in her service as her secretary. Moreover, since his narration of the battle of Charleroi is from the perspective of 1919 when he returns to the battlefield with her, it is made obvious that neither the heroism of the charge, nor a healthy consciousness of the debased reality of war, have made any impact on the decadent social order of the peace.[20]

The narrator's own initial role of heroic warrior has been outlined above. Drieu is as concerned as in the case of Mme Pragen to reveal the hollowness of this myth through which the narrator views the war. The narrator himself comes to understand that the objective result of the charge is the senseless death of hundreds of his comrades (p. 80). The unreality of his nostalgic dream is further exposed by the irony of the rhetorical questions: 'Where was the flag? Where are the flags of yesteryear? And the trumpets? And the colonel? And his horse?' (p. 80). Drieu employs a range of comic devices, of which bathos is the most significant, to deflate these myths. A single example must suffice; the charge is lyrically evoked in a powerful rhythmic crescendo: 'I was shouting, running forward ... With my arms I gathered the men up. I wrested them from the ground and threw them forward';[21] but it is pulled up short by the bathetic: 'There was nothing in front of us' (pp. 73–4). In Drieu's view the nostalgic perpetuation of anachronistic dreams is debilitating; restorative action must avoid such role-playing.

The 'comédie' of the title, however, is not to be confined to the question of role-playing and the ironic contrast of dream and reality. In Drieu's view man acts out his destiny in different contexts which determine whether his performance will take place in a tragic, epic or comic mode. In an absurd world man's performance can only be comic, in a sense close to 'derisory' ('comédie' tends to have pejorative overtones). War, which should be the *décor* for a dramatic figuration of man's heroic and generous nature, is a disillusionment: 'One fights to express something ... to give a performance.' But 'this particular performance was a flop' (p. 84). The reality of the war, which had served to undermine the myths, is revealed as a degraded, essentially comic reality, which itself must be negated if Man is to be reborn.

In the 'Voyage des Dardanelles' the 'comédie' lies neither in role-playing nor in the ironic discrepancy between dream and reality; for the dream has disappeared and has not been replaced by any faith in the future. Perspectives are confined to the present. In the aimlessness, the absurdity of his situation, man's enactment of his destiny has lost its dynamic and dramatic forms – which the charge had represented – and has subsided into a formless stasis. The mood is one of demoralisation which generates the darker comedy of derision. Drieu significantly adopts a quite different style for much of this episode, one reminiscent of Céline in its cynicism and self-disgust. Its slangy, broken syntax is intended to convey the fragmentation and absurdity of contemporary life.[22] But this slang differs radically from the usual slang of soldiers' speech in war fiction and has a quite different function. It is also significant that the narrator's squad now includes both a former acrobat and a clown and that he himself is seen busking to pay for his drink (p. 192). Scenes of mob intoxication and aimless riot pervade the episode, imbuing it with a coarse humour. The narrator, it is true, does eventually attempt to break free from this static, demoralised world. But his lone attempt to silence an enemy machine gun comes too late and the episode ends with the narrator awakening next morning 'in a shell hole' (p. 227). Far from escaping from the 'comédie' of the world through such an instinctive resurgence of heroism, his act is itself, in its ineffective and short-lived nature, to be viewed in part with irony; at the most such a nostalgic spasm of heroism may preserve the narrator from the leprosy (p. 252) of demoralisation. It is no real way forward, for the shell hole is a reminder of its counterpart at Charleroi into which the charge tumbles when its impetus is broken and from which 'we have never managed to get out to continue our advance' (p. 77).[23]

Heroic zeal is treated with still deeper irony in the concluding episode, 'La Fin d'une Guerre'. This relates the narrator's temptation to risk his life again in a wholly gratuitous last visit to the front lines. The *élan* is here a mere theatrical gesture (p. 299). It is in all respects an ironic contrast to the charge at Charleroi: the narrator has no intention of fighting, walks rather than runs and is alone. This time his zeal is finally broken by his encounter with the man wounded in the face; he leaves the front never to return.

The novel ends on this negative note; there is no way back to an ideal in the past and no explicit orientation towards a future in which nobility, and hence tragedy, will again be possible. The *Comédie* is rather a work of demystification, preparatory to some future cultural renaissance. Drieu limits himself to furthering awareness of the anti-human nature of modern war and the modern world; the comedy, even farce (p. 304), of the work is an expression of this dehumanisation. Tragedy is impossible when men no longer express their passions in direct confrontations. Drieu may yearn for the epic and the tragic, but these are not real options since they depend upon faith[24] and faith is absent from the *Comédie* and, in Drieu's eyes in 1933, incompatible with the modern world. This comedy of disenchantment, one might suggest, becomes inescapable from the moment when the charge is halted and the narrator separates from his men. That destruction of meaningful action creates a fundamentally ironic distance between the self and the world of war. Whether or not Drieu's innate talents were lyrical and epic as he sometimes claimed,[25] his vision of the world was in fact compatible only with satire. Drieu came closer to reality when he envisaged his work as that of a satirist, a Daumier rather than a Delacroix.[26]

It must already be apparent that the *Comédie* is no representative novel of the First World War. It does contain many of the habitual scenes, from the excitement of mobilisation to a gruelling night march and the officer shot in the back by his own men; but these do not begin to compare in descriptive power to similar scenes in many of Drieu's predecessors. His concern is not with realism in the sense of accurate observation and detailed description. His realism lies in a distillation of the experience of war in which non-essential elements are evaporated away, leaving behind a concentrated spirit – the significance of the war for modern Western culture. This explains the absence of other no less universal experiences, ones which Drieu himself had known, such as relaxed off-duty group conversations, contacts with friends and relations, etc. These simply do not accord with his interpretative framework with its emphasis on the atomisation inherent in mass society.

This wider interpretation of the war's significance, which distinguishes the *Comédie* from most earlier fiction of the war, relates it at the same time to important contemporary trends in the French novel, in particular to the many works which diagnose a disease of modernity spreading malignantly through the body of Western civilisation. This diagnosis is also an accusation. The works of Bernanos, Giono, Céline and Guilloux at this time constitute a 'trial of bourgeois civilisation in its entirety'.[27] In so far as the war is widely seen as the most horrific manifestation of that disease it is natural that these writers should use it as evidence in the trial. Works such as Giono's *Le Grand Troupeau* (1931), Céline's *Voyage au bout de la nuit* (1932), Drieu's *Comédie* and Guilloux's *Le Sang Noir* (1935) represent a tendency for the War no longer to be 'viewed in isolation as a thing in itself'.[28]

The anti-war novel, early predominant in France, seems to divide at this time, through the combined effects of distance from the war and a deepening social crisis, into two more distinct forms, both of which offer a larger interpretation of the war's significance. The rather helpless, if defiant, note of protest of much early war fiction is either subsumed in a wider and more coherent critique of our civilisation; or the defiance is sharpened into a more precise analysis of the political system held to have produced the war and a more positive conception of what could replace it. This is the contribution of Aragon's *Les Cloches de Bâle* (1934).

To simply submerge the *Comédie* in the current of literary history, however, is to neglect its originality. Amongst its most distinctive features are the retrospective elements in its narrative point of view and its essentially antithetical nature; for, however much it is a warning about modern warfare, it also contains a dream of ideal combat which, although inapplicable in present conditions, remains in its essence inviolate. Through the *Comédie* we are able to witness a transformation of the heroic mode of war fiction,[29] under the pressure of reality, into pacifist protest.[30]

The fact that Drieu was himself divided helps to prevent the *Comédie*, despite its warning function, from suffering from the illeffects which the 'will to prove' may produce. He has no simple answers; emotionally torn himself, he cannot be over-dogmatic. His structural and narrative techniques, moreover, in their constant shifts of viewpoint and scene, serve to fragment the narrator's conceptual analysis of the war and to integrate the fragments with the narration of a concrete episode in his war experience. Where theoretical discussion does predominate, in 'Le Lieutenant des Tirailleurs' and 'Le Déserteur', the dialogue form reflects Drieu's divided attitudes. Finally, since the *Comédie* is limited to critical perspectives and eschews speculation about solutions it remains steeped in the experience of decadence which is a visceral reality for Drieu.

La Comédie de Charleroi which, in its very lack of vivid description, in its images compressed to the point of abstraction, in the importance of its ideological framework, would seem endangered as fiction by such didactic essay-like elements in Drieu's approach, is not in the end much weakened by these. Indeed the uniqueness of the work is largely derived from them. In almost all respects it is a thoroughly unified work. Structure, narrative and stylistic techniques all contribute to the exposure of the debased nature of modern war and society, the recognition of which, in Drieu's eyes, is an essential precondition for any renewal of the human spirit. If the *Comédie* has been so rarely examined both in itself and in terms of its place in the evolution of first world war fiction, it is because the unity and the wider implications of this apparently loose collection of war stories have been almost wholly disregarded.

8   Against Nature: Jean Giono and *Le Grand Troupeau*

W. D. Redfern

While composing *Le Grand Troupeau* in 1929 (it was published in 1931),[1] Giono noted down that a dominant theme should be the duty of participants in war to survive, 'faire la bête': to play the dumb animal.[2] War is against nature (both human and non-human, which are tightly bonded in Giono's vision). The key verbs in the fight between nature and war are *mâcher* and *gâcher*. They suggest on the one hand digestion and on the other pulverisation; absorption and wastage. Their visceral loathing of war makes Giono's people spew it forth, whereas they embrace sensual and emotional drives. Not that such opposites are polar, and indeed overlap is a recurrent phenomenon in this novel. Though Giono would have us believe that 'living naturally' is a simple matter of recognising self-evidences, much ambiguity clearly inheres in the whole concept.

A decade after his permanently scarring experiences in the First World War, Giono interrupted work on his cycle of lyrical peasant novels known as the 'Pan-trilogy', in order to express out of his system all that in war had entered him against his native grain. The dream-like, atemporal, though often frightening world of the peasant tales for a time made room for an apocalyptic universe of senseless destruction. Concern with individual or small-scale plenitude yielded for a space to the wider plight of whole peoples caught up in war. While ambivalent on some issues, Giono's vision is consistent. And so elements of his earlier work (the hallucinations and fetishism of *Colline*, for example) recur in *Le Grand Troupeau*. Giono is a utopian, and utopians are especially conscious of what they are rejecting in the constituted world. *Le Grand Troupeau* contains his anti-utopia and his proposed anti-dotes.

It starts grandiosely with the forced descent of a massive flock of sheep from the hills to the plain, in midsummer. For the locals this unseasonal *transhumance* is a palpable sign that life is being turned back to front by the war. The villagers witness the departure of mobilised men and the passage of displaced sheep, so that from the start human and animal collectivities are conjoined in the same image. The advent of the huge flock progresses from a distant smell to clouds of dust blotting out the sun and the deafening noise of large-scale woe. An ass-colt sucks; a ram expires in agony: life and death are juxtaposed starkly, as throughout the novel. The description of the dying ram curiously resembles that of a birth: 'He opened his thighs and let go a bundle of black blood and guts' (p. 551). The flock surges on. As with men at war, if one keeps going the rest follow. The flock is water flowing, but also dough (p. 561). Suffering thus contains what is life-giving. Giono's system of compensations is hinted from the beginning. The shepherd leaves in the villagers' care a prize ram, for collection in better times.

Le Grand Troupeau swings regularly between general and particular, front and rear. On the battlefield the two representatives of the peaceful home plateau, Joseph and Olivier, experience in their different sections the lethal absurdity of war. Whereas home is roots and security, the theatre of war is total instability. A soldier picks up the motif of a mashed humanity: 'We're like a great damned pile of mortar and somebody at the top has got the trowel' (p. 704). Note the vagueness of the charge. The stress falls on chaos: bewildered soldiers, loosed farm-stock, transformed and unrecognisable topography. War murderously parodies Giono's peacetime cosmos where the emphasis is also on com-mingling; but in war the absurd ousts the meaningful. Giono is concerned only with the effects, all evil, of war, and not with this war in itself, its causes or purposes. The paradox of all wars, that most sane men hate them while going along with them, was a compromise that Giono would not practise. War is an essentially totalitarian phenomenon, and Giono the conservative anarchist could do no other than reject it totally. He refused to prettify it naively like Apollinaire, or to glorify it fascistically like Montherlant.[3] Guns are cannibals: 'The machine-gun purrs as it eats into the soft flesh of something warm and living' (p. 619).

If war itself is wilfully pitiless, it embraces pity, which is most fittingly embodied in a grossly overworked front-line doctor operating in appalling conditions. Less fittingly in Joseph. Presented initially as a ferociously possessive man who on leaving home gives strict instructions for his wife Julia, his sister Madeleine and his bitch-dog to be closely watched in case they stray, and who later writes egoistic, petty-minded letters from the front, Joseph is improbably transfigured into a man of compassion. The knapsack of fatigue weighing down this non-combatant scout and liaison-agent is more plausible than the Atlas-load of pity. He becomes more interesting, because less false, when a wound amputates his arm and he is consumed by a fear of death invading through this breech in his wholeness. In his case suffering isolates, but in the rear-lines hospital the legless guide the eyeless, and a blind accordionist consoles all the wounded. Although Giono periodically remembers his title and inserts images comparing soldiers to a flock of sheep, overall he shows war more through the eyes of the individual and seems little interested in the social provenance or composition of groups. He allows for comradeship but rarely for unanimism. Conversely he does not generalise hatred. Even the officer-class is shown no real hostility. A captain who goes off his head and talks to shadows is treated with great tenderness. Throughout the Germans are seen not so much as the enemy but rather as 'the other flock of men'.

Dropping his revulsion from war for a spell, Giono provides in one section of this novel a scene of quite horrible beauty which describes the fastidious carnage of dead soldiers by rats and crows, a gastronomic feast which adds new dimensions to Hemingway's 'A Natural History of the Dead' in *Death in the Afternoon*. Like eclectic gourmets, the rats select beardless young flesh; they savour the aroma and like diners wipe their chops clean before continuing. The corpses are compounded with the soil and their own supplies: blood, wine, earth and bread – a potent brew. 'The damp red crust of soil was dripping with human juice, like bread dipped in wine' (p. 621). All this of course secretes a baleful truth: the land and its creatures can grow fat on human nourishment, just as man lives off the land. Giono has no word of distaste for these carrion-seekers, whose behaviour is rendered as entirely natural. Some readers might feel doubts about this obsession with bloodletting, the opening of entrails and the erotic undertow of such spectacles. No doubt Giono would have loathed a real gladiatorial show, but his own imagined gore, a strange overspill from his zest for life, captivated him. There is in the whole episode a curious medley of serene olympian distance and excited dionysiac involvement; it is the writing of a greedy but choosy epicure. If death has such a sweet, densely rich smell, can dying itself be so important or awful? Giono's attitude hovers. It is a weird vision which recurs in later books, and in which it is hard to disentangle the protest against the obscenity of dying from a far from morose delectation. In Giono's hands the life-force takes contrary forms, generosity and self-gratification.

Each time the novel swings back to life at home, we see this latter impulse in Julia, whom Giono conceived as a happy and healthy animal. In the fullest sense she *embodies* the theme of 'women without men'. In Joseph's absence, her appealing flesh reacts strongly to the highly charged erotic goads around her; straight sexuality, bestialism and autoeroticism are in her headily confused. With none of D. H. Lawrence's residual complexes, Giono sings of the body's demands more fully than any other major French writer. In him there is no

Cartesian severance of body from brain. Julia indulges the pressing temptation: 'It's no good closing your eyes and stiffening yourself up from top to toe, because the urge knows its way around your body and, anyway, I like it and, besides, it's a free country' (p. 567). Sex, food and drink are to her all one glory. Giono writes with conniving comprehension and evokes beautifully the twin joy and burden of being a woman and having breasts. (He is never limited, like Hemingway or Malraux, to the all-man's-eye view.) Giono drools over what stimulates her. She is ripe, 'like a peach trembling beneath a bee' (p. 647). After feeling brief hot shame on straddling a boy in a game, and after being dominated by the butcher's domination of her dangerous sow, Julia teams up with the equally hungry flesh of a deserter. Spontaneous sex later becomes premeditated, when she oils the door-hinges. Giono offers no disapproval for she is driven, like all his creatures, not to miss out on anything, to respond to 'the song of her entire flesh' (p. 647). It is almost as though she were paying homage to Joseph, in answering the call of life while he is fending off death. The whole episode is one of the very few places in Giono's uninihibited work where one of his people is unfaithful to a partner. But even so the main stress in this novel falls on the optimistic belief in the possibility of authentic and lasting liaisons.

One such is that between Olivier and Madeleine. Olivier is largely silent, except for words of caring. Haunted by the horrors he has seen (the eye of a corpse staring at him turns out to be a bit of brain), when home on leave he grabs at life in its most succulent form. Madeleine, a translucent girl who offers herself for total communion, had stolen Olivier's red belt as an erotic talisman. On his return they translate the symbol into joyful fact, in an act of mutual physical charity. When Madeleine becomes pregnant, Julia, dreading Joseph's anger, attempts a homespun abortion, an act which in this novel dedicated to ripeness is inevitably seen as unnatural. For his part, in the general rout at the front, Olivier flees with a comrade, accepting that it is no longer his war.

Pastoral retreat is not uncommon in war literature, if only on the stereotyped level of the 'warrior's rest'. In *Le Grand Troupeau*, the country home is however more of a true counterweight to the war, and in fact the switching between the two avoids the monotony of many trench-confined war novels. Giono writes not as a peasant (he worked in a small-town bank before taking up professional writing, and his father was an artisan), but as a champion of and learner from the peasantry and country life. In all the scenes of battle in this novel, there is always some tangible presence of nature. In one fantastic sequence, Olivier gratefully accepts the lesson of the microcosm from the ghost of Regotaz, who holds a crackling pinecone to the youth's ear as a reminder of his natural home: 'It flowed through him like a sparkling stream; it filled him like a forest. He could feel soil on his lips, and the wind blew through his head' (p. 682). This recalls the true connection between man and habitat, in the midst of the chaos of war which severs them. Regotaz, a lumberjack turned tree-protector, embodies another variation on pacifism, on leaving well alone, and is one more of Giono's healer-figures. Well cannot indefinitely be left alone, of course, and on the plateau weeds begin reclaiming the land inadequately cared for by the women. Even here, while acknowledging the necessity for human control over natural growth, Giono allows himself a residual sense of joy at the emancipation of the land. The plateau children live an idyll picking wild flowers, while the official harbinger treks from farm to farm announcing the death of menfolk. 'When you drink your breakfast milk on the step the almond blossom drops into it. . . . Well, we've got some excuse for not always thinking about death the way we should' (p. 586). Giono identifies with such comprehensible selfishness. 'Obey the great call'; this sums up the joyous acceptance of necessity by Giono's people. There is danger here, naturally. Like the Norwegian novelist, Knut Hamsun, whom he much admired at that time as a heartening writer, Giono seems tempted often to take refuge from personal accountability in the blind surrender to natural imperatives. Truth is not constant in the lie of the land.

Against the grain of historical likeliness, Giono views peasants as natural pacifists. He sees them as the true universal beings, closer to peasants in other countries than to industrial workers in their own. His arcadias are not melioristic but given over to the preservation of simplicity, and hence largely static. The key myth-figures are Noah and Robinson Crusoe, and the crucial dictum that of Voltaire: the world is a shipwreck and it is every man for himself. Thus the plateau-dwellers of *Le Grand Troupeau* bemoan the times they live in and flaunt their own parochialism and resistance to officialdom. In cracker-barrel fashion, war to them 'is not worth the life of a man and all that he can rake towards himself in the way of happiness and peace by his own toil' (p. 617).

Throughout, the despair of those shipped off to war is combated by the hopefulness of those left on the land. Various bridges connect the two: leave, the reminders of a peaceful countryside at the front, the imprints left by departed men on their marriage-bed or on their favourite tools. But perhaps the chief example of consoling presence-in-absence is the ritual (invented and possibly stemming from a play on words about salt) of the wake without corpse. The fire is put out, the ashes heaped in the hearth, a pile of salt placed in the middle of the table and a peasant intones: 'His friends will remember this man who was the salt of the earth' (p. 594). Later, salt is used to cleanse Madeleine's baby, thus again linking birth and death in cyclical patterns. 'The poet must teach hope, if he wants to earn a place alongside those who work with their hands',[4] Giono wrote in the early thirties, when he clamoured the need for 'remedial' literature. Indeed, he set himself up early as a kind of horse-doctor, offering rough antidotes or at least palliatives (placebos, his enemies would say), charms against misfortune. Apart from ethical preference, his very sensibility leads him habitually to foist on to things as they are his own instinctual system of compensation, substitution or displacement.

The shepherd introduced at the outset returns to the centre of attention at the end, when he comes to collect the ram. He returns to underline trust in the present and future, and to bless Madeleine's new-born with the gift of optimism. When he expresses in Whitmanesque strophes the wish that the child should be one who leads rather than a follower, he is urging self-reliance more than leadership qualities, for Giono's absolute anti-totalitarianism made him hostile to any cult of the Chief. The triumphant rotundity of the half-pagan, half-biblical phrasing fails to camouflage the loose sentimentality of the thinking. It is written in the optative mood, whereas most of the novel is in the indicative. Losses are in fact not negligible. Joseph has been lopped of his working arm, and for Julia it is almost as if he had been gelded. Madeleine's first twin, a girl, is defective in limb, the result of the botched abortion and of Joseph's vengeful brutality. Olivier's mutilation was controlled, in order to avoid the definitive severance from all he values. Giono's economics are optimistic: each loss is outweighed by a gain. Madeleine's second twin, a boy, is whole. In Giono's self-regulating universe nothing is ever wasted. His serenity can seem obtuse in that he can never pass up the chance, like his carrion-crows, of profiteering from any event. All the same, the hopefulness at the end of *Le Grand Troupeau* is bought more dearly than in some of his more idyllic works. Perhaps he should have had the courage of his dubiety and opted, as he planned at one stage, to make his shepherd-hero a true solitary, sceptical towards the perverted values of his fellowmen, instead of mindlessly blessing them as total innocents. In his haste to denounce official wars, Giono was at that time insufficiently ready to admit the permanent hostilities between civilians.

Giono rewrote this novel painfully several times, and its structure gives some clues as to what is fake and what convincing in this amalgam where nature and anti-physis compete. In writing it, Giono clearly felt the need for a literary self-renewal, as well as hoping to tame a traumatic experience. He expressed the urge to model his writing on Bach, whose 'mathematical constructions' he admired; on Breughel and his capacity for portraying simultaneous actions; and on the sensual intensity of Cézanne (as in the sculptured rendering of Julia's body). Aiming to convey both the disruption of war and the continuity of country life, he settled for a succession of tableaux. The result is an episodic novel, held together by certain constants (e.g. the chorus of aged peasants), rather than an organic whole, which was ruled out by the very premise of the novel. The dominant tense is the graphic present, which makes the events related both more immediate and yet more timeless. The movement of the narrative is essentially discontinuous and proceeds by lurches. An inveterate storyteller, written or oral, Giono can manage every tempo from near-stasis to hell-for-leather frenzy, but in this novel, except for scenes of panic flight, both peasants and trench soldiers mainly and predictably plod.

Amidst so much pattern-making (Front and Home, War and Nature, Death and Birth), some of the contrasts are gratuitous, even meretricious. Madeleine's attempted abortion takes place to the accompaniment of the touching noises of a ewe tending her lamb. Others are more telling, for instance the description of the army butchery just prior to that of the operation-tent. The dominant motif of the flock itself is ambiguous. Who or what does the exhausted lead-ram, or indeed the good shepherd, represent? The treatment of animals similarly hovers between sentimentality, when Giono belligerently puts the reader on his honour to respond as a compassionate being, and warm perception, as when the narrator weds the animals' presumed awareness of what they are losing by their forced march: 'The taste of familiar grass, the night-wind nesting in the wool round their ears' (pp. 546–7).

This readiness to speak for the speechless is central to Giono's style, which is also his world-view. Throughout, the life of nature goes on, mocking or making up for the mad slaughter between men. Giono intentionalises fire, wind, sounds, smells, flora and fauna. Even negatives come alive: 'You could hear the electric crackle of silence' (p. 620). Yet, for a 'force of nature', as he has often been justifiably called, Giono can be at times far too bookish: 'Cléristin gazed at the animals' story, at what the great flock was writing in letters of blood and pain on the ground' (p. 550). Where most writers practise a stop-go economy, Giono favours galloping inflation. Often there are more words than sense. Giono will have none of analytic breakdown, which he sees as a form of autopsy, and plumps instead for that 'marvellous excess' that he rejoices to find in classical Antiquity, in Rabelais, Shakespeare, Cervantes and Melville. He writes largely, like Balzac and Zola, in the superlative mode: sounds strike the roof of heaven, movements originate in the depths of time. This can clearly beget false images. Here is Giono led astray by the idea of a dead farm: 'The bones of the decaying farm were scattered in the meadow, and crows pecked at the empty eye-sockets of its windows' (p. 606). But he can equally well be exact in his notations: 'She pulled off her stockings as if she were skinning a rabbit' (p. 568), or simply charming: 'The trees danced around their shadows like tethered goats' (p. 663). Above all, he is pugnacious, he refuses to apologise. Impatient and aggressive, he makes rapid elisions between different sense-impressions, and is unafraid of mixing metaphors. With Julia notably, we have seen how Giono crams together diverse elements, until his creations are literally fit to burst. Even in madness or when mutilated, Giono's people remain entire, so that the projected theme of 'the haemorrhage of the personality' never really comes into play.

The First World War is often thought of as a linguistic melting-pot, where men from different countries, regions or walks of life devised a *lingua franca* for easier communication. Dialogue in Giono's texts before *Le Grand Troupeau* had exhibited an often precious kind of French, knowingly tinged with Provençal and making little effort to mirror the speech of actual peasants. In this novel, by way of homage to an important if hated reality, he brings in contemporary colloquialisms of a recognisably military flavour, especially that mixture of insult and camaraderie. On the whole, however, Giono's people in his early work perform more engagingly than they talk.

'The series of books beginning with *Le Grand Troupeau* will be called Apocalypse'.[5] Cataclysms and millenarist febrility come naturally to Giono (and there is indeed a recurrent strain of apocalyptic guff in all his work); as a devotee of Pan and Dionysus, he responds fully to epidemic situations. True, in *Le Grand Troupeau* war is imaged as the murderous beast of the Apocalypse, and Giono makes a vague use of chapter-headings from St John and Jeremiah, not always closely linked to what follows and rather distasteful, besides, in a self-professed epicurean pagan. The battle scenes are a mixture of obscurity and brusque fulgurations, just as the style oscillates between the gnomic and the florid. Through all runs the consistent tone: insolent, ruled by that *gourmandise* which is the principal mode of Giono's sensibility.

Le Grand Troupeau was the first of Giono's novels to divide critics into enemy camps. Robert Brasillach in the right-wing *Action Française* attacked Giono's political premises, which pacifist-minded reviewers approved.[6] It has sold around 100,000 copies in the original. It was published thirteen years after the end of the war, but writing it was not a case of assimilation of experience, for Giono disgorged his. Possibly the writing of his fictionalised 'autobiography' *Jean le Bleu* around the same period led Giono to live backwards for a time in order to examine his past experience. He had begun his literary career by creating a world elsewhere, and only gradually did he come to oppose it openly to the world around.

His actual experience had been full enough: Verdun, Chemin des

Dames, Mount Kemmel. He stayed a second-class private and was decorated only by the British for the unwarlike act of helping a blinded British officer to escape from a burning hospital where he was himself being treated for gas-affected eyelids. He suffered all the horrors known to more combative soldiers. In one text, he describes without hysteria the shallow crater crammed with starving wounded men and excremental filth in which he survived several days under continuous fire. Naturally, what he wanted after that was 'To clean off all the filth, to touch objects with a skin scrubbed spotless'.[7]

In writing *Le Grand Troupeau*, Giono felt severely hampered by the weight of his remembered experience. He said of the model for Captain Viron: 'He was too real, and it handicapped me. To get him right, I had to strip him of virtually everything.'[8] This confession tells us much about Giono's preference for using observed reality as starting-blocks or a trampoline. Socialist Realism would have been his cup of hemlock. His novel pays little heed to the real chronology of the war, and there is such an air of timelessness that the reader might wonder whether it is specifically the First World War on show. Giono is not dealing with the experiencing of war in any wilful sense, but only in the passive mode of imposed suffering. The real war was of course not globally meaningless, though it was senseless to very many individuals. And it is the individual, indeed the individualist standpoint that Giono chooses. This does not mean that he offers a false image of war. On the contrary, *Le Grand Troupeau* contains authentic experience powerfully rendered: 'Life in the mud, sleeping underground, our fear of open spaces and our need for cubby-holes and hide-outs.' It captures above all the malleability of matter in conditions of heavy bombardment: 'The constant transformations of the landscape, the sky, the light, the mashing together of soil and men, it all made for a total lack of reality.'[9] This last phrase tells us much about Giono's impulse to reshape given material and to mould from it a hallucinatory hyperreality. In contrast with Barbusse and Drieu la Rochelle, Giono is neither solemn nor frivolous; he is other, lyrical.

In *Le Grand Troupeau*, we never see Giono's chosen few kill anyone, though several are themselves killed or maimed. His text supports his native pacifism. His urge has always been to retreat, to believe that courage means running. Coupled with this goes a radical refusal of nationalism. During the thirties, his pacifism became more militant, as threats to world peace proliferated. His professed aim in writing was: 'To bludgeon readers with freshness, health and joy. The man who is swept up in the torrent of rich living can no longer understand war.'[10] In fact, he tended to vacillate between preaching non-violent civil disobedience and vague talk of revolt (e.g. urging farmers to withhold wheat from warmongering governments). He argued that life is too uniquely precious to be squandered on unknown future generations or for the sake of fake ideologies. Far from being cannon-fodder, men are the raw materials of their own wills. He attacked national leaders, war-mongering writers like Drieu la Rochelle or Montherlant, or those who like Romain Rolland lived to accept war as a defensive measure. He published messages to the peasants which few of them probably read; he denounced war unremittingly. He fancied himself at that period for a position amongst what Lévi-Strauss has called 'the supranational brotherhood of supermen': Alain, Gandhi, Einstein.[11] The logic of his unconditional pacifism made him pro-Munich, and he broke with the Left at that time. At the outbreak of the Second World War he was to be imprisoned, presumably for his pacifist pronouncements. In all that period, this nucleus of individualist wilfulness could be and was a preacher, but never a true proselytiser.

Giono's anti-war feelings were not always pacifist. Against the growing dictatorships of Right and Left, he dreamed at times of peasant *jacqueries* which would combine destruction of the old, and regeneration of even older civilisations. The gloatingly sadistic quality of his imagination emerged ever more nakedly, until it became apparent that for him to kill is also natural (Montaigne too wondered whether Nature herself had implanted in us an impulse to be inhuman). Giono's evolving attitude to war is indeed a good index for his changes of stance in general on human affairs. Recently, in *Le Désastre de Pavie*, though admittedly evoking a Renaissance war, he could adopt an amusedly olympian standpoint towards war as a 'divertissement on a grand scale'.

More than in his explicit anti-war propaganda in the thirties, Giono's entire fictional work, expressed didactically or not, portrays the rich benefits of peace, especially those of living at peace with oneself. He is, and our very term for it is archaic, a yea-sayer. Dealing mainly in self-affirmation (his own and that of his heroes), he seldom bothers to make his people ordinarily likeable, lovable or even admirable. 'The men from round here are no saints. Saints have never made the land bear fruit. Most of them are arrant egoists.'[12] His vision is non-tragic, and it belongs to the Platonic and Nietzschean traditions of a faith in an Original Oneness. Any tragic events in his fictional world are an off-shoot, an afterthought, an unavoidable concomitant, rather than a postulate. His eudemonism is bloody-minded in its resistance to that misery-mongering so prevalent in literature this century. For him pleni-tude can be attacked, like a citadel, but it antedates and most often survives its assailants. In *Le Grand Troupeau*, his hatred of war and his incurable optimism are intimately entwined. It is a moot point whether, overall, the system of compensations (the stopgaps and replenishments) minimises the horrors. It is a moot point also because

Giono's voluminous girth refuses to fit neatly into academic pigeonholes. I myself believe that Giono is too radically utopian to tell us much of value about war itself, but that he offers a more appealing picture of anti-war, of peace, than many another writer, Generally, he sees the writer as a creative liar. But in this novel, he does not lie about the war; he gives the lie to it, he gainsays war. Despite its faults and omissions, *Le Grand Troupeau* reiterates passionately Giono's major lifelong theme: the intransigent pursuit of their heart's desire by committed soloists, in their alternative society.

9   Projections of Everyman: The Common Soldier in Franconi, Wiechert and Williamson

Holger Klein

Gabriel-Tristan Franconi (1887–1918), Henry Wiliamson (born 1895) and Ernst Wiechert (1887–1950) share many features besides a limited affinity to Fascism. All came from petit-bourgeois backgrounds, were bent on literature, followed the call to arms without reserve, began as privates, fought with distinction and ended up as subalterns. Moreover, in these novels, they chose to transform their war experience in a specific way: *Untel de l'armée française* ('Someone or other in the French Army'), *The Patriot's Progress*, *Jedermann* ('Everyman') – the titles indicate an attempt to typify, to present a universal image of the common soldier in the First World War. This essay tries to analyse the techniques the three writers use to achieve their common aim and to gauge the success of the books as representative records and as works of fiction.

Franconi wrote with little distance from events and kept so closely to his experiences that Dorgelès could exclaim: 'Make no mistake, Untel, that is Franconi himself, this story is his own.'[1] There are significant differences however. Born in Paris, Franconi was twenty-seven in 1914, a happily married poet, enthusiastic littérateur and innovator.[2] Untel appears to be younger, is associated with the country *and* the metropolis (pp. 1, 63), his marriage is only mentioned at the end (p. 257). Franconi suppresses his service with the artillery (1914–15); by inference, Untel shared all the important engagements of his infantry regiment (pp. 71, 142–3) which is drawn from various regions. He is not promoted but emerges as a *chef de bande* due to personal magnetism and enterprise (pp. 220, 225, 241).

The book appeared as a serial late in 1917.[3] Date and mode of publication help to explain many features. Several of the forty-three chapters saw separate publication[4] and most are extremely short, revealing by their openings and endings their separate inception and the readership addressed, which is further clarified by asides – notably the chapter 'Explanation of some Army Expressions' (pp. 161–6), and numerous literary allusions. Essentially the whole is a mosaic of scenes and portraits with no real narrative thread. Two episodes indeed are unconnected with Untel[5] and serve, like the transformations of biography, to enhance the representativeness.

The literary achievement of the book thus rests with the quality of the individual vignettes. They contain many well-written passages both in the narrator's cultured, lucid diction and the soldier's colloquial language, the two often blending surprisingly well. There are impressively profiled scenes, especially the panoramatic 'Barbed Christmas' (pp. 87–91), the sequence of attack and wounding (with striking images, e.g. the field dressing station as a 'shelter to which the battered army thronged like a poor flock whose burning eyes have discovered the gate of heaven', p. 100), the sarcastic account of medical boards (pp. 126–8), the village fete behind the lines (pp. 197–200), and the flight of the doomed pilot whose plane lifts itself against the sky like a 'Japanese doll' (pp. 245–8). Still more remarkable is the fantastic gallery of characters: Donquixotte, the eternal grocer and optimist, Citoillien the revolutionary cobbler, Lulusse of Charonne, the agile and garrulous company cook, Pollux the film star, Lazare Carnot, the noble savage in person, and many more. One does not see much of the actual fighting (six chapters, two more containing some action); one is shown instead a veritable tableau of a nation in arms.

Yet there are few entirely successful chapters – those least affected by the pervasive propaganda strain.[6] At the end of a home service period in Brittany, for example, Franconi creates a perfectly visualisable situation: a beautiful evening, Untel and the quietly mad La Bruyère sitting in a small café. But he ends with the remark: 'In this way he learnt to rebuild, whilst playing truant, the loving and joyous soul which the warrior needs' (p. 140). Phrases like this abound. Even Lulusse, one feels, stirs his pots in constant awareness of what contribution to the war effort his soups represent. They did, no doubt, but the emphasis on a conscious patriotic response to the needs of France frequently jars with the narration of events and evocation of atmosphere.

Apart from direct statements the propaganda effort takes three main forms. It guides the selection of characters. The men are all splendid, nice even in their foibles. The N.C.O.s are superb, including Tap-Tap, the terror of the bull ring (pp. 156–60). The officers are exemplary (pp. 54–5, 69–73, 151–5). There isn't a soul along the front line that is not heroic[7] Correspondingly, there is hardly any animal imagery, so frequent in other novels, and the martyr imagery is balanced by a sizeable number of images evoking heroes, from St George with the dragon (p. 56) to the Gauls of Vercingetorix (p. 251).

Selection also applies to events. After all, 1917 saw France even less successful militarily than the preceding years. One remembers the events which inspired Faulkner's *A Fable* for instance. All this is absent from Untel. Indeed the episodic structure, forced on Franconi by external conditions, facilitates his 'seeing it through' message. A continuous narration could hardly have helped alluding to the overall situation, whereas local successes no doubt occurred and offered, interspersed with interesting character sketches and moving or amusing anecdotes, the right material for presenting the unbroken spirit of the troops and their lovable ways to the people at home.

Lastly the propaganda attacks those at the rear who were not doing their bit. Contempt of lead-swingers, anger at profiteers and alienation from those at home are frequent in war literature. Here they become an overriding concern, crowned by the elaborate parable of Trebizond (pp. 179–89). In all, as a record of the soldiers' experience from 1914 to 1917, *Untel* strikes not as false certainly, but as incomplete and one-sided.

The greatest indignation is directed at artists and writers. Already before the War Untel had dismissed the artistic 'establishment', pictured as feckless, self-inflated, -ism-mongering, in terms close to the later concept of 'degenerate art': 'A sculptor of genius died from cold in his studio while the unjust and stupid crowd admired Archipenko constructing horrible dwarfs with plates of sheet-metal' (p. 32). Discharged from hospital, Untel spends his leave in Paris and now combines the aesthetic rejection of modern abstract art with the warrior's fury at artists like Mortné (another speaking name) who simply opt out of the war (pp. 109–11). And he is 'irritated by these aesthetes who make him esteem more than ever the peasants of his squad with their slow and serious reasoning, their healthy life, their sensible ways' (p. 117). Anti-modernism, xenophobia and racism merge in the outburst:

> Chinamen with crumpled faces, enervated and misanthropic Russians, phrase-mongering Roumanians, a whole cosmopolitan fauna seduced by incoherence and disorder, were discussing the problems of modern art. Big-rumped Jews ... obsessed with aesthetic and social questions, keen to uphold their wandering race, were enthroned in martial poses, condemning without any consideration our institutions and our works. (p. 117; cf. pp. 118, 184)

Even without details like 'fauna' (pre-empting later totalitarian biological imagery) or the physiological generalisation about Jews which one finds again, e.g. in Hitler's crude drawings showing racial traits in *Mein Kampf*, the proto-fascist tenor is clear. And, as so often, the condemnation of modernist art goes hand in hand with that of the political party system (cf. pp. 27, 223).

Untel's representativeness now assumes a crucial role. He is described as 'the perfect image of an unquiet period' (p. 19), as 'the exact type of a generation' that passed, in their enthusiastic search for perfection, through all ideas only to dismiss them, to a vision of the fatherland supported by common love of the native soil and common interests (p. 28). Untel is fundamentally a man of action (pp. 27, 218, 221) and thus like the officer Gustave, the figure most resembling him, ideally suited for the war, that supreme time for heroic activity and adventure (e.g. pp. 78, 126, 222). And he is just one example (p. 222; cf. pp. 246, 252). His soul, in the closing sentence of the book, embodies the 'whole, young, ardent and generous soul of the French Army'.

It is against this background that the frequent thoughts about life after the war must be seen. Untel is more shocked by what he finds at home than by anything observed at the front. Gratefully acknowledging the sympathy of the common people he notices some reconciliation of opposing interests in society. However, he cannot believe this will outlast the war (p. 107). Moreover, the fatherland might prove ungrateful as it was to the 1870 veteran (pp. 122-5). And there are so many whom the war has not changed or who have deteriorated. By contrast, change and reconciliation of opposites – bourgeois and worker as embodied in Donquixotte and Citoillien (pp. 44-9), town and country (p. 221), even the republican spirit and monarchism as represented by the Belgian King Albert (p. 175) – is the universal experience at the front. Indeed, a new communal spirit is born under the great test in the trenches (p. 171), a new mysticism and faith (pp. 84-6). And this 'holy fusion' forged under fire (p. 258) will not perish but will force a 'new law' (pp. 171, 224) on post-war France.

The visions of the 'new society' are curiously ambiguous. On the one hand they amount to nothing more than ensuring just rewards for the old combatants who will be a powerful constructive element in society (p. 171). There will be universal love (pp. 46, 112), everyone having the right to happiness (pp. 255-6) and the basic needs of life – 'A cottage, a heart, and freedom', as the title of the last chapter puts it.

On the other hand, obstacles to this paradisiac situation are anticipated and measures envisaged to overcome them which dangerously smack of other things. The predominant version[8] recalls in part Sassoon's 'Fight to a Finish': a sanitary cleansing of the streets will take place to remove parasites and profiteers (pp. 189, 231). The old interests, factions and lobbies which dominated the Second Republic will not be allowed to continue in power (p. 223), the war will, if necessary, be continued as a revolutionary war (p. 172; cf. p. 111) leading to a 'new feudalism' with natural leaders of soldiers such as Untel as the 'aristocracy of tomorrow' (p. 223). The continuation of the war at home also recalls the end of *Le Feu* although Franconi is far from any concept of class struggle. In fact, *Untel* was seen by some as a counterblast to Barbusse.[9] This projected new society will not be achieved through either parties or classes (p. 258). It is just this vision of a classless, social and national uprising that inspires misgivings, although the overtones of this new gospel are filled with greater humanity than was eventually shown elsewhere. There is a strong element of *joie de vivre* here, of mutual respect and love based on liberty (pp. 130, 207, 258). And of course Franconi cannot be blamed for idealistically envisaging in his book what the fascisti groups, the *Freikorps* and Nazi storm troopers later carried out in grim practice. Nevertheless one feels uncomfortable at reading:

> There were ten thousand, twenty thousand Untels . . . who affirmed before history the nation's will to live. They were a glorious band of brothers . . . the spirit of these bands worked miracles . . . Certainly, this *esprit de corps* will be formidable to the future; it has replaced the organisations of parties and classes, and no human force will now be able to withstand it. The bands are established; they have their leaders who are powerful because beloved by the followers. . . . (p. 223; cf. 254.)

Untel looks to the future with a warrior's and a poet's imagination, fired by an invincible conviction that he will be there to share in the liberation and the permanent leave with its new struggles and new peace (pp. 131, 259). His creator and *alter ego*, Franconi, died in action in July 1918. It is futile to speculate how he would have reacted to the actual peace and what followed – although the career e.g. of Drieu la Rochelle might offer a potential analogy. Of his sincerity there can be no doubt, nor of his personal valour. Neither can one doubt that by temperament, artistic and political outlook he was predisposed for fascist ideas which, developed by the war, shaped *Untel*.

On its publication in book form (1918) *Untel* was awarded the Prix Monthyon by the Académie Française. As a writer Franconi was destined to remain a figure of promise – not inconsiderable, judging by his control of style, the power of some images and the ability to create profiled characters and visualisable scenes.[10]

The Great War fundamentally influenced Henry Williamson even to his late association with the British Union of Fascists and beyond.[11] It also dominates *A Chronicle of Ancient Sunlight*. This *roman fleuve*, planned as long ago as 1927 and finally published from 1951 to 1969, contains in the story of Philip Maddison most of Williamson's previous writings[12] and indeed everything he has experienced and felt, 'all autobiography transmuted by what Keats called The Imagination'.[13] *The Patriot's Progress* seems to be peripheral to Williamson's work.[14]

Yet there are correspondences of detail between it and the five novels of the *Chronicle* which cover 1914–18.[15] Moreover: the rejection of a society which produced the war, emerging basically unchanged to steer towards the next, is common to both works. Also they aim at the same effect albeit by diametrically opposed methods. In *A Chronicle* representativeness is achieved through the magnitude of the context in which an idiosyncratic character is placed; in *The Patriot's Progress* it is achieved by the creation of a colourless figure, a non-character, set in selected circumstances of marked typicality.

The plans for Williamson's 'history of the last fifty years'[16] go through the very volumes of the sequence like a red thread, the inner balance required for starting it being at last achieved at the end of the fifteenth novel. By contrast, the impulse for *The Patriot's Progress* came from outside. In 1928 J. C. Squire, then editor of the *London Mercury* suggested Williamson should write a story around a series of lino-cuts by the Australian-born artist William Kermode.[17] Yet this is no hackwork;[18] the two really collaborated. The book appeared in 1930. A look at a similar collaborative effort, Raymond Escholier's *Le Sel de la terre* with woodcuts by Louis Neillot[19] brings out even more clearly the high degree of integration achieved in *The Patriot's Progress*. While the story eventually dominated the lino-cuts, its texture is adapted to theirs. The combined effect is well described in Williamson's image of the German 'pill-box' – thick concrete walls within an old farmhouse. 'His lino-cuts would be the shuttering to my verbal concrete' (Preface).

In contrast to *Untel* where every character has his own history and personal features, the people in *The Patriot's Progress* are functional entities, sketchy props that are suddenly there one moment and gone the next – all except the padre (p. 176), Wishart ('Daddy Washout') who is explicitly introduced as a stretcher-bearer (p. 130) and later picks out John Bullock's mangled body from the surrounding dead (p. 174), and Bullock's successive chums Ginger and Nobby Clark who are obliquely introduced but linger in his mind after their deaths. The flatness of the central figure, 'A clerk in the City of London', the broad-brushed background of people and the continuity of events free the reader's attention for a hardly mediated, unbroken confrontation with the war, which is the only true agent in the story. Thus 'Reality in War Literature' which Williamson demanded of himself and others,[20] becomes possible in a specific way. At the same time these factors create a massive sense of uniformity – reality has been fixed in large set blocks.

The title already suggests this with its allusion to Bunyan's *The Pilgrim's Progress* and the medieval morality background. The name John Bullock is a modern national equivalent to generic names like

'Christian' – or indeed Everyman. The chapter headings, 'First Phase' to 'Fifth Phase', have the same quality. So has the very setting of the print which in its accurate, harsh columns of large letters seems to evoke 'concrete'.

The general impression of the style is rough, hard and solid, corresponding to the lino-cuts. Syntactically this is achieved through the predominance of short sentences conforming to the simplest standard sequences: subject-predicate or subject-predicate-complement.

> The C.S.M. came along with the rum. Jokes began to be heard about the trench. Captain's orders – No one to fire from the trench, or show himself, or dig. The sun brought some cheer. Breakfast was two biscuits and half a tin of bully. No water. Ration party lost. Shells came over; they crouched and cringed for half-an-hour. (p. 106)

This passage also shows two main variations: the brief, grammatically incomplete phrase and the larger sequence tightly controlled by the parallel subordination of additional units. This can extend to some length without loosening the structure: ' "Mind that shell-hole! Pass it down", was whispered, spoken casually, hissed with tension, carefully passed on, ignored' (p. 55). Often narration merges into speech (e.g. p. 74) or thought:

> They went on slowly past the field gun batteries. The long bright shafts of whitish light smacked the air, the shells screamed away just over their helmets. Each narrow light-blast was like concentrated moonlight. Surely the Germans would see them. His mind flung about in panic. Stop firing, for Christ's sake. Blinding light, paa-aa-ang of shell screaming away eastwards. The mud pulled at the top of his skull, hurting and wrenching it. How much farther? (p. 192)

One also notices the use of technical terms and soldier's slang (without Franconi's 'explanations'). Most striking are physical sensations and energetic verb-metaphors (e.g. 'smacked' – similes are rare) and generally the use of precise, expressive vocabulary: 'Some time later John Bullock was trying to fill sandbags with mud, heaving them up on the parapet, squelching shapeless bags oozing and dripping, falling down and splashing' (p. 116). We are given reflections and emotions – 'John Bullock enjoyed his first night in the trenches' (p. 58), etc. But sensory perception and physical action predominate – 'John Bullock saw' (p. 58), 'John Bullock crept' (p. 58), 'John Bullock heard' (p. 61) – most strongly when he lies wounded on the battlefield:

> Rough and smooth. Rough was wide and large and tilting with sickness. He struggled and struggled to clutch smooth, and it slid away. Rough came back and washed over him. (p. 171)

The use of onomatopeia is more successful here than in many war novels.[21] Among the early readers T. E. Lawrence particularly stressed original images like 'the gangrenous light of dawn began to spread over the German lines' (p. 116; Preface), and Arnold Bennett the powerful, effectively phased battle descriptions.[22] One must see these things within the strong, unified whole. They are made of the same materials as the rest.

The three middle Phases, in France, each show John Bullock pulled deeper into the maw of war, which is working more and more violently until it crushes him and spits him out. They are bracketed by the first (pre-war existence and preparatory processing) and the fifth (retrieval, after-care), which indicates – as does the near-identity of the lino-cuts on p. 4 and after p. 194 – resumption, minus one leg, of the pre-war existence. Stasis governs the only major movement: the archetypal way out to the front and back to the point of departure. In my end is my beginning, with a vengeance.

The overall hard oneness is so strong that it neutralises under-currents of development like the increasing power and destructiveness of the war in the succession of Phases Two, Three and Four, and the gradual formation of the soldier John Bullock indicated by the names John and Bullock, variously used as 'inside' and 'outside' view alternatives to the full name during Phase One, being finally welded together at the end of that Phase (pp. 25 ff.) to a stereotyped formula. Another development is the evolution of 'Roll on Duration' from the famous enlistment term, which recurs like a refrain, marking for example the end of Phase One, to be discarded after the death of Ginger at the end of Phase Three: 'The cry was no longer Roll on, Duration. The first seven years will be the worst, they said to each other, avoiding, in the semblance of jest, the reality on which their minds refused to dwell' (p. 119).

This is an example of the narrator speaking not from John Bullock's point of view but his own. Throughout the book John Bullock is the 'reflector' (though not in a Jamesian sense). What he experiences, feels and thinks is what the reader gets. Yet – although John Bullock is once raised above the others as being more alert (p. 51) he is clearly incapable of such remarks as that quoted above. In its narrative situation the book stands between Manning's *Her Privates We* and John Richard's *Old Soldiers Never Die*.[23] The omniscient narrator uses John Bullock as the centre of perception, but there is no doubt as to whose are the magnificent descriptive powers rightly prized by Bennett.

One further development beneath the surface is that this narrator from Phase Three onwards intervenes not only more often but also more noticeably, giving a summary of events from May to September 1917 (p. 126), portraying thoughts of other figures (the padre, p. 154;

officers, p. 152) and interrupting John Bullock's journey back by showing his father at home reading aloud patriotic newspaper passages
(pp. 181–3). The other intrusions can easily be integrated. This scene
cannot – it is so obviously interpolated to create a sharp emotional
contrast and sticks out also through the visual effect of whole pages set
in italics. Here (as in the isolated remark 'thus our hero's thoughts',
p. 128) control has slipped and the unity of tone is temporarily dis-
turbed.

In general the distinction between the narrator's and John Bullock's
point of view is used subtly and effectively to convey the attitude to
the war. John Bullock's opinions vary according to the soldier's circumstances: he joins, 'anxious lest the war might end before he saw some
of the fun' (p. 7). The anguish at leaving England makes him ask
'What were they all doing here?' (p. 39);[24] in the excitement of the
train journey through strange country he feels 'this was the life' (p. 50).
Having got used to dirt and death he enjoys an undisturbed bowel-
emptying and returns 'thinking that the war was fine' (pp. 65–6).
Later only the hope of a Blighty wound keeps him going (p. 125).
He works up courage to go to a brothel 'before he was bloody well
snuffed out' (p. 133). The experience leaves him cold, hollow and
resigned:

> Drubadrubadrubadrub. More slaughter up there in the mud. Poor
> sods. His turn soon. What did anything matter? You had to die
> sometime. . . . Well, what odds if he went where Ginger was, and all
> the boys. (p. 146)

He drinks himself silly, doubts God (p. 147, cf. 157), reaches camp
drunk and is caught. Waiting for his sentence

> he felt that life was dark and hopeless. During the instant that the
> Colonel glanced through his crime-sheet he saw the war as something
> he had never fully thought of before: something that kept millions
> of men like himself in slavery. (pp. 151–2)

He gets fourteen days of Field Punishment No. 1 and 'At last he had
realised the War. He wouldn't come back from the attack. Roll on, the
attack!' (p. 153). Afterwards at Le Havre hospital his feelings are
reduced to 'he wasn't sorry to be out of it' (p. 189). His stump heals
and

> He grew fat and happy and lost all interest in the war. Never wanted
> to hear of it again. It hadn't been such a bad time, taken all round;
> he wouldn't have missed it, really. They said you could do a lot on
> an artificial leg. (pp. 191–2)

Thus John Bullock not only arrives back at his point of departure externally, but also mentally. The cruelty and horror of the process escape the victim. They are visible to the reader and, as in Oliver Goldsmith's 'Distresses of a Common Soldier',[25] are brought home more forcefully through the ultimate unawareness and unconcern of the protagonist. This also keeps him true to his character as representative of the ordinary man. However, as it were in compensation for tying John Bullock's moments of insight to phases of commercial sex, excessive drink and physical constriction, Williamson grants him one great moment: when the cigarsmoking prosperous old man benevolently assures him England won't forget the soldiers' sacrifice, he replies: 'We are England' (p. 194).

There is pathos here, as Lawrence noted, but also accusation. This last scene of London celebrating victory on Armistice Day and the last lino-cut show that nothing has really changed. The sense of tragedy and bitter irony in the title-allusion to the *Pilgrim's Progress* emerge fully in this ending. After all, Christian in Bunyan's tale reaches the Heavenly Jerusalem at the end of his wearisome journey.[26] The contrast is expressed in the hopes of the one figure capable of a sustained view – *not* John Bullock, but the padre: 'He was one of those rare men who carried the real war on their shoulders ... After the war it will be different, he used to think: out of this great agony will survive a new spirit' (pp. 154–5). The padre believes that 'Christ had come again to the world, arising in the comradeship of men crucified on the battlefields!' (p. 176). There and then the narrator adds: 'He died of nervous exhaustion soon after the Armistice.' What survives is the same society dominated by the same interests as before, personified in the fat old man who even now has not had enough: 'In my opinion the Government is weak. We ought to have driven the Hun back into Berlin and given their country a taste of what they gave France' (p. 193).

Looking back on *The Patriot's Progress* in 1959 Williamson criticised its anti-staff bias (Postscript). There are such passages, but no more than usual in many war books. The real bias emerges from the design and arrangement of the story and the lino-cuts. This message is not far removed from that of the war novels and the two immediately following in the later great sequence.[27] The visual and verbal image of a meaningless, destructive mechanism which Kermode and Williamson created amounts, in Bennett's words, 'to a tremendous, an overwhelming, an unanswerable indictment of the institution of war'.

Wiechert, a married writer and schoolteacher by 1914, was like Williamson nearly destroyed by the war though he, too, recovered from his physical wounds.[28] In what he later called 'paroxysms' he tried to rid himself of the war's 'poison' in two novels – *Der Wald* (1920, published in 1922) and *Der Totenwolf* (1922, published in 1924) which seem breathtaking anticipations of the entire Nazi nightmare. An inverted 'Wolf of Death' followed with the Christian sufferer *Andreas Nyland* (1926).[29] After two egocentric, destructive, basically a-human extremes: the blonde beast and the fanatic saint, Wiechert's recovery is manifested in the creation of a *man* who mirrors his assumption of a deeply conservative, countrybound and religious-humanitarian stand (which after 1933 progressively brought Wiechert into conflict with the regime).[30] A trilogy was planned (later superseded by the *Jerominkinder*) of which we have two volumes: *Die Kleine Passion*, a fascinating, mainly realistic if sometimes melodramatic childhood story set (as is usual with Wiechert) in his corner of the world, the lonely fields, woods and lakes of southern East Prussia; and its continuation, the war novel *Jedermann* which appeared in 1931 and won the Schünemann Prize in 1932.[31] It is a seminal book for the whole of Wiechert's middle and later work.

The first thing one notices about this 'Story of a Nameless One' (sub-title) is that he *has* a name, and unlike Untel and John Bullock it is complete and individual: Johannes Karstens. He also has a distinctly unusual history – son and step-brother of criminals, he lives under his divorced mother's name at her ancestral farm. He joins up with two classmates: Klaus Wirtulla and Percy Count Pfeil. And his first encounter with the Army is an examination by the doctor with whose wife he had a love affair while still at school. There is obviously no attempt here to achieve typicality through a generalised background; the namelessness must be understood differently.

The design of the story on the other hand clearly underscores representativeness: the three classmates volunteer right at the beginning. The action covers the whole war and embraces both the Eastern and the Western Fronts. This was indicated by Wiechert's own experience, of which a good deal is incorporated;[32] but compared to the autobiography the move West is significantly shifted to the middle of the war – 1916 – to include the Somme (pp. 417 ff.). The soldier's experiences are comprehensive, no major aspect is left out.

The principle of representativeness also applies to the characters. Like many others, Wiechert concentrates on the squad which, as opposed to Untel's and John Bullock's, has clear contours and a continuous existence. We can visualise the squad leader, Corporal Hasenbein ('Haresleg'), Gollimbeck, a small trader like Donquixotte (but presented unsympathetically), Lorenz and Schröder, two utter brutes, and Josef Megai, the sad, luckless but courageous Jew.[33] Then there are the three classmates: Klaus, the childlike, slow, bed-wetting, unhappy son of a railway gatekeeper; Johannes (like Untel 'younger' than his author – Wiechert makes him a student), the pensive and poetic man of the soil; Percy, the impeccable, intelligent and energetic aristocrat; and finally a new man: Heinrich Oberüber, a sober, practical and robust vagrant. These four friends form a 'kernel' within the squad (p. 400) and are central to the story. Johannes has a special position. We know most about him and everything is seen from his point of view with no overt authorial intrusion. However, he is *not* Everyman. One could argue that the Everyman-figure has been folded out into these four men collectively to represent the soldier: they are a fair cross-section by class and temperament, as well as by rank and fate: Oberüber and Klaus remain privates, Johannes (ineligible for a commission because of his family circumstances) is made an N.C.O., Percy is commissioned and later leads their platoon; Percy is killed, Klaus loses his legs, Johannes is seriously wounded but recovers, Oberüber gets off nearly unscathed.

However, the namelessness[34] – exponent of universality – which runs through the novel as a *leitmotif* has even wider dimensions. The war strips *everyone* of their individuality of which the name is the external sign. At first this seems to have encouraging and comforting effects (pp. 309, 313, 317 f., 364). The last echo of this occurs when Johannes, feeling alienated at home, longs for his comrades. The very experience however inverts the feeling: 'They have made us so weak ... that we can only live in numbers ... only the squad can survive, not the single man' (p. 444).

The sense of loss, deeper than death itself, had set in very early (p. 308, cf. p. 341). Johannes notices the levelling effect of their outfit and thinks: 'One must save the face from out of the uniform' (p. 327). This is of course impossible, the war stamps them all:

> ... believe me, this is not the war. This is death, but death is not the war. The war, little Klaus, is that our hearts are empty. Do you understand? That we have no mother left, no home, no name and no face. (p. 421, cf. pp. 389–90, 402, etc.)

In the works of the war machine – variously figured as a mill, a mine, etc. – they are reduced to material, to one great mass of suffering. An early vision of hundreds of thousands gliding quietly to the earth (p. 354) is expanded to include places, equally nameless, even love. Finally everyone Johannes meets has the same face, into which merge all the faces he has ever seen (p. 473). He tries to determine this universal face in vain until it comes upon him looking at a shelled village:

> Out of all the gable-ends, ridges and roofs, the face of the village was slowly forming for him, a grey, suffering, dilapidated face like the face of the soldier for which he had been looking for so long. A face showing defencelessness and resignation in which the history of the war was written, more clearly and more moving than in the

grave profile of heroic deeds and individual deaths – the face of humanity rather than of man. (p. 479)

And yet it is only part of them, Johannes feels, which is thus stereo-typed. Something childlike remains underneath. This split of the personality is earlier on perceived as a hope: war will not destroy them completely (pp. 391–2). On their return, however, in the mirror-scene in Königsberg, the 'Everyman-face' becomes a burden for the future:

> They will always have someone walking by their sides, strange and yet familiar, who follows them from the mists of the past, a grey, universal, nameless figure. (p. 515)

Interposed in this process of recognition, which has universal relevance for the novel, there are two other, more personal themes: the accusa-tion of God (the archetypal father-figure) after the mutilation of Klaus which throws Johannes into an abysmal crisis coming to a head in the rejection of Abraham's sacrifice (p. 453);[35] furthermore the clearly regressive reliance on his mother, culminating in a curiously twisted pietà-scene (pp. 448–9). This element is however balanced by other mother–child relations and a generalised though still remarkable glorification of the mother-figure (p. 375).[36]

Besides the working out of these major themes other, more formal devices strengthen the novel's cohesion. The single perspective ensures continuity and unity of tone. It also facilitates great shifts in focus which the comprehensiveness of experiences makes necessary. Com-pared to Williamson, where the profile of events is lessened for the sake of the overall effect, there are great changes from significant event extensively described (with concomitant arrest of movement) to rapid flux of time and action. Thus the first day in the recruits' lives fills a chapter (pp. 326–46). Afterwards the weeks of training merge into one another. The first time Johannes directly kills (ironically John Bullock had never seen an active enemy soldier) is shown in a long moving scene (pp. 386–9), after which the continuous fighting becomes blurred in memory. The changing narrative tempo becomes even more marked by pauses of reflection and emotional response which appear natural in Johannes, the student of philosophy and incipient poet. The death of Corporal Hasenbein, for example, is presented in great detail (pp. 410–16). With his blood his life story pours out – he was a school-teacher, had children and an interest in bees. When he is dead, Johannes realises that this was a simple, innocent man; he was too severe, too intent on his dignity, but mainly because of his ridiculous name. He had never done any real harm – and now he had been killed by someone like himself on the other side. The one death illuminates many others and reveals the nature of war. Such moments of insight also have structural significance, most clearly around the centre of the book.[37]

The structure generally is strong and balanced. As in *The Patriot's Progress* each phase or chapter marks a definite state. The whole is framed by the gathering of family and friends at Johannes' home the night before army life begins, and a similar gathering at the end after the war has cruelly hit them.

Wiechert's style in the immediate post-war novels has great force, suggestiveness and, as it were, a dark brilliance where it does not patently lapse into the absurd. With the *Kleine Passion* he abandoned his heavy and explosive, quasi-baroque diction. *Jedermann* continues this quieter, more poised style, retaining however the richness in striking images that Wiechert commanded from the beginning, and adding symbols of determinant significance for the whole work. The fate of Klaus had been foreshadowed mainly through his taking the communion 'for all of us' as Johannes had involuntarily said (p. 363, cf., pp. 374, 463). There is also a presentiment of Percy's death, but this event seems more natural. He was the most suited to the war. But it is symbolic that of the four central figures he should die. The death of this nobleman, in whom the old world had remained intact whereas it had been dying off morally long before, seals the end of an era. Wiechert underlines this symbolism through the ritual determination with which Johannes and Heinrich cart Percy's body back across the Rhine to bury him – reminiscent of an important early work in Germanic myth-building: Felix Dahn's *Ein Kampf um Rom* (1870), which ends with the final retreat of the Ostrogoths carrying their dead last King, Totila, away with them.

The visit to the Countess completes their last mission and ends the war for them. 'What is left?', Johannes asks in despair (p. 511). Heinrich's answer – Nature – had been prepared long before: 'The earth is not engulfed in the maelstrom of the time, not shaken by the eruptions of man. It has kept its law, its face, its gesture' (p. 315).

With its law and face (which it preserves despite temporary disfiguring) the earth is the real counterforce to the war. With this assurance Johannes had set out. At the height of the crisis his deepest anguish arose from the feeling of alienation from nature even more than from man (pp. 438–9). As the cataclysm works itself out, Johannes' link to the soil re-emerges. He eagerly responds: 'We are going to plough, Heinrich' (p. 517, cf. pp. 522, 533). It is symbolic that he, the only one coming (at least in part) of farming stock should survive, bring Heinrich, the homeless one, home to the farm and take once more under his protection, this time effectively and permanently, Klaus who is the symbol of man's wounded but indestructible innocence.

Two other symbols have paved the way to making this return a
renewal. During the strange loneliness and silence of the last days at
the front, when everything else seemed to end with the war, Johannes
comes upon a tied-up dog like a 'pledge from God' (p. 481) and an
old musical box with a magically tender tune. Both the dog, symbolising animate nature, and the musical box symbolising the cultural
heritage have in their turn been foreshadowed in earlier passages
(pp. 305, 341–2, 363). They correspond to Johannes' dual nature: the
future poet (pp. 354, 454, 533–4) descended from the land who will
never, as Heinrich soberly reminds him, be a farmer in the literal
sense. However, just as he grasps the significance of the earth as a
counterweight to the war, he feels that the *anti-leitmotif*, the 'Every-
man-melody' (pp. 521–2, 531–2), a musical correlative to the 'Everyman-face' can be overcome by art. He takes the dog and the musical
box home, concrete symbols of what is left.

The novel closes on a Messianic note. Johannes has finally grown up,
he releases his mother from her burden, thus freeing her to pursue her
own fate. And he unites the circle of survivors with his idea of a new
task: ending the hatred and beginning once more with love (p. 531).
Healing and helping become the new theme – more fully developed in
his spiritual 'successor', Jons Ehrenreich Jeromin, whose war service
is Wiechert's third re-creation of 1914–18.[38] The last scene of *Jedermann* in its visual and verbal entirety symbolises in sharp focus the
contrast between the old and the new. Heinrich and Johannes have
helped Klaus 'outside' and carry him back to the house where the
celebration of Christmas Eve is in progress. Heinrich announces them,
reverting lightly to the military mode: 'Squad Karstens, three men.'
Klaus smilingly corrects: 'Squad Johannes, two-and-a-half men' (pp.
537–8).

The name Johannes itself assumes symbolic meaning. The great
model of the Baptist is evoked when Johannes is called a 'messenger'
(p. 530). Nothing illustrates the distance from Wiechert's first shaping
of the war in the *Totenwolf* more clearly: the apostle of destruction has
become the follower of him who announced the new age of Christ.
An arduous pledge. In view of subsequent events in Wiechert's life it
reads like an omen – something of which Wiechert must have been
conscious, perhaps a little too conscious, when he chose to resume the
name Johannes in his account of Buchenwald, *The Forest of the
Dead.*[39]

The analysis of these books reveals some basic similarities. All three are
based on personal experience and its transformations contribute to the
representativeness of protagonist and story. In all three novels the
third-person narrative is chosen as the less immediately personal one.

However, the actual shaping of the central characters and their fate is very different both in content and fictional technique.

In none of the books does the attempt at universality entail objectivity. All three are heavily biased, the difference being that Wiechert and Williamson integrate the propaganda much more than Franconi. The projected attitudes differ profoundly: Franconi depicts a character naturally adapted to the war whose propensities are confirmed and developed by it. The response invited is admiration and the desire to emulate. Williamson gives a perfect case history of manipulation, the intended reactions are indignation and anger. Wiechert's Johannes becomes a leader only in the movement away from the war. Like *The Patriot's Progress*, *Jedermann* is an indictment of the war, but the dominant note is sorrow, the message hope. Overtly Williamson restricts himself to the demonstrative mode, while Franconi and Wiechert add (opposed) exhortative dimensions: *The Patriot's Progress* merely presents what has been done, *Untel* expounds what should be done, *Jedermann* shows what might be done.

As far as representativeness means comprehensiveness Franconi's bias leads to a wide but one-sided selection of characters and scenes; Williamson's account is much more comprehensive in spite of its concentration on John Bullock. Wiechert's *Jedermann* has greater scope and balance than either. In depicting the common soldier at the front, *Untel* effects least, simply because there is little of that and what there is lacks concreteness and sensory impact. Both *The Patriot's Progress* and *Jedermann* convey the reality of the fighting soldier's experience forcefully, but by radically different means: Williamson relies on direct, mainly external and physical, impressions with a minimum of mediation and reflection. The multiple chaos that is war in action assumes a material presence which remains unparalleled in war fiction. John Bullock is shown, so to speak, *inside* the machine. In Wiechert the impressions are always mediated, there is physical impact, but the emphasis lies on the emotional and intellectual response. Through the medium of Johannes Karstens there emerges an image *of* the machine and its effects on man. The two books complement each other.

Only in Franconi do the affinities to fascist thought enter into the war novels discussed, and here in a form one might call idealist prefascism, showing among other things the romantic traits Sérant has stressed in other French writers who survived to participate in actual fascism.[40] *Jedermann* marks Wiechert's final severance from a phase that, while not including accession to fascist movements certainly shows their spirit. Williamson's association with fascism dates from after *The Patriot's Progress*. In its outraged accusation of society it portrays a position from which a man might clutch at anything appearing to preserve some of the values he cherishes. Williamson's and Wiechert's veering, however peripheral and temporary, towards fascism in response to the war may well be paradigmatic, no less than the eventual position of permanent nostalgic disillusionment in the one, and of pious (but ultimately retrograde) renewal in the other.

10 Journalism into Fiction: *Im Westen nichts Neues*

Brian A. Rowley

All Quiet on the Western Front (*Im Westen nichts Neues*) is one of the most surprising phenomena in the history of literature. Its commercial success was unparalleled: in fifteen months after publication, 1,040,000 copies were sold in Germany, and total sales in all languages – there seems to be no bibliography of translations, but there were apparently 32 of them[1] – were more than $3\frac{1}{2}$ million in the same period.[2] World sales to date have been estimated at over 8 million.[3]

But the novel was not simply a best-seller. It also became a focus of intellectual and, indeed, of political life. Immediately upon its appearance, it provided a *casus belli* for the battle, in the Germany of 1929, between militarists and pacifists, right wing and left. Its author's name became such a household word that a contemporary article on the great seventeenth-century novelist, Grimmelshausen, appeared under the title 'The Remarque of the Thirty Years War'.[4] The novel was immediately parodied;[5] and no less than nine books about it and its author appeared in Germany in 1929 and 1930.[6] In Russia, the translation sold so well that the Soviet Government feared for the ardour of its armies and banned the book.[7] In America, in 1930, *All Quiet* was made into one of the early talking films, directed by Lewis Milestone;[8] but after disturbances at its German première, in December 1930, the film was banned by the German Government – whereupon Rowohlt rushed out a 'book of the film'.[9] When the Nazis came to power, the novel itself was among the books ceremonially burnt in the Opernplatz in Berlin, on 10 May 1933.[10]

Remarque appears to have been caught unawares by this furore. In an interview with Karl Vogler, in the summer of 1929, he said: 'How was I to know that I would become, so to speak, the voice of the many? Success took me by surprise . . . It will be hard to write anything else after this success.'[11]

Certainly, such a success was not presaged by Remarque's earlier career.[12] Born Erich Paul Remark in Osnabrück on 22 June 1898, he was the son of a retired seaman, turned book-binder; and, when the war broke out, he was attending the local Catholic training college. He volunteered in 1916, and served until the war ended. Afterwards, he taught in a village school, later becoming a salesman and, eventually, in 1923, a journalist. On 14 October 1925, he married a divorcée, Ilse Winkelhoff, née Zambona (they were divorced in 1932, and remarried in 1938). As a young soldier, he had already started to write, and his first poems and essays were published in 1918; from 1923, he adapted his name to the form Erich Maria Remarque and produced, as a journalist, numerous articles on sport, travel, and good living – one of which, 'On the Mixing of Expensive Brandies', has been highlighted by critics as symptomatic of his career at this stage.[13]

All Quiet is sometimes regarded as Remarque's first novel; but in fact he had written two earlier ones.[14] *Die Traumbude* ('The Den of Dreams', 1920) presents an aesthete alienated by the aftermath of the war, in a mannered style: it was bought up by the publishers of *All Quiet*, in March 1928.[15] Remarque's second novel, *Station am Horizont* ('Halt on the Horizon', 1927-8, published in the periodical *Sport im Bild*, of which he was then editor), is more fluently written; but its content reflects the brittle side of the 1920s. Neither novel showed much sign of what was to come.

All Quiet on the Western Front was written in Berlin, in the autumn of 1927. Rejected by several publishers, it was finally accepted by Ullstein;[16] and, after being serialised in the *Vossische Zeitung* between 10 November and 9 December 1928, it appeared in book form, slightly revised, on 31 January 1929.[17]

Remarque's later career is also relevant to any assessment of his best-seller. Troubled by the publicity and controversy it aroused, and fortified by his royalties, he left Germany, and in 1931 bought a villa at Ronco near Ascona in Switzerland. In 1937, he was deprived of his German citizenship, and in 1939 he emigrated to the United States. After the Second World War, he again lived in Switzerland, and did not return to Germany except for brief visits. In 1958, he married again, this time the film star Paulette Goddard. He died at Locarno on 25 September 1970.

In the forty years following *All Quiet*, Remarque published another nine novels; none of these sold less than 150,000 in Germany, and three were moderate best-sellers: *Three Comrades* (*Drei Kameraden*) (1938); *Arc de Triomphe* (1946); and finally *The Night in Lisbon* (*Die Nacht von Lissabon*) (1962). This hardly suggests that Remarque was a 'one-book man', that it had really been 'hard to write anything else'.

Remarque's career thus suggests that the reasons for the success of *All Quiet* are likely to be somewhat more complex than is commonly supposed.

On the one hand, timing is obviously of significance. The interval of

ten years since the war was short enough for the memories of participants not to have faded, but long enough for the ex-servicemen to have
recovered from their immediate post-war desire to forget. At the same
time, the developing political situation at the end of the 1920s made
modern war into a live issue: with the establishment of Fascism in
Italy and the emergence of National Socialism in Germany, violence
as an instrument of policy became ever more likely, and opinion
polarised between Germans who looked to militarism to restore their
prestige, and those who clung tenaciously to their pacifist hopes. By
beginning the serial publication of the novel on the eve of the tenth
anniversary of the Armistice – 10 November 1928 – the house of
Ullstein was deliberately tying the novel in to this political controversy.
In this sense, *All Quiet* is one of a group of novels whose reputations
fed on their times: Ludwig Renn's *Krieg* (*War*, 1928) in Germany;
Manning's *Her Privates We* (1929) in England; Hemingway's *A Farewell to Arms* (1929) in America.

But not all these were best-sellers; so Remarque's success was due also
to the book's intrinsic qualities.[18] Some of these, we may feel, are
journalistic rather than strictly literary. The particular blend of suffering, sensuality and sentiment suggests that Remarque had gauged
public taste. The horror and degradation of war is represented, but it
is shown with irony, wit, and even humour. To a large extent, this is
made possible by the choice of a group of characters who are close to
the reader. And this again depends upon Remarque's command of a
clear but lively, indeed pungent style. All these features owe something
to journalism. Yet this is not to deny the book's very real literary merits.

Let us look at some of these aspects more closely. The sensuality, for
example. 'We have lost our sense of other connections, because they
are artificial. Only the facts are real and important to us' (pp. 26–7).
And sensual comforts are facts, just as much as war's horrors. Remarque
loses no time in foregrounding these comforts in Chapter 1. The novel
starts with food ('a belly full of haricot beans and stewed beef', p. 7);
with tobacco ('for every man, ten cigars, twenty cigarettes and two
sticks of chewing tobacco, that can't be bad', p. 7); and with sleep
('war wouldn't be so bad, if only we had more sleep', p. 8). But the
soldier's idea of comfort doesn't stop here: the 'decencies' of ordinary
society have been left behind, and so, when the novel opens, Remarque's
heroes spend two hours sitting in the sunshine on little portable
thunder-boxes, talking and playing skat (pp. 13–16); and Paul comments: 'Here in the open air this business is a real pleasure to us . . .
To the soldier, his belly and his digestion are more familiar than they
are to anyone else. Three-quarters of his vocabulary is taken from that
area . . .' (pp. 13–14). Scatological terms certainly do appear in the
characters' vocabulary – though less often than they would have done

in real life. Again, in Chapter III the nakedness of Himmelstoss before his whipping is made explicit.

Unlike defecation, copulation is only lightly suggested in the early chapters. Paul's fellow-soldier Leer has 'a beard and a great liking for girls from the officers' brothels; he swears they are required by army orders to wear silk shifts and, for customers of the rank of captain and above, to take a bath beforehand' (p. 9). In Chapter v, one of the answers to the question, What would you do if the war ended today? – that by Haie Westhus – revolves around women (pp. 81–2). But the main sex-scene is kept for Chapter VII when – ironically after Haie Westhus's fatal back-wound has been reported – Leer, Kropp and Paul swim naked across a canal at night to visit the three French-women they have propositioned. After the food they have brought has been eaten, the six of them make love:

> There are rooms close by . . . How different all this is from things in the other ranks' brothels, which we're allowed to visit and where there are long queues. I don't want to think of them; but unbidden they pass through my mind, and I take fright, for perhaps one can never ever forget such things.
>
> But then I feel the lips of the slim, dark girl, and I push myself towards them; I close my eyes, as if to shut it all out – war and horror and vulgarity – to wake up young and happy . . . And I press myself all the more deeply into the arms that enfold me; perhaps a miracle will occur. (pp. 151–3)

The sexuality is unmistakable; but so is the restraint.

The fact that *All Quiet* was read for its indecencies was recognised from the start. 'Many read it mainly for its improprieties', writes an early commentator;[19] and the impact made by the latrine-scene in Chapter I and the sex-scene in Chapter VII may be gauged from the emphasis on them in the parody *All Quiet at the Gates of Troy.* This was certainly a reason for the novel's success. Yet Remarque never lets indecency become obscene, still less pornographic. More important, he is able to show, because of the point of view of his narrative, that an emphasis on creature comforts is part of the soldier's psychology; less trivially realistic, that it is part of his defence against the otherwise unbearable brutality of war. This is illustrated, in the farcical mode, by the goose-roasting sequence in Chapter v after the horrors of the wire-laying fatigue in IV; and in the lyrical mode, by the love-scene in Chapter VII after the battle-scene of VI. And finally – as Paul's love-scene with his brunette suggests – it is a mode of experience through which the soldier's contact with the deepest springs of life, threatened as it is by war, can be renewed. All these points are made in Paul's meditation earlier in VII, which concludes:

But our comrades are dead, we cannot help them, they are at rest
– who knows what faces us? what we want is to lie down and sleep
or eat as much as we can get into our bellies, and drink and smoke,
so that the hours are not empty. Life is short. (p. 142)

Sensuality in the novel functions on many levels.

The same is true of external nature. When the three walk back along
the river-bank after their love-scene:

The night air cools our hot bodies. The poplars tower up into the
darkness and rustle. The moon is in the sky and in the water of the
canal. We do not run, we walk side by side taking long strides.
(p. 153)

The poplars here are counter-images to war; but they are also priapic
and, thereby, metaphysical, even religious symbols. A simpler contrast
is produced by the scene after the soldiers leave their trucks, in the
wire-laying episode of Chapter IV:

Mist and gun-smoke lie chest-high over the fields. The moon shines
on them. On the road, troops are passing. The steel helmets give
back dull gleams in the moonlight. Heads and rifles stand out above
the white mist; nodding heads, swaying rifle-barrels.

Nearer the front the mist ends. The heads become figures here;
coats, trousers and boots emerge from the mist as if from a pool of
milk. (p. 60)

Mist and moonlight make a backcloth for the devastation that is to
follow. One of the most reverberant examples of this technique of
juxtaposition is provided by the passage when Paul leaves the hospital
after Kemmerich's death at the end of Chapter II:

Outside the door I feel the darkness and the wind as a kind of
salvation. I breathe as deeply as possible, and feel the air warm and
soft, as never before, against my face. Thoughts of girls, of meadows
in flower, of white clouds flash suddenly through my head ... The
earth is permeated by forces which flow into me through the soles
of my feet. The night crackles electrically, the front thunders dully
like a concert of drums. My limbs move supplely, I feel my joints
are strong, I pant and blow. The night lives, I live. I feel a hunger,
greater than that of the belly alone. (pp. 38–9)

Liedloff suggests that the motif of the 'butterfly' provides a particular
instance of such juxtaposition.[20]

Nature, too, then, restores the lost contact with life. The intimate
connections between war and nature are reinforced by Remarque's use,
from time to time, of a grammatical device – a kind of zeugma which
links, without overt comment, experiences from the two spheres:

It smells of tar, summer, and sweaty feet. (p. 45)

Then, once again, there are only the rockets, the singing of the shells, and the stars . . . (p. 68)

On the success of Remarque's rendering of the brutal reality of war there has been, from the beginning, more agreement than on most other issues. Some details, certainly, were challenged: notably the screaming of the wounded horses, in Chapter iv (p. 66). But other critics were quick to point out literary analogues in Fenimore Cooper – incidentally one of the authors Remarque recalls admiring in his teens[21] – in Liliencron, and in Zola;[22] whilst a veterinary surgeon confirmed that horses do indeed scream when in pain.[23] It was also, more widely, argued that war is not always so brutal and so ignominious as this novel depicts it; but that is to miss the point that trench warfare in Flanders in 1914–18 is not war in general, but a particularisation of the brutalising tendencies inherent in all warfare to a point of no return. And this sort of warfare *is* captured by Remarque's sober realism, more successfully than ever before; as Friedrich Fuchs wrote when the novel's sales reached a million: 'I can only explain it like this: you can read here, for the first time, what it was really like out there.'[24] This success, which lies at the heart of Remarque's achievement, was summarised by the Expressionist dramatist Ernst Toller, in a review that became famous:

No modern writer has more magnificently evoked a battle, a gas-attack, hand-to-hand fighting, a visit home on leave; I shall never forget the hail of fire over the graveyard, or the dying of the helpless wounded horses . . .
This is how German soldiers lived in the trenches, and French ones, and British ones.[25]

How does Remarque manage to evoke the reality of battle? Let us look at a passage from the graveyard section (in iv) which Toller praises:

The fields are flat, the wood is too far and too dangerous; there is no other cover but the graveyard and the mounds. In the dark we stumble in, each man is at once glued to the back of a mound as if spat there.
Not a moment too soon. The darkness becomes insane. It heaves and rages. Blacker darknesses than the night, hugely bulging, rush towards us, over us. The flames from the explosions flicker across the graveyard.
Nowhere is there an escape. In the flash of the shells I risk a look at the fields. They are a sea in turmoil; the jets of flame from the shells jump up like fountains. It is impossible for anyone to get across there alive.

The wood disappears, it is pounded, torn, shredded out of existence. We will have to stay here in the graveyard.

In front of us the earth bursts. It rains clods. I feel a jolt. My sleeve is torn by a splinter. I clench my fist. No pain. But that doesn't reassure me, wounds never hurt until later. I run my hand over the arm. It is scratched, but whole. (pp. 69–70)

For the most part, a blow-by-blow account of successive events. Only at a few points – 'The darkness becomes insane'; 'a sea in turmoil' – does the language heighten and interpret. For the rest, no understatement certainly; but no exaggeration either. Even the description of the annihilation of the little wood – 'it is pounded, torn, shredded out of existence' – convinces us that its rhetorical accumulation is no more than sober truth. This consistent and determined factuality is the key to Remarque's total success in depicting trench warfare.

In the 1929 interview with Vogler, Remarque claimed not to have read the war novels of either Barbusse or Unruh;[26] and his descriptions do not give the impression of deriving from literary models. It is rather that his experience as a journalist has taught him how to select facts and convey them in a style that heightens, rather than blurs, their impact; and that this journalistic skill is here put to literary use.

To say this, however, is to remind ourselves that truth is a matter of style as much as of content. The style of *All Quiet* has been more praised than analysed. A striking feature of the syntax is the prevalence of simple – one-verb – sentences, and of compound ones without co-ordinating conjunctions, or at most with 'and'. Complex sentences with their subordinating conjunctions and, in German in particular, their less immediately penetrable thought-structures, are correspondingly scarce. It is this characteristic, no doubt, which led Richard Katz to speak of '... the lapidary style ... Each sentence expresses shortly and clearly *one* idea.'[27]

On the vocabulary side, Remarque, we have seen, grounds his language on the precisely factual word. Yet he also has a command of overtones: as O. M. Fontana observed when the novel appeared, 'Erich Maria Remarque has what Ludwig Renn lacks: words – words that give more than a photograph – words with all the fine resonances and movements of the soul, of atmosphere, of the inexpressible, imperceptible as these are to the factual sense – in short, poetic words.'[28] Some of these effects, we have noted, spring from juxtaposition, of war and nature, or of the physical and the spiritual; others from metaphor, which is kept simple and sensuous. Liedloff comments on the colloquialisms and 'soldier-language expressions' (p. 394). Remarque also has a line in brash similes:

> He [Tjaden] is thin when he sits down to eat, and when he gets up again, he's as fat as a pregnant bug . . . (p. 9)

> Even his [his dying Kemmerich's] voice sounds like ashes. (p. 20)

> When Kat stands back at the hut and says: 'We're for it –', well, that's his opinion; but when he says it up here, the phrase has the sharpness of a bayonet in the moonlight, it cuts through our thoughts . . . (p. 58)

Liedloff comments on such features: 'Such expressions are proper in the actual conversation but bothersome in the narrative because they disrupt its unity.' A few lines later he speaks of 'Remarque's opinion' (p. 394). But he misdirects himself here. What he sees as a weakness is in fact a strength, as Klein has already argued (pp. 503–4). The style of the book is not Remarque's style, and the opinions are not Remarque's opinions; at least, not in the first instance. From the beginning of Chapter I until two paragraphs from the end of Chapter XII, the novel is narrated by the central figure, Paul Bäumer. This narrative stance provides Remarque with a realistic context for a naive and simple style, which is part of the novel's popular appeal; but also for a fragmented, uncoordinated syntax, and for the use of the present tense with its immediacy; these features thus become part of the famous 'frog's eye view' of the war. He is able to give the short-sighted comments on events of Paul Bäumer himself, and through him of the other characters, without the need to provide an omniscient narrative perspective – indeed, with a requirement *not* to do so. In short, style and point of view are matched, and both reflect the incomprehensibility of war.

The choice of a first-person narrator does however create one possible problem. The two concluding paragraphs have to stem from a new, apparently omniscient third-person narrator, whose intervention is needed after the first-person narrator's death. Strangely, however, the novel does not suffer from this change of viewpoint; nor from the absence of any explanation of the mechanics by which it came to be set down – an absence which distinguishes *All Quiet* from Goethe's *Werther*, with which in narrative standpoint as in other ways it has close affinities.[29] The introductory paragraph preceding Chapter I may, perhaps, best be considered as a kind of epigraph, or even foreword, rather than as part of the novel proper; which may be another way of expressing Klein's parallel (p. 490) with the short captions at the beginning and end of films.

Narrative viewpoint leads us on to consider characters. *All Quiet* focuses on Paul Bäumer, his former classmates, and – to secure some age-variation – a few fellow-soldiers of different background, notably Stanislaus Katczinsky. Klein's argument (p. 489) that the central figure is closely connected with only *two* others (Katczinsky and Kropp), however, seems to have been influenced by a desire for symmetry with *Her Privates We*; at least as strong a case could be made out for Tjaden as for Kropp, and the model in *All Quiet* is not so much a triangle as a series of concentric circles around Bäumer, with Katczinsky on the innermost of them. But Klein rightly points out that Remarque's choice of characters successfully solves the problem of identity which faces the authors of war novels (p. 507, n. 25), whilst at the same time creating a curiously unrealistic cross-section of the fighting troops, with no senior officers and hardly any junior ones or N.C.O.s (p. 502). This again is a powerful determinant of the sense of alienation which pervades the novel.

Paul Bäumer, sensitive, an intellectual and an artist by inclination, trying without complete success to grow a thicker skin, may be seen as a distant descendant of Werther, with whose semi-anagrammatic name his own name may have affinities.[30]

Narrative viewpoint and the focus on the central character are also closely linked with structure. At one level, the work is divided into many small sections, separated by asterisks: 92 of them, which gives an average length, in the original edition, of about three sides. This again is a feature that makes for easy reading; but, combined with the predominance of the present tense, its also makes for a realistic effect — that of a journal entry or a brief conversation. A journalistic approach has been adopted for aesthetic effect.

Yet the fact that the novel has twelve chapters suggests that its underlying structure is not that of a string of casual jottings. Liedloff's analysis (pp. 396–9) starts from the observation that Chapters vi (38 pages) and vii (48 pages) are much longer than the other chapters (average 19.6 pages); and he argues that these chapters are the centre of the book: vi, because it is the fullest depiction of battle in the novel, and vii because it shows the characters relaxing after their period in the line. Liedloff's suggestion that the novel is built around these two chapters is resisted by Klein (pp. 490–2), who argues that the structure is cyclical: Chapters vii to xii repeat the sequence of i to vi, with one important difference — there is no escape at the end of the second series. Another, small-scale, example of the cyclical principle at work would be Chapters iv and v, the wire-carrying followed by the goose-roasting. The novel operates structurally, in fact, on an alternation between the cruelty and despair of the battle-scenes, and a gradual return to life during periods in reserve. Chapters vi and vii are the major instance of this alternation; but, ironically, the fact that Paul and his friends escape from this battle is not a guarantee that they will escape from the war; the second half of the novel moves inexorably to their destruction. This process, which is intensified by the changeover from single events to iterative formulae, to which Klein has drawn attention (p. 492), is also accompanied by seasonal changes. Like *Werther*, *All Quiet* occupies two summers and two autumns, handled in such a way that Chapters I to VI seem to be all in summer, and Chapters VII to XII all in autumn: like *Werther*, if less formally, this novel too is in two contrasting books.

The progression of the novel is thus one of increasing alienation from any world but that of war. This alienation is implicit, and indeed explicit, at the beginning, but the characters still behave as if they can escape, whatever they may say. Paul himself hopes for a miracle in the love-scene in Chapter VII, but it is hard to believe that he finds one, except for the existential moment. And the sterility of his leave: coming, as it does, after the big battle, it should celebrate his safety, but instead it confirms his despair. So the structure of the novel articulates its themes.

The most basic of these is the monstrous unacceptability of modern trench warfare – manifest especially in Chapter VI. A second theme is the moral bankruptcy of leaders who have encouraged young men to volunteer for this holocaust – expressed already in the discussion of their form-master Kantorek in Chapter I. Yet a third theme is the suggestion that, when the war is over, something must be done to change the world we live in – intimated, for example, in the Duval scene in Chapter IX. More important is the 'lost generation' theme, already sounded in the book's epigraph:

> This book is meant neither as an indictment nor as a confession. It is meant only to try to report on a generation that was destroyed by the War – even when it escaped the shells. (p. 5)

The sense of comradeship which awareness of belonging to a 'lost generation' engenders is yet another theme. And finally, there is the existential theme of the assertion of self, in the face of the nothingness of war, through sensual experience and through contact with nature – a theme which gradually fades from the novel as alienation becomes more pervasive.

The narrative standpoint of *All Quiet* does not allow these themes to be fully reconciled with one another, or even to be fully articulated. It is also true, as many critics have observed, that Paul Bäumer and his friends are not, as he claims and the novel implies, representative of the effect on all soldiers of trench warfare and its horrors. And yet, it is wrong to demand, either, as Remarque's Nationalist critics did, that these victims should have been more heroic, or, as Marxist critics do,[31] that they should have been more consciously revolutionary. What Remarque achieves is more true to life than either of these: a depiction of mean sensual man, crushed by circumstances and yet preserving his humanity in unexpected ways. It is this that, ultimately, captured his readers; and it is this, and the unobtrusive formal mastery with which he achieves it, that is at the heart of his literary value. Like all major writers, he shows us what is wrong with our world, not how to put it right.

The Embattled Style: Ernst Jünger,
In Stahlgewittern

J. P. Stern

The central themes of Ernst Jünger's writings – throughout the period
of the Weimar Republic at all events – are death, total war, and the
depersonalisation of modern man; and by virtue of these themes he
established a literary reputation which, in its first phase, was that of
spokesman for the front-line soldiers of the Great War.[1]

Ernst Jünger was born in 1895 in Heidelberg, the eldest of five
children, into a well-to-do middle-class family, who soon moved back
to his father's native region of Hanover. Before long, however, the
atmosphere of his home proved irksome to the boy's adventurous
nature: at the age of seventeen, his fancy full of the literature of
adolescence, he decamped for Marseilles and the Foreign Legion. After
a few hazardous weeks in North Africa he was reclaimed by his father,
but not for long. The episode was but a prelude to the great break:
'Grown up in the spirit of a materialistic age, we all had a great longing
for the unusual, for the great danger.'[2] It was 1914 and Jünger, a boy
of nineteen, joined the 73rd Hanoverian Fusiliers immediately war
broke out; in this regiment he served for over four years, first as a
cadet, then from 1915 as a lieutenant.

For four years of the bloodiest war the world had known he fought
in Northern France and Flanders. Brief periods of leave, brief spells in
hospitals with wounds – these were the only interruptions. Most of the
time he commanded platoons of shock-troops and reconnaissance
parties, his name becoming an epitome of courage and recklessness.
'Tempered in a storm of steel', he was wounded seven times, and
highly decorated. And he came back – to a country defeated by her
enemies, torn by internal strife – wholly out of sympathy with the
moderate left-wing views that were gradually gaining ground in the
young Weimar Republic.

But he had not only fought; he had also kept a journal, ruthlessly
true and as precise as he could make it, of these four years of war. First
published in 1920, *In Stahlgewittern* became the most popular book of
its time, thrusting its writer overnight from the comparative anonymity

of a heroic soldier into the limelight of fame. The theme, the times, the country and the man were such as to make this more than a mere literary success. In a number of articles, some of them under a pen-name, he was slowly finding his feet in the world to which he had returned, slowly asserting his position as the spokesman of a generation that had staked its all, sacrificed all, and had gained nothing. These articles contain the usual amount of invective associated with the writings of early National Socialists, the usual promises of a new world to give meaning to the sacrifices of the war, the familiar metaphysics of nationalism and of the German mission in the world, the diatribes against Social Democracy, the farrago of resentments against the 'paper-war' and profiteers, the specious contempt for 'political parties'.[3] They differ but little from the writings of the 'Movement' itself (it was at this time that the National Socialists began to call themselves by a 'dynamic' term, 'die Bewegung', relegating to Social Democracy the term 'das System', which in the course of many years of propaganda hardened into a term of abuse). But while in the writings of National Socialism there is from the first a conscious appeal to the working classes with their specific material problems, Jünger's articles call simply and consistently for the exercise of force, for 'das Elementare', the primordial passion of violence in men. It was this direct appeal to power through force which enabled him to give his admiration, quite impartially, not only to the nationalist saboteurs of the Ruhr ('the men who are in love with dynamite'), but also to the German Communists of the late twenties, whom he found ready to embrace 'a positive and martial will to power'.[4] And it is probably this directness which rendered his appeal ineffective in practical political terms.

Ernst Jünger took his discharge from the German Army in 1923, having previously contributed to its Service Manual a chapter on the tactics of infantry platoons during advance under enemy fire. In the same year he matriculated in the University of Leipzig as a student of botany and zoology, also attending lectures on philosophy. Impoverished like everyone else in Germany by the inflation, he was able to make a living and to travel extensively on his Army pension and on the income from his writings. He married, probably in the middle twenties, and his first son was born in 1926. By this time the war-experience had been repeatedly scrutinised and three further books issued directly from it: in *Der Kampf als inneres Erlebnis* ('Battle as Inner Experience'), he gives a close and fairly systematic descriptive study of 'trench mentality'; *Copse 125* is the detailed account of a comparatively small though savage encounter with the British Army in an area between Arras and Ancre known on English maps as 'Rossignol Wood'; and finally, in *Feuer und Blut* ('Fire and Blood') he returns to the German offensive of March 1918 to give 'a small section of a great battle', the only battle of that war which he thought indicative of the shape of things to come.[5]

Jünger's stay in Berlin, after 1927, marks the culminating point of his overtly political activities. It seems that he was not, at that time, without political ambition. But the Berlin of pre-1933 days was so full of political intrigues, fantastic conspiracies, utopian clubs, nightmarish violence and corruption, so full of the most improbable combinations of doctrines and party affiliations, that the full extent and details of these activities are difficult to ascertain. He seems above all to have associated with a small group of men whose doctrine of 'National Bolshevism' aimed at a *rapprochement* with Russia against the West. Romantic notions of a hierarchic military-cum-syndicalist state were in the air, an élite of workers and soldiers was expected to usurp power and rescue the Reich from decay. . . . This is the background to *Der Arbeiter* ('The Worker' or, in Jünger's extended sense, 'The Technocrat')[6] which was published on the eve of Hitler's assumption of power, as a manifesto of the new hierarchic movement, the new aristocracy of work. In practical terms it was an attempt to 'dish the Whigs' (the Socialists' concern with the working classes) by establishing an élite of 'Workers' (the word imbued with more than ordinary meaning) whose means of securing power were identical with the end for which power was to be secured: this end and means were contained in the conception of '*total mobilisation*'. This conception marks Jünger's most distinct intellectual achievement. It is perhaps not surprising that when the National Socialists came to power they adopted the whole doctrine – premises, method and conclusions – to form, whenever required, an 'intellectual superstructure' of their own programme. Jünger had by this time become the most important and most influential of those writers who had not emigrated. In his turn he did little to protest when the National Socialists made use of his work and of his reputation as a soldier for their own ends.[7] He never, on the other hand, became a Party member or even a fellow-traveller, preferring the position of an outside observer.[8] And this was to remain his vantage ground throughout. He did not protest when the Weimar Republic was brought down, for he still considered (as Thomas Mann had done a dozen years earlier) that all democratic régimes were 'out of touch with the elementary realities of human destiny, which is tragic' (thus seeking inside the political and economic arrangements of a society that which, both in the Christian and the existentialist view, man must face outside organised society, alone). This is a view to which, were it put a little less abstractly, a man like D. H. Lawrence might well have subscribed; but Jünger, it seems, had a better chance than Lawrence of being taken seriously. And when 'pristine violence' became a fact he saw that it was not what he had wanted; the National Socialists' rise to power, he later considered, was 'the ametaphysical solution, the purely technical execution of Total Mobilisation'. He foresaw and greeted the end of the régime of terror, although he cannot have failed to recognise some similarity between Hitler's description of the S.S. – '. . . hard as Krupp-steel, as tough as shoeleather, as fast as greyhounds'[9] and his own utopian conception of the 'Worker' with the iron mask of duty and the cold heart whose sole aim is achievement. *On the Marble Cliffs* (1939) (which was a thinly veiled allegorical attack on the National Socialist régime), and the first part of his new war-diary, *Gärten und Strassen* ('Gardens and Streets'), 1942, covering a little less than the first year of the war, were banned by the German censorship and, towards the end of the war, his pamphlet *The Peace* was circulated clandestinely among young German soldiers on the Western Fronts. And finally, when the Second World War was over, the British occupation authorities banned his books in their zone while translations of them were being printed in London.

Even though in his later works Jünger rarely comes back to the Great War (except to speak of it in general terms), nevertheless its atmosphere, its language, the scale of values it imposed upon him, the shock and the numbing of sensibility remain firmly imprinted on his mind. A brief history of the text shows the significance it had for him.

From 1920 to 1943 there were twenty-five reprints of the *Storm of Steel*, embodying some five or six revisions. First, during the late twenties, the narrative scenes are shortened, stripped of redundancies, and of one or two expressionistic conceits; then, in the early thirties, the live experiences of the battle-field come to be embedded in that 'philosophising' which in due course becomes one of the hallmarks of Jünger's style; and finally, all generalisations are stripped of the personal element and increasingly abstracted from it, until the final version (1942, contemporaneous with *Der Friede*) emerges as the most economical and at the same time the harshest statement of all.

The need to concentrate one's criticism of the book on its use of descriptive and evaluative language is dictated by the limitations Jünger himself imposes on his literary undertaking. There is here no plot or coherent line of action – except the 'action' of front-line warfare, which is experienced as conduct wholly governed by 'impersonal' and 'anonymous' forces beyond any single man's control. There are few detailed character portrayals, and none that remain unrelated to their military functions. The sequence of the book's twenty chapters is simply Jünger's war itinerary and list of battle engagements, from the chalk dugouts of the Champagne (January 1915) to his last sortie against the English on the road from Bapaume to Cambrai (August 1918). And the book closes with the award to him of the highest German decoration, the order of *Pour le mérite* dated 22 September

– thus avoiding any need to mention the German defeat of November 1918.

What moulds Jünger's style is, first and foremost, the war itself and his decision to adopt an attitude of assent toward it. Since he considers anti-war writings – he has in mind writers like Remarque and Barbusse – to be the decadent products of a wistful humanism, he decides to accept war as a positive experience, as the touchstone of human conduct. This assent is in no way facile; passages like the following (from the German offensive of March 1918) show the great force and economy of his writing, his honest and successful endeavour to set down all he can, his avoidance of false heroism, and his ability to express something of the tremendous and shattering impact of the experience:

> Again it shrilled through the air; everyone had the tautening feeling: this one's coming over! There was a deadening, tremendous crash; the shell had burst in the midst of us.
>
> I picked myself up half-dazed. From the large crater the belts of machine-gun ammunition, set on fire by the explosion, were shining with a glaring pink light. It illumined the sulphurous fumes of the explosion in which a dense heap of black bodies was writhing, and the shadowy forms of the survivors, who were scattering in all directions. At the same time rose a many-voiced horrible roar and cry for help.
>
> I will make no secret of the fact that after a moment's numb terror I took to my heels like the rest and ran aimlessly into the night. Not until I had fallen head over heels into a small shell-hole did I understand what had happened. To hear and see no more! To get away, far away, to hide in some hole! And yet the other voice called instantly, 'But you're the company commander, man!' So I forced myself to go back to the dreadful place.[10]

The precision of this passage relates not merely to outer events; in the two words 'schwelender Qualm' Jünger not only indicates the exact nature of the explosion, in which the fumes themselves continue to smoulder, but the words 'sulphurous fumes' also express an atmosphere of evil; these, he is saying, are the fumes of hell.

But 'in this hell is all manner of delight'. Again it is (to put it briefly) the veracity of the description which gives Jünger's passages an authenticity I have found nowhere else in the literature of war:

> The firing on the horizon in front of us was flaring up more and more densely, its light reflected high in the clouds as a blood-red flashing. It formed a long dancing chain and at last melted into one glowing wall. What was the significance of a single battery in all

this? The reports of its shells were lost without a trace in a fabu-
lous tumult, in a thousand poisonous hisses of trajectories intertwin-
ing above our heads into a narrow-meshed net, and in a glowing surf
which surrounded us, like Greek fire, as a contiguous element. But
our faces were turned West, and motionless we stared into this fiery
wall. We were no longer afraid, for this spectacle was so great that
no human feeling can come up to it. We were waiting, for there was
no doubt that this prodigious waste of material must be followed up
by the deployment of men. And then I saw next to me Officer-Cadet
W., a very young man, bend down and grasp a bottle of wine, which
a party of carriers had brought up for him the night before and
which was to be saved for tomorrow's hot hours of noon. I saw him
lift it to his lips, drink it at one deep draught and laugh as he threw
it over the parapet. And I understood the meaning of this act: he
foresaw that tomorrow he would no longer be able to drink it. Yet
there was in this simple action so rash a daring and so self-evident a
superiority that suddenly I had a feeling of great release – I would
have liked to embrace him, and suddenly I had become quite light-
hearted.[11]

The opening here is slower; the 'Greek fire' an unnecessary conceit:
and (to give a more exact though less kind translation) in the phrase
'the spectacle of a greatness to which no human feeling can rise'
Jünger is projecting the notion of determination or size on to something
expressly indeterminable. But here as in so many other places, he
is trying to express, even through a maze of contradictions, the strange
experience on the borderline of death. And in his use of the word
'feeling' – first unattainable, and at last attained through the act of a
boy's recklessness – he achieves just this effect. The end of the passage
issues in a brief, wholly unsentimental acceptance of this mood of suicidal courage.

And this assent is certainly a part of our own world. The life of
heroism and recklessness, of suspended responsibility, of violence
rewarded by visible, tangible effect, of self-assertion and endurance in
the face of annihilation – all this several generations of Europeans have
accepted, propagated and enjoyed irrespective of national frontiers. In
dozens of situations, on scores of pages, Jünger has essayed the expression of the moment of action, and no one has excelled him in this. The
tension before, the triste after: the comradeship of danger: respect for
the enemy: contempt for the staff at the base: boredom between operations: the casual, hectic pleasure-hunting of leave: the safety of routine
– of all these things Jünger speaks in a language whose authenticity
forces us to recognise them as true, as a part of our own world, as
enlargements, indeed enrichments, of our experience. In so far as single

and isolated war-situations are concerned Jünger's war books are unrivalled.

But no experience is single and isolated, none stands on its own. And it is in the connecting of these experiences that our rejection of Jünger's writings will set in. To him, this moment of ecstasy, this life of fear-and-courage, this violent venture is the true touchstone of a man. What values are in man, of what goodness, truth and beauty he is capable – here, and here alone, are they shown forth and proved. But this assertion, central to his work, is false. It is false, not merely because practical experience shows it so: as for instance in the demoralisation, the 'loss of moral fibre' which sets in as soon as an army of such warriors as he describes is withdrawn from the battlefield, all too often proving itself incapable even of the small decencies of life, let alone of the great 'values'. The assertion is false in a less contingent sense: because this 'highest moment' is within the context of Jünger's sensibility wholly *dis*connected. It is, in fact, not the 'highest' moment at all; it is *the* moment, reducing the rest of experience not merely to relative but to absolute insignificance. For this *negative* mystical experience the soul cannot prepare itself by either loving God or men, or contemplating the world, or resisting its temptations. This moment is to life what an earthquake is to a city. With all values of the spirit invested in this singular experience of consuming ecstasy, all that is left for the rest of life is detached intellectual curiosity, an attitude of mind which ultimately engulfs the ecstasy itself. Thus the theory of the 'existential moment' becomes the triumph of the *voyeur*. It is the ironical fate of this kind of *littérature engagée* that it operates perpetually on the brink of mere cerebral sensationalism.

This curiosity (which many critics have confused with a live capacity for responding to the mysteries of man and of nature), this avidity to see how men behave under the threat of death, this *partial* and 'uncommitted' but *constant* response to every situation, is the source of Jünger's consistency. Abstract cruelty and aestheticism turn out to be not opposites, but different aspects of a single, defective mode of experience. There is no contradiction in the sudden toppling over of the one into the other, in that sudden tilting of the scales which so often takes place in Jünger's books, in which the observer's attitude remains constant while it is merely the object under his glazed eye that changes. It is this defective sensibility which is fundamental to Jünger's ideology of the existential moment.

There is little doubt that Jünger is conscious of this predicament – conscious that the literary style, too, is a pointer to the quality of the non-literary experience. And there are two ways in which he tries to repair the flaw in his system. The first is simple enough: at a given point he abandons the system. Thus his description of one of the battles at Langemarck (July 1917) is briefly interrupted by an account of how, in the thick of it, he suddenly came upon his younger brother, who had been wounded, and how he ordered five of his few remaining men to take the boy back to a field ambulance (1942 edn, pp. 175 f.). Now nothing could be a more human, a more natural thing to do than this brotherly service; yet in a word such as Jünger extols, this act is nothing but a dereliction of duty. The Lt Jünger we know would challenge at pistol-point any subaltern who proposed to do what he is doing. And if we call this act human and natural, it is merely because Jünger has failed to convince us of the validity of his system, from which such an act is excluded.

But there is a second 'solution' of his dilemma, which Jünger adopts more frequently, and which becomes indeed a permanent feature of his style. Contemptuous of 'mere' literature, whose standards are other than those of the existential moment, he tries to break and bruise for himself – a soldier turned writer – a way into the system: he attempts to emulate this violent venture, this life of fear-and-courage, with pen and paper. He refuses to recognise that to extol the desperate heroism of 'the stand in the lost trench' is one thing, while to take up this stand is another. And by deliberately loading his style with military metaphors he endeavours to bridge the gulf between words and events in the world at large. But this endeavour defeats its own end. For the result of this preoccupation with metaphors is mannerism, which fails to bring the experience to life; its result is not a *littérature engagée*, but, inevitably, its exact opposite–aestheticism:

> ... the taking up of the pen remains always a supreme venture, and requires a harder trial and scrutiny than that of leading armies into battle.[12]

But a piece of prose is not a 'military exercise',[13] nor do 'guns speak', except by way of a worn-out metaphor.[14] In committing this fallacy and in clinging to it, Jünger contributes in his own particular way to one of the major (and wholly unheroic, indeed truly 'decadent') confusions of our age. Perhaps it may be true to say that as long as a stable and live metaphysical tradition ensures the recognition of a purpose in all experience, no one kind of experience is felt to be less real than another. What is certain is that, once this balance is upset, men's lives become a scramble for 'reality', in which each kind of experience tries to steal the other's fire. To the ensuing confusion Jünger contributes at every point: history is mistaken for the past (or even for the present); theology for faith; philosophy for rule of life; psychology for the soul; political theory for politics; and literature for moral precept – in brief, words for deeds.

Given Jünger's preoccupation with war, the result of this confusion is an 'embattled style', the essence of which lies in its author's inability to sustain generalisation without abstracting it from living experience. Sometimes he succeeds. Thus in the passage (quoted above, p. 116) which describes the explosion of ammunition-belts, the following paragraph is interpolated since the 1934 edition of *The Storm of Steel*:

> But above all the rolling movement of the dark mass in the depths of the smoking and glowing cauldron, as in the hellish vision of a dream, rent open for a second the uttermost abyss of pain. (p. 240)

In this scene a limit of individuation is transcended, and expression of what is beyond it is attempted; and if literature is at all capable of yielding direct descriptions of war, here are its limits too. More often, however, Jünger goes outside them. With almost unparalleled cruelty he intertwines the languages of war and peace, nowhere more harshly than in the insensate understatements of clichés from which all feeling, all life has gone out; describing a skirmish with hand-grenades, he writes,

> In this manner we broke a few decisive vertebrae off the spinal column of the enemy's defence. (p. 240)

The complex horror of this sentence is not easy to characterise. It issues from a mind that has shut itself off from all conceivable imaging, from all external experience and all possible happenings, and gropes blindly among a mass of dead words. The sentence is preceded by the words '... und so den Widerstand abzutöten' (and thus to paralyse all resistance); here abstraction reaches a dead end: having lost all notion of the real meaning of the verb, he now uses it as part of the abstract intellectual jargon it has become; but what he is talking about is the real thing.[15]

It is not only his choice of words, his cruel metaphors and calculated understatements, that go into the shaping of this 'embattled style'. For his purpose Jünger makes use of a number of different constructions which have this in common, that the generalisation or assertion or command expressed in them exceeds, in a tumorous fashion, the context from which it sprang. And this excess, which is an act of the will, is offered as a kind of substitute for the defective response to live experience, leaving behind it gaps for a reader to pitch and lurch through, at the author's whim. The overwhelming impression this style makes is not one of heroism, or of courage-and-fear, but of cold contempt. Contempt for those who do not 'follow'; for those who do not accept, or who oppose, the scale of values adopted here; for those who have not renounced 'the old orders'; contempt, in brief, not for death but for all life that is lived on any other but the 'existential level'.

Of this language of contempt, full of abstract cruelty, we may not claim ignorance. It is familiar enough. The terminology of recent wars – its 'mopping-up operations'; 'expendable troops'; 'cleaning parties'; 'softening of resistance'; 'saturation raids', and the rest – is still sufficiently well remembered to prevent us from indulging in false distinctions: what Jünger is expressing is not confined to one nation at war. But this language is not, or at any rate not yet, the language of literature. It may be the appropriate style of communiqués and staff-officers' memoirs; it may even be the language of those 'blood-brotherhoods' of front-line ex-enemies which Jünger praises so highly as the bearers of the true tradition of chivalry. But literature is capable of speaking this language of contempt only by making an issue of it, by deliberately exposing it and showing it up for the defection from live experience that it is. Ironically and on a narrow scale, this is what has been attempted in Henry Reed's *Lessons of War* and in the posthumously published diary of Felix Hartlaub.[16] Whether, in this mode of writing by indirection, a man of genius, a man endowed with the range, human warmth and metaphysical passion of a Herman Melville may yet find it possible to write a war novel to match Karl Kraus's war drama *The Last Days of Mankind* must remain an open question.

In literature we are all on this side of death. And this view of literature, far from implying that it must shirk the theme of death, means only that its account of death is always in terms of that which is living. Where literature speaks of death, as in the poetry of the Metaphysical poets, the German Baroque, or the novels of Melville or Tolstoy, it can do so successfully only by projecting living experience beyond its own ken. In this projection literature comes to look upon death, without shirking its terror, as a mode of living experience. In other words, literature in this enterprise requires the services of a man whose senses are ceaselessly akindle with their response to living creation, whose ardour will bring out the force and majesty of death by showing as abundantly as can be what it is that we shall soon be leaving. This, and this alone, is the theme's challenge to the literary imagination, and this its indirect method. As to modern warfare, the full realisation of one man's death – the 'diminution' I experience from one man's death – is enough, is perhaps all that can be attempted. This, but nothing less than this, is enough. Short of it lies abstraction; and, indeed, all that contempt can express is not this *death* of one man fully realised, but the *decay* of the life of the senses, the drying-up of the sources of sympathy and love. Nothing, in the literature of war, is more difficult to express without sentimentality than this love. But where an author succeeds, as, for instance, does Manning:

... the sergeant-major looked at the dead body propped against the side of the trench. He would have to have it moved; it wasn't a pleasant sight, and he bared his teeth in the pitiful repulsion with which it filled him. Bourne was sitting: his head back, his face plastered with mud, and blood drying thickly about his mouth and chin, while the glazed eyes stared up at the moon. Tozer moved away, with the quiet acceptance of the fact. It was finished. He was sorry about Bourne, he thought, more sorry than he could say. He was a queer chap, he said to himself, as he felt for the dug-out steps. There was a bit of a mystery about him; but then, when you come to think of it, there is a bit of a mystery about all of us. He pushed aside the blanket screening the entrance, and in the murky light he saw all the men lift their faces, and look at him with patient, almost animal eyes. Then they all bowed over their own thoughts again, listening to the shells bumping heavily outside, as Fritz began to send a lot of stuff over in retaliation for the raid. They sat there silently: each man keeping his own secret.[17]

there the bluster of contempt is wholly extinguished, and the escape into 'philosophical' *obiter dicta* abandoned. No such individuation occurs in Jünger's book – it contains, as I have said, no characteristics unrelated to their warlike functions. Instead there is a grey mass of abject figures, portrayed without any of the pity that is the source of individuation:

> There now begins one of those endless discussions about war which I have listened to *ad nauseam*, hundreds and hundreds of times. It is always the same, only as time goes by the bitterness grows. The men attack this vital question with a religious earnestness, only to run again and again against the walls of their horizon. They will never find the solution, for the very vantage-point of their questioning is wrong. War is to them not an expression but a cause, and in this way they seek on the outside what is only to be found within. Only the appearance, the crude surface, is significant to them. However, one must understand them. They are materialists through and through, and I, who have lived among them for years, hear this in every word. They are really material, the material which, without their knowing it, the great idea consumes to reach its great aims.[18]

In the writings of such men as Léon Bloy, André Gide, Corvo or Jünger, contempt is claiming an entry into literature; but its place there must remain precarious. Now in some of Gide's and Bloy's work this contempt is to some extent redeemed by love, but such a combination is not usual. In Jünger's writings contempt is paired with respect, which is an abstraction from love. But neither contempt nor respect is live enough to sustain the theme of death. In the respectful admiration Jünger has for the 'new race' of warriors with their 'supple, lean, sinewy bodies, sharp-edged faces, eyes petrified under the helmet by a thousand

terrors'; for the worker-warriors of these and of future wars, 'techni-
cians . . . in oil-stained overalls . . .: in such types Vulcan the worker is
already beginning to permeate the martial figures'; for the 'lithe tigers
of the trenches, masters of dynamite'[19] – in the admiration and respect
he expresses for this *type* of man, he is withdrawing from a full response
to the impact of war. This type has its precise counterpart in our own
world; and to what extent it is capable of literary realisation, and to
what end, remains to be seen. But that this type is least capable of
expressing the 'living experience' of death, of this there can be no
doubt; for its whole meaning and subsistence in Jünger's writings lie in
its deathlessness. This 'Worker' is an Achilles with both heels perfectly
invulnerable, a Siegfried on whom no linden-leaf has dropped, a Super-
man without the exacting moral conditions of Nietzsche's vision;
nothing about him is capable of feeling that terror and *apprehension*
which give death a great part of what meaning it has for us.

Not, indeed, its whole meaning. And in his search for a fuller meaning
of death in war, the Jünger of the forties turns to the concept of sacrifice, already adumbrated in the twenties, in the hope that a fuller elaboration of it will yield an answer. In *The Peace* (written between 1941
and 1943) he develops the view that a stable and just settlement in
Europe and in the world can issue only from the 'seed of sacrifice',
'from the great treasure-hoard of sacrifices . . . that have been accumu-
lating in every country'. To this it might be objected that such a conception of the foundations of peace is no better than those vague though
insistent exhortations which in England come under the heading of the
'Dunkirk spirit'; that such exhortations issue from a fundamental confusion of what war and peace are about; and that such a confusion,
deplorable enough in the heat of party politics, is intolerable in a serious
enquiry into the matter. But we need not go so far. In his full-dress
definition 'sacrifice . . . [is] that action in which even the least and simplest of men [can] unrestrictedly make his move',[20] Jünger's cliché shows
him at heart incapable of conceiving it on any other level than that of a
game, and a solemn game at that. But sacrifice, if it is to have any
distinct meaning, if it is to contribute to the meaning of death in war,
cannot be defined in the language of a game.

We glory in sacrifice not for the death it is but for the light it sheds
on the living truth, which is of this world too. It has nothing in common
with the lifeless abstraction of a chess-board, especially not if it is to be
'interpreted theologically, according to the saving gospel' ('. . . theo-
logisch gesprochen, nach Heilsworten . . .'). For then it involves not a
'move', at all, only an abdication: 'I shall no longer act or suffer, to
the sword's end.'[21] But it is clear that Jünger's arrogation of the concept
of sacrifice is in the end hardly more than a piece of rhetoric, a plunging
among mean words and high sentiments.

Yet it is worth adding that his conception of sacrifice as a self-validating good, and his conception of the necessary hardness and destructive nature of any validation of man, are not idiosyncratic beliefs. On the contrary, they are what he and all major German writers share with the ruling ideology of the age, the ideology of National Socialism; more than that, it is by virtue of these conceptions that the first forty-five years of this century form an epoch in German history and give it a distinct historicity of its own.

Jünger is indeed a representative figure: the double defection we witness in his writing moves in a perfect circle: the failure to respond to sacrifice (or war) as an event in the world at large makes Jünger look for it as an event in the world of words: nor would he seek it there if this world were fully alive to him: and a failure to respond to the world of words incapacitates him from expressing the experience sacrifice (or war) as an event in the world at large. From this double defection *vis-à-vis* the living experience of words and deeds issues Jünger's 'battlement style'. Its source, briefly, is the iron in the soul.

But all this must not deflect our attention from the importance of the questions Jünger is asking, and asking more directly and pertinently than any other writer of his generation; nor do his deficient answers dispose of them. In his habit of abstraction and in his contempt, even in his false system of values, lies Jünger's acceptance of responsibility for the things our age stands for. Here, paradoxically, is his Cain-like commitment to his own and his contemporaries' deeds. Given this age, given this man's central experience, and given also his decision (for it is, however diffuse and gradual its detail, a decision forced on him by the limits of his gift) to speak the language of his age, abstraction of the kind we have described is perhaps the only possible response, and certainly we have had no fuller response to the theme of cruelty and depersonalisation in the modern world. In expressing it, Jünger is breaking up a literary tradition of many centuries, and placing his own writings on the borderline between literature and abstract documentary reporting. In this he comes closest to writers of George Orwell's type. To what extent Orwell's *1984* is a true prophecy is of no interest to anyone except the insatiably curious. The importance of the book lies in its detailed and almost unrelieved cruelty, in its writer's final inability to respond adequately to the horrible situation (real enough and common enough in our world) which he has consistently and convincingly constructed.

Whence this failure? It must, of course, still remain true that, in so far as our situation is not unprecedented, the traditional resources of literature will be adequate to it. The attempt to find a meaning for death in war is no more unprecedented than the attempt to find a meaning for the lust for war. What do we, what can we make of it all?

As long as men can remember they have been asking this question. And the only answer they have ever known (not found: for there is nothing here that can be acquired) lies not in abstraction from, but in the love of, the living detail of divine creation:

Where is the steed? Where is the man?
                    Where is the giving of gold?
The places of feasting? Where is the pleasant hall of old?
Alas for the bright cup! Alas for the man of war!
Alas for glory of princes! How the time goes o'er,
It vanishes under night's shade, as it had never been.[22]

But writers like Orwell, Malraux and Jünger suggest that there are aspects of our situation which *are* unprecedented; that the memory of the steed, of the man, of the giving of gold is dim, distant and unreal; that the expression of death through the glory of creation is impossible since creation has ceased to be glorious; that the experience of men as targets of phosphorus-raids, as inmates of concentration-camps, as objects of experimental medicine, as passengers of tube-trains, as objects of social anthropology, as calory-consumers, as 'expendable material'[23] cannot be sustained by traditional literature – and yet that these aspects of our experience cry out for direct expression. Are these men right? Is it their own defection from a live sensibility, or, more crudely, their literary impotence, which sends them to search among cruel abstractions for this expression while literature that forms a continuity with its own past still holds the valid answer? Or again, are they wrong because the only possible response to this situation is not utterance at all, but prayer? Perhaps this last question comes nearest to the truth, so that at last 'nothing is left of the unsayable except not to say it'.[24] And all attempts at new formulations, at a new style, at a new expression are then voices of children in the dark: all are then attempts at escaping from a final challenge to silence. And at this conclusion, all criticism of Jünger's work would simply resolve itself into an ultimate demand that, if he has really experienced that which is unprecedented in our situation, he should be contented with silence. But there is in him, as there is in all men except saints, a will to self-assertion, to utterance and expression. It is not admirable, this will of Jünger's, it is neither good nor does it even contain the capacity for recognising what is good; it is crude, though masked and varnished. But it is real, it is the only living thing behind the abstraction, part of our common world. For this reason, and also because through its very rawness and false rhetoric this will points *per impossibile* to the silence beyond it (though not to the prayer), we must consider, and try to evaluate, Jünger's language as an interim expression of our age. Contemporaneity is no virtue; rather is it a sign of recognition, a token of Cain-like brotherhood.

12   Humanitarianism and Law: Arnold Zweig, *Der Streit um den Sergeanten Grischa*

W. G. Sebald

Arnold Zweig was 27 years old and a budding *littérateur* when the First World War broke out. Up to then he had read German, Philosophy, History, Psychology, Economics and Fine Arts at various universities – obsessed, it seems, with that strangely diffuse craving for erudition so characteristic of the shallow and eclectic tendencies of the Wilhelmine era. Zweig had not during these academic years acquired any insights into political developments. He recalled later that the First World War had taken him completely by surprise as the manifestation of some higher historical order that by its very nature precluded all doubts and questions.

> Facing each other were the great military powers and their clash, as history lessons had taught us all along, was to be regarded as an inevitable concomitant of living in this world. We had been brought up to look upon and accept their eruptions as 'natural' occurrences.[1]

To this generation, as Paul Klee recorded in his diaries, the war appeared to be 'the words of the history book made flesh',[2] the final proof required by the historiographers of imperial Germany. The philosophy of free enterprise and aggressive evolution had, in a sense, always implied war as a catalyst of historical development and when after far too extended a period of peace war did actually break out, enthusiastic identification seemed the only appropriate attitude. It was thus that 'the world of yesterday', overwrought by feverish desires, mistook its end for its liberation. On 1 August 1914 the bourgeoisie felt that it had been released from the bonds of a restrictive society and relished the prospect of an heroic summer.

The literati, no matter what their erstwhile allegiance, had been infected by the general intoxication and in a show of depressing uniformity they turned overnight into an army of serviceable chauvinists. Hofmannsthal and Werfel, Rilke and George, Thomas Mann and

Döblin, Dehmel and Hauptmann – all contributed in their own way to the heightening of the national mood. Where the country's preceptors stepped thus into the limelight, lesser talents could not afford to take a back seat; their numbers were legion and Arnold Zweig was among them. He produced impassioned reviews of such tracts as Max Scheler's *Vom Genius des Krieges und der deutsche Krieg*[3] and wrote war stories, examples of a new literary genre in which grotesque fantasy and propagandist purposes entered an unholy alliance. In December 1914 the *Schaubühne* published Zweig's story 'Die Bestie',[4] 'which in its mixture of bloodthirsty details and a cultivated narrative style provides a classic example of aestheticisms degeneration into barbarity'.[5] It is quite obvious that the abstruse violence of Zweig's story is intended, above all, to denigrate the arch-enemy; yet at the same time it informs war with a quasi-mythical aura. In this story three German soldiers who have taken up quarters in a Belgian farm are killed by a vengeful peasant, bled to death and slaughtered. In relating this monstrosity the author, who is clearly inflated with the self-conceit of a sacrificial priest, deems himself to be performing an impressive augural ceremony but, as ever, this kind of soothsaying is a far cry from a true elucidation of the future.

In the first two years of the war the satirical journal *Simplicissimus*, which in 1914 had abrogated criticism and polemic in favour of rabid jingoism, printed nine more war stories of Zweig's and a tenth appeared in the *Merkur*. Zweig's literary production up to 1916 is representative of the intellectual corruption that had affected the great majority of German and, to be sure, European writers at that time. In his case it is pardonable only because it figures as the prelude to a painful process of readjustment which was to occupy him for the rest of his life, a process which began in 1916 when Zweig, an ordinary private, came for the first time face to face with the horrors of war on the battlefields of Verdun. That Zweig, as opposed to Jünger, did not take this concrete experience as an occasion for mythical speculation concerning man's 'natural' aggressiveness but felt challenged to penetrate and analyse the absurdity of war, remains the decisive ethical difference between the two writers.

In 1917 Zweig was transferred from the Western Front to serve as an editorial assistant in the information department at the Army Headquarters in the East. In this new and official capacity he came across examples of explicit anti-war literature for the first time. He read Barbusse's *Le Feu*, Leonhard Frank's *Der Mensch ist gut* and René Schickele's *Weisse Blätter*. At the same time he gained detailed knowledge of the gross injustices for which the war and more particularly its administrative mechanisms were responsible. *Grischa*, which brought Zweig international acclaim, dates back to an authentic case witnessed by him during that period. He outlined the plot as early as 1917. In 1921 he dramatised the story without, however, achieving any sign of public recognition. The novel then was written in 1926/7 and first published by the *Frankfurter Zeitung* in instalments. The actual book came out in 1928 and gained immediate popularity; it had to be reprinted in numerous editions and was translated into seventeen languages.[6]

The recognition of the fallibility of martial law and its corrupt administration which travestied any acceptable idea of justice lies at the heart of *Grischa*. It is also the turningpoint of Zweig's development as an author and chronicler of the First World War. His extensive fictional *oeuvre* consists of a cycle of novels at the centre of which, both chronologically and thematically, stands *The Case of Sergeant Grischa*. The cycle as a whole was to bear the title *Der grosse Krieg der weissen Männer* ('The Big War of the White Men').[7]

For over thirty years Zweig worked to complete this ambitious scheme which like the oversized novels of Mann, Musil and Broch represents an attempt to write the definitive account, the *summa* of the bourgeois era and its spectacular decline. Georg Lukács complained that Zweig's undertaking did not sufficiently reflect the political development of the German people and that it was engrossed merely in the further education of a bourgeois intellectual, the problems of adaptation caused by the hesitant awakening of Zweig's *alter ego*, the clerk Bertin.[8] And indeed, the novels of this cycle hardly ever give the impression of a conscious attempt at political articulation. For the most part it strikes one that Zweig's main concern is a quest for self-knowledge after the well-proven fashion of the German *Bildungsroman*. The careful and gradual education of the hero is a reflection of the cautious political development which Zweig himself underwent during the twenties.

Like the great majority of liberal intellectuals with leftish sympathies Zweig was disposed to wait and see, not to act. It is characteristic that he showed traces of radicality only towards the end of the war when for a brief time it may have appeared as if one had nothing to lose. In the summer of 1918 twelve poems by Zweig were published clandestinely. They were informed by the programmatic pathos of the proselyte who dreams of a sudden metamorphosis of the political world and entertains the most extravagantly illusory visions of an imminent revolution. At the end of the war Zweig was also for some time a member of the Wilna soldiers' council. However, when he realised that the transition to a new order could not be effected in practice as smoothly as in poetry, and when revolution proper broke out in all its stark reality, Zweig felt called upon to distance himself from this turn of events through a critique of revolutionary power. On 23 January 1919 the *Weltbühne* published an essay which Zweig had dedicated to the memory of Karl Liebknecht and Rosa Luxemburg. In this essay he expresses his vague confidence in the indomitable humanitarian spirit whilst declaring revolutionary power to be an aberration.

In the second half of the decade the judiciary and executive forces of the Weimar Republic increasingly began to put pressure on writers who showed radical socialist or communist leanings. For Zweig, as for many others, the immediate result of this change in circumstances which implied a threat to bourgeois liberalism as well, was a certain *rapprochement* between revolutionary theory and his own more moderate views. In 1926 he published the novella *Der Spiegel des grossen Kaisers*, a kind of testimony to his basic socialist conviction. Inherent in the historical style of this tale is a didactic intention: the grandiose and yet run-down Palermo of the Emperor Friedrich II can easily be recognised as an intended likeness of capitalism in its terminal phase. It is out of this critical attitude that Zweig's decision to recast the Grischa play as a novel was born.

In *Grischa*, one of the most significant works of German anti-war literature, war figures only marginally. Nowhere do we find here descriptions of battles in panoramic style such as Jünger produced with so much tell-tale gusto and which even in pacifist works tend to assume an air of sensationalism. Zweig's novel focuses not on the 'objective' developments but on the subjective emotions and reflections of people affected by those impersonal forces. It relates the story of Sergeant Grischa Iljitsch Paprotkin. Grischa is a complete natural, a kind of noble savage who breaks out of a German prisoner-of-war camp because 'inside' he cannot find room to breathe.[9] Hiding from German patrols in almost inaccessible forests he comes across Babka, a hardened and yet astoundingly female partisan. Babka is quite taken with Grischa's childlike naivety which arouses her repressed maternal instincts. Grischa's unreflected desire for freedom and Babka's determination to fight for it enter into a kind of mystical union. One could almost describe Babka as an allegory of political awareness and courage, as the natural mother, to use Marx's image, of natural man. They live together for a short while and when Grischa's innate restlessness makes itself felt again, Babka sets him free providing him with the papers of a dead soldier. Later on Grischa is picked up by the German military police; he claims to be a deserter and states that he has been moving about behind the German lines for weeks. In admitting this he is quite unaware of an order passed recently by the military authorities which lays down that any deserter who does not give himself up within three days shall be courtmartialled as a spy and, if found guilty, executed on the same day. Bertin, the clerk, in one of his comments explains that this order is not really concerned with the question of military security.

He sees it as a political manoeuvre designed to intimidate the German troops.

> Every fool knows there is no espionage about it. What they are really afraid of now is that the men will be infected by ideas. They want to prevent the spirit of revolt, which after years of agony has seized upon the Russians at last, from spreading to the German Army. (p. 127)

Grischa is sentenced but his execution is postponed as he succeeds in proving that the espionage clause does not, in fact, apply to him, Sergeant Paprotkin, who escaped from a German prisoner-of-war camp. The divisional court martial, on behalf of General von Lychow under whose jurisdiction Grischa comes, shows itself prepared to annul the death sentence. However, the commander-in-chief on the Eastern front, General Schieffenzahn, who issued the order to execute deserters suspected of spying, refuses to repeal the verdict. He is bent on making a political example of Grischa's case. Although General von Lychow represents the supreme court of appeal in his territory and has the letter of the law on his side, he does not have the power to enforce it. The power lies with General Schieffenzahn even if he, legally speaking, has no right to intervene in the case of Grischa.

Between the two parties, between law on the one side and power on the other, there ensues the controversy concerning Sergeant Grischa which in its convolutions defies the hapless victim's attempts to comprehend it. As is to be expected Schieffenzahn's power finally asserts itself over von Lychow's more legitimate intentions. In a last effort to save Grischa General von Lychow calls on Schieffenzahn in person and in this decisive encounter Zweig, with considered pathos, pitches the principles of power and law, embodied in the two men, against one another. Lychow argues with all the force of conviction he can muster.

> He said the matter had gone far beyond a mere question of jurisdiction. It was a question of plain justice – whether in Prussia there was to be equal justice for every man, as the Bible says: 'One scale, one measure, and one weight shalt thou have for thee and for the stranger within thy gates. I the Lord have spoken it.' (p. 283)

Lychow shows himself to be profoundly moved by the authority of these Biblical words. Schieffenzahn, however, remains unimpressed. He throws in that 'the art of war, looked at from a technical point of view, seems to be intended to put God in his proper place. I prefer . . . to take the plain blunt view of the situation: the State creates justice, the individual is a louse.' (p. 284) Lychow replies: 'The State creates justice, does it? No, Sir, it is justice that preserves the State. . . . When a state begins to work injustice, it is rejected and brought low. I know, as I sit here under your lamp fighting for the life of this poor Russian, that I am fighting for something greater than your State – I mean for mine!' (pp. 284 f.) After a number of further objections on the part of Schieffenzahn, von Lychow, normally a somewhat reticent character, summons what articulateness he has left for an ultimate sally.

Nothing in the world could justify a State setting in motion the mighty machinery of the law against the innocent, and so destroy a nation's sense of justice. The national sense of justice... was the symbol of Divine justice, and if it is thrown on the scrap heap on political grounds, no one could tell whether, as a result of such an outrage, in the eternal sphere of the Divine justice sentence might not be passed on the State itself: *Mene, tekel, upharsin* might be seen faintly glimmering on the wall of a room in which a General was using his pitiable logic to bring God's commandments into contempt. (p. 286)

The great theme then of Zweig's novel is the question of law and justice. And much of the substance of the book consists of the helpless human emotions which are engendered not only in Grischa but also in the other figures involved in his case. The reader's attention is focused above all on those who attempt to uphold the idea of justice, on General von Lychow, the old-style Prussian *Junker* with a temperament reminiscent of Fontane's resigned heroes, on Winfried, his pragmatic adjutant, on Posnanski, the Jewish officer from the judge advocate's staff, and on Bertin, the mouthpiece of the author. But the other side too is presented with insight and discrimination. The portrait of Schieffenzahn, through which Ludendorff's physiognomy can easily be discerned, is far removed from the danger of turning into a caricature. Schieffenzahn's power-political fixation becomes understandable as a compensation for the humiliations which he, as an upstart from the bourgeois *juste milieu*, had to endure during his military career. The technocratic perfectionism with which he governs his sphere of influence is the style that helped him to the top and now enables him to call officers of the old school to heel even if, like von Lychow, they happen to have justice on their side. For Schieffenzahn the case of Sergeant Grischa Paprotkin is no more than an opportunity to put this to the test.

It is not as if Zweig had arbitrarily seized upon a single aspect of the war in portraying these people exclusively in relation to Grischa's fate. Rather Grischa's case serves as a paradigm for the notorious connection between politics and crime, law being seen as the *tertium comparationis* between the two factors. Where law is swept aside, so Zweig's novel tells us, politics becomes criminal and the society of men reverts from civilisation to barbarity. Only at one remove therefore is *The Case of Sergeant Grischa* a book against the war; in the first place it is a protest against the manipulation of law through which the Weimar Republic destroyed its own foundations. As early as 1919, in an open letter to Riesser, a member of the Reichstag[10] who had thought it opportune to praise German judges as the most impartial in the civilised world, Zweig speaks of the corruption of German justice. He refers to Riesser's statement as an example 'of the idiotic self-adoration by which the liberal bourgeoisie made itself, at least partially, responsible for the war' and draws attention to the 'infinitely corrupted administration of the law'[11] in Germany and in particular to the débâcle of law and justice under the aegis of the High Command on the Eastern Front which he knew from personal experience. Zweig's formulations are anything but exaggerated. The administration and application of the law in nineteenth- and twentieth-century Germany always tended to distinguish between the social classes when it came to meting out punishment. If in the early part of the nineteenth century this was only to be expected, the second half of the century might have shown a distinct improvement in this rather biased practice. However, after the abortive 1848 revolution the bourgeoisie adopted increasingly defensive tactics against the Fourth Estate and one generation later Bismarck's antisocialist laws finally cleared the ground for class justice in Germany. The war then offered further opportunity to manipulate the law according to what appeared politically expedient and after the revolution had come to an end in 1919 the standards of German justice degenerated still further. Seven thousand revolutionaries were imprisoned whilst the murderers of revolutionaries often went unpunished or were treated to a kind of honorary sentence. The agents of the white terror incriminated in the Kapp-Putsch, in the Ruhr struggles and in the suppression of the workers' uprising in Saxony had little to fear from the courts. No less than 354 political murders committed by the radical Right earned a total of merely ninety years' imprisonment, whereas twenty-two deaths laid at the door of workers and soldiers resulted in ten death sentences and a total of 248 years' imprisonment.[12]

German literature began to protest with some degree of preoccupation against this kind of lopsided justice when the trials of revolutionaries were increasingly replaced by trials for literary high treason. Kaul's *Kleiner Weimarer Pitaval*,[13] a sombre record of political justice under the Republic, lists 137 such trials in 1923, 516 in 1924 and 561 in 1925. Although some of these cases may have been petty affairs they were no less symptomatic of the general trend. Hans-Albert Walter writes about this issue: 'In countless instances literary works of radical democratic, socialist or communist content were impounded and prohibited, their authors prosecuted, committed to trial, sentenced or at least defamed and vilified.'[14] During the second half of the decade this witch hunt was stepped up further still,[15] whilst authors who publicly displayed fascist sympathies could have blatantly propagandist works printed without the censor's interference. The danger, inherent in this development, even for bourgeois authors, had thus become quite tangible and some of them reacted with plays and novels warning that further depravation of law and justice would have fatal consequences. Mühsam's *Staatsraison* (1928), Rehfisch's and Herzog's *Die Affäre Dreyfus* (1929), Bruckner's *Der Verbrecher* (1928), Wassermann's *Der Fall Maurizius* (1928), Ottwalt's *Denn sie wissen, was sie tun* (1931) and Feuchtwanger's *Erfolg* (1930) all appeared in the wake of Zweig's *Sergeant Grischa*.

This novel is an attempt to describe war and the mindless annihilation of human life not as the irrational eruption of a cataclysmic event but as the direct issue of a perverted sense of justice. It thus fulfils a threefold function: in portraying the life and death of one guileless individual who is murdered for reasons of political rancour, Zweig demonstrates in understandable dimensions what war meant to millions of similarly hapless victims. At the same time he pronounces a verdict on those of his immediate contemporaries who were about to legitimise murder as a political weapon and warns of the imminence of a new war which is bound to emerge from a system contemptuous of law and justice. In all this Zweig's strenuous concern with right remains ethical rather than political, that is to say, he does not spell out an overtly ideological message. Yet it is also true that the author of *Grischa*, having recognised the fatal tendencies of what went by the name of democratic stabilisation in the Weimar Republic, was now prepared to consider marxist doctrines more sympathetically than at the beginning of the twenties. Bertin, at any rate, his representative in the realm of fiction, speaks of war as a means of preserving outdated class-structures. And when at the end of the novel – the date is November 1917 – an enginedriver stops his train in spite of the protests of a number of officers safely tucked away in a first-class compartment, so that a breathless private may scramble aboard (pp. 447 ff.), we gather from the tone of the episode that this journey home may also be one into a better future.

If Zweig, notwithstanding his obvious sympathies for the left, refrained from express political statements, then this was not least because such direct interference might have done damage to the texture of his story. And Zweig was a storyteller before he was a politician. He once confessed in a letter to Paul Huys that he had been taught the art of narration through his mother's habit of reading Grimm's fairy tales to him.[16] At the hub of his novels – and *Grischa* is an excellent example here – we usually find a simple legend, the description of an unassuming and yet heroic and exemplary life much in the style of the *Vita*

Sanctorum. That is to say Grischa does not act, he only endures. As he comes into contact with what to all intents and purposes is an antagonistic system, the legend of his life unfolds and takes on epic dimensions. We move from the forests into the towns, from nature to civilisation and all of a sudden a vast number of subsidiary characters appear, the friendly and the hostile as well as the indifferent spirits of the novel. These figures are, as a rule, highly realistic. Be it Täwje, the Jewish joiner or the leninist *agent provocateur* Sascha, be it a German nurse or an ordinary private, they are all made of the stuff of realistic fiction which is mimesis. Recognisable as they are in psychological, social and linguistic terms their existence, dictated by the economy of the novel, remains curiously undynamic. Yet their interrelations constitute the epic network, the pattern of the *tragédie humaine* from which Grischa cannot escape. This, however, does not imply that Zweig's attitude is fatalistic. He makes it abundantly clear that the political and thus the human quality of a system is determined by those who are capable of manipulating it. In Zweig's description of the hierarchic order of society Grischa's function is that of a touchstone; his reduced existence illustrates the prospects which life affords for those who find themselves at the bottom of society's structure and who simply have to bear the pressures imposed on them. Zweig's verdict on the established system is expounded by the fact that Grischa's first contact with the German army bureaucracy is the beginning of his end and turns the remainder of his life into a fateful progress.

As Grischa's doomed existence draws to its close, the reader finds himself increasingly under the spell of the story, turning the pages in an almost frantic effort to keep abreast with its developments. The eternal epic question 'and then?' is continuously at the back of our mind and tends to obscure the wider implications of Zweig's novel. Indeed pace and rhythm are an extremely important element in Zweig's work quite generally and in *Grischa* in particular. It may be of interest here that Zweig, who throughout his life had trouble with his eyesight, usually dictated his novels and this at a rate of some fifty pages a day. Not unlike the narrator of an illiterate age he was almost completely dependent on the flow of his narrative. Naturally, this only served to stress the negative teleology of *Grischa* still further. There is, however, also another pattern in this novel which, by contrast, might be described as its positive teleology. Towards the end of the book Zweig manages to offset the fatalistic tendencies implied in his story by showing Grischa to be completely attached to his fate. In endless excursions Grischa's uneducated mind eventually comes round to the idea that his death, however unwarranted it may be in one respect, is also an act of expiation for the killings which he, albeit almost unwittingly, committed as a fighting soldier (p. 152). The cross of the order of St George which he had received for outstanding bravery finally overtakes him as the priest who has come with the execution squad once more confronts him with the symbol of a crucified life (p. 431). The message, then, of Zweig's novel is essentially pacifistic. Grischa sees his life as a sacrifice, not to the Gods, but to a better future, a future without violence and destruction. Babka, although all her plans to free Grischa have foundered not least because of his resistance to her schemes, is pregnant with Grischa's child. And this child, Grischa confidently hopes, will be born into new times, for is not his own death the unmistakable omen for those who ordained it? (pp. 326 f.)

Juxtaposed to this progressive vision are Grischa's escapes into the realm of his dreams. Again and again we find him wandering among the images of his mind's eye, a protagonist in a panorama of forests, plains and animals. These strangely unreal sections of the book seem to be something like psychoanalytic fairytales; Grischa is as much at home among their scenery as we are puzzled at their appearance in the context of a realistic novel. Zweig, as we know, thought very highly of Freud and underwent analytic treatment at various stages of his life.[17] Presumably archaic memory was as important to him as political vision. The tension between regressive and progressive utopia in *Grischa* can be understood as a pointer to utopia proper where all tensions will be resolved, where man is naturalised and nature humanised. As a citizen of this utopian republic Grischa holds out hope in the end. Just as eighteenth-century philanthropists imagined they saw children of nature in those who suffered the weight of oppression, so Grischa who is destroyed by the machinery of organised life around him becomes the epitome of natural man whose irreversible fate reveals the almost metaphysical malice of communally administered 'justice'. In this Grischa proves to be a relation of Melville's Billy Budd; but unlike the innocent sailor he is not raised to the heights of the cross in a final symbolical scene. His liberation from a life of travail is free from religious or existentialist overtones. In his death Grischa's features are relaxed into a hippocratic smile, the smile of a purely materialist serenity. Through the testimony of a life accomplished in this way Zweig believeded that he had revealed to his readers the prospect of a more humane world – a gesture of pious hope which he like Grischa had learnt from the Chassidic carpenter Täwje. Täwje too, in his consolatory remarks, refers Grischa to a materialist world to come. From among the treasures of his midrashim he selects a tale illustrating the pleasures of life in paradise in which 'the seadragon Leviathan ... was slaughtered by Jonah, and served up, as *gefillter fisch*, at the tables of the blest' (p. 375).[18]

13   The Last Days of Austria: Hašek and Kraus

Robert Pynsent

Most Czech First World War literature concerns the establishment of a Czechoslovak state. For all its horrors the war was in the end positive. Sassoon's bird suddenly burst out singing rather more meaningfully for Czechs and Slovaks than for the hung-over British, French, or Germans. Few Czech writers of war fiction had no political axe to grind and not many of them could squeeze any humour out of the war. Few tried to create characters, to give any sort of psychological interpretation of their warring heroes' actions; usually their heroes are ideological types. After the aristocratic individualism of the 1890s the war provided an opportunity to become anti-individualistic, to write collective novels demonstrating the collective labour-pains of the new state. To do this sincerely was a problem, since most Czechs had been either indifferent to the war or more or less *kaisertreu*, defending by word and deed the Habsburg Monarchy.

Whether they concern the hinterlands (e.g. Hora, *The Hungry Year*),[1] the fronts (e.g. Weiner, *The Fury*)[2] or the life and opinions of the Czechoslovak Legions (e.g. Medek, *The Legionaries' Epopée*),[3] most war novels have a good word for T. G. Masaryk ('Daddy Masaryk', 1850–1937), the first president of the new state, satirise Austrian bureaucracy and war propaganda, and show what frightfully good soldiers the Czechs were, whichever side gave them their sausages and mash. The most important common characteristics however are horrific anti-semitism, the culmination of a tendency widespread in nineteenth-century Czech literature, and Neo-Revivalist patriotism. Neo-Revivalism was an anti-aesthetic trend starting in the 1880s, which sought to refire the ardour of the Revival in the early nineteenth century and to convince the Czechs of their historic mission. Most writers' judgement of the War was based on the extent to which they thought it gave the Czechs an opportunity of justifying their existence and demonstrating that they were not a nation of efficient little servants and bureaucrats.

With the exception of a few middle-aged Liberals, writers, true to the Czech tradition of committed writing, were far from being detached about the war. On the other hand, they were immensely interested in facts. There is nothing quite so political as a fact. The facts of the hinterland situation were politically most important for the inhabitants of the new state. In the atmosphere of the twenties and thirties message-conscious writers needed to remind the nation of their privations during the last, totalitarian days of Austria. It may be that this need reflects the Czech martyr complex, the Czech search for national martyrs and their glorification. The evident persecution of the Czechs during the war furnished these patriotic masochists with a bumper heyday. The names of politically unreliable Czech authors were often expunged from textbooks. Mention of the Kingdom of Bohemia was not allowed in school history books. Czech folk songs were banned, and not even a box of matches or a woman's dress could bear the Czech national colours. At the beginning of the war such trivialities were important, but as the war continued the greatest problem became the lack of food, clothing and heating fuel. Hunger made an unpleasant situation a trifle unbearable. Shopkeepers, industrialists and farmers became racketeers; the poorer were driven to begging and stealing. War-material suppliers made immense fortunes. The wives of soldiers were unfaithful. Hinterland life became an ugly demoralisation. Life at the front revealed the same demoralisation as life in the hinterlands. The donning of a uniform turned men into animals who murdered innocent civilians, tortured, raped – sometimes wiped out whole villages because an officer or an N.C.O. was a little angry or frustrated. Czech writers, like writers of other nations, took horror and pain and cruelty and love all very seriously. But then along came a beaming little bibber called Jaroslav Hašek (1883–1923).

Hašek[4] was the son of an unqualified schoolmaster, who later became a clerk in an insurance company. He died when Hašek was thirteen and the boy left school and became a pharmacist's apprentice, but in 1899 went to the Prague Commercial Academy and began writing while studying there. On completing his studies he became an insurance clerk, but was soon dismissed, and by 1904 he was a member of Prague bohemian and anarchist circles. In 1909 he began editing the popular zoological magazine, *Svět zvířat*, and in 1910 he married a well-heeled *bourgeoise*. Shortly after his marriage he lost his job because he had begun inventing animals to the dismay of his respectable readers, and shortly after that his father-in-law retrieved his daughter from him. For the 1911 elections Hašek created a new political party, the 'Party of Moderate Progress within the Limits of the Law', and delivered pompous speeches, parodies of serious electioneering. In the same year he started a dubious dog trade which he called the Cynological Institute. In February 1915 he was called up and joined the 91st Infantry Regiment in Budweis. He soon went with his regiment to the eastern front and, having been promoted to corporal and won a medal for gallantry, in September he went over to the Russians. After a period in a prisoner-of-war camp he began editing a Czechoslavak periodical in Kiev and writing satires and patriotic articles. At the beginning of 1918 he left the Czechoslovaks and joined the Red Army and by September 1919 he was political commissar of the Fifth Army. While in Siberia he married a Russian. In December 1920 he returned to Prague; he was in the unenviable position of being both a traitor and a bigamist, and no doubt these new labels helped him forget his sober, respectable behaviour in Russia and go back, as he did, to a more natural life of too much drink and a great deal of practical joking.

When he was in Kiev Hašek's attitude to the war was similar to that of most left-wing Czechs there, and we need to look at something of his journalistic work[5] there to realise that post-war *Švejk* contains elements of self-parody. He likes Daddy Masaryk as much as the rest, at least until May 1918, when in an open letter he rejects Masaryk's conception of revolution. Like the right-wing Rudolf Medek (1890–1940) he preaches a politics of revenge.[6] Like Medek he sees the war and especially the forming of the legions as the spiritual reawakening of the Czechs. Like Medek he emotionally refers to Czech soldiers as 'molodci', the Russian for 'fine lads'. Like the rest he makes antisemitic statements. Like many he points out the demoralising effect of war, for example in his picture of stretcher-bearers stealing the valuables of the wounded. The satire we have in these articles and anecdotes has a different tone from that of the post-war *Švejk*; here it is angry, bitter, and often becomes little more than sarcasm, for example in his stories of Prague secret policemen and informers and of Czech informers in the prisoner-of-war camps. His satire on Austrian officers is less sarcastic, but equally inspired by hatred. One of the officers he describes has his mistress embroider 'Gott strafe England' on her suspenders. His attacks on the Habsburgs are as violent as Kraus's. He loathes Franz Joseph, whom he considers a medieval plague, and despises Charles who, he hopes, will become a jockey and die in a horse-race. The Russian period, when Hašek attacks others for that lack of seriousness which had hitherto been the hallmark of his own life, acted as a catalyst. It turned the literary prankster into a major novelist.

That process can be best seen in the development of the character and function of Josef Švejk. First we have five Švejk stories in *The Good Soldier Švejk and Other Strange Tales* (1912).[7] These stories, written in a primitivist style at variance with all contemporary Czech literary trends, are straightforward anti-military satire. Second, we have the amorphous sketch of a novel, *The Good Soldier Švejk in Captivity* (Kiev, 1917),[8] which is a significant patriotic left-wing contribution to Czech war literature concerning army morale in the hinterlands and on the eastern front. It is highly tendentious. Finally we have the unfinished four-volume picaresque novel, *The Good Soldier Švejk and his Fortunes in the World War* (1921–3),[9] a plotless firework display, whose message, if it has a message at all, is a double message, that the war had been a grotesque, ridiculous, undignified horror and that Czechs should not take themselves or the war so damned seriously; it is a great relief after the boredom of most Czech war novels, though even *Švejk* has its own unforgivably boring passages. In each of the three versions Josef Švejk has a different social background: in the *Tales* he is a cabinet-maker of no fixed address; in *Švejk in Captivity* he is a brotherless shoemaker with his own shop and a bed-sit behind the shop; his main interest in life before the war was his guinea-pigs; in *Švejk* he is a shoddy dog dealer, fairly well read, with a daily help and a brother who is a grammar-school master.

His social development is, then, parallel to Hašek's own social development. When Hašek was a drunken anarchist, Švejk was a jobless artisan out to enjoy himself. When Hašek was experiencing his Russian *embourgeoisement*, Švejk was a patriotic shopkeeper. When Hašek was dousing his wartime respectability in gallons of drink, Švejk was a *bourgeois manqué*. The Švejk of the *Tales*, when called up for military service, went willingly because he thought the army would be good for a lark. As in the later versions he has a sweet smile. This sweet smile, his exaggerated deference to his superiors, and his literal carrying out of commands make him a frequent guest in the glass-house. In the *Tales* he is uncomplicated; he is simply a lucky fool and a pain in the neck, who gets a medal for surviving the total destruction of an arsenal in which he was working smoking his pipe, and who breaks all world records by not knowing how to fly and just waiting for the fuel in his aeroplane to run out.

In *Švejk in Captivity* he is a little more complex; the reader already has to work harder, has on one or two occasions to decide whether Švejk is just a plain idiot or an accomplished confidence trickster. What is more, Švejk is suffering from the Czech martyr complex: 'He was in something like an exalted state of martyrdom, of content, golden-hearted martyrdom'; 'the expression on Švejk's face was one of divine peace; it showed both resignation and that spirituality we see in pictures of martyrs'.[10] He is an automatic Austrophile who develops paranoia as a result of a dream in which he lops off Franz Joseph's nose. Like the later Švejk he tells anecdotes, but in *Švejk in Captivity* a great many anecdotes, mostly sarcastic, are not told by Švejk at all, are simply interpolated by Hašek to make the work as much a political pamphlet as a work of fiction. Like the later Švejk he spends a brief time as batman to a padré, and then becomes devoted batman to an infantry officer. The officer here, Dauerling, is violently anti-Slav, initially loathes Švejk but in the end takes a liking to him. He is, like all the officers, a fearful coward. Švejk, however, and here it looks as if Hašek is making fun of bravery in battle, is wholly unperturbed by life in the trenches. He does the quivering Dauerling's morale no end of good by deferential reports on the state of battle like 'Sir, have to report, sir, that they are going to make mincemeat of us.'[11] In the end Dauerling asks Švejk to shoot him in the arm so that he can get away from the front. Švejk shoots him – and kills him by mistake; then he wanders over to the Russian side. The third version of *Švejk* is more complex still, more open to various interpretations.

Criticism[12] on *Švejk* is mostly concerned with interpreting the figure of the good soldier himself. This criticism is often extreme in its loathing or loving of the inanely smiling bletherer. Nationalists like Arne Novák[13] (1880–1939) saw in Švejk an obscene travesty of Czechness. Some measure of the importance of such interpretations may be assessed from the fact that in 1925 the Czechoslovak Army authorities banned the book from all barracks, that in 1928 the Polish translation was confiscated,[14] and that F. Karikás's Hungarian translation, published in Paris, was not allowed into Hungary.[15] Communists like Julius Fučík[16] saw in Švejk a mocking saboteur of the *bourgeois* morality. A group of Soviet writers and journalists, however, seeing E. F. Burian's production (1935/36) could not understand why the Czechs should boast about such a figure as Švejk rather than Žižka.[17] An intelligent socialist account of Švejk is one of Brecht's diary entries from May 1943, when he was writing his *Schweik in the Second World War*, a feeble play whose hero fails to be Švejk, although Brecht clearly understood what Švejk was; he sees in Švejk 'the genuinely unpositive attitude of the common people, for whom there is only one positive value: themselves . . .'[18]

Švejk is an anti-authoritarian clown, an idiot only by virtue of his relentless acceptance of an oppressive moral order. The novel is a petty *bourgeois* sexual fantasy where the *femme fatale* is the state or the military authories as representatives of the state, and where the spurned lover is Švejk. And Švejk is constantly pinching the *femme fatale*'s bottom. Pinching a woman's bottom is an undignified act, but a *femme fatale* with her bottom pinched by such a spurned lover as Švejk is even less dignified. Perhaps the best examples of this are Švejk's encounters with the ranting paragon of Austrian authoritarianism, Lt Dub. Švejk's relationship with his own officer, Lt Lukáš, is an anomaly because here is authority fundamentally, albeit after considerable pain, accepting Švejk's anti-authoritarian absolute obedience. Lukáš is the necessary anchor-point for the *picaro*:[19] he is Švejk's Squire Allworthy.[20] Society's reactions to Švejk, in the bourgeois and officer figures of the novel, are otherwise uniformly negative. That is, unless those figures happen to be as tight as owls. And we do have the homosexual colonel who is briefly taken by Švejk's sweet smile, and, if one counts the anarchist volunteer Marek as a member of the officer class, he is another exception. Marek, who comes nearest of all the characters to being a self-portrait of Hašek, may be interpreted as Švejk's *alter ego*, the intellectual application of Švejk's behaviour.[21]

Švejk's movement from place to place is not as important as usual in picaresque novels. At each station of his journey he meets the same mores, though perhaps in slightly different versions. Hašek intends thus to show the geographical extent to which Austrian military incompetence and stupidity stretched; it does, however, make for patches of boredom. The one movement from place to place which is important is Švejk's excursion from Tábor to Budweis via Horažd'ovice, Strakonice, Vodňany and Písek, and that is because it is a satire on the equally foolish excursion of the Czechoslovak Legion in Russia.

Švejk's movement through the novel, his movement through bureaucracy, is a satirical representation of the movement of Czechs through the War. Right from the beginning the Czechs, like Švejk, had to come to a compromise between being both *kaisertreu* and good Czechs. Švejk is an ardent soldier, and yet he is a pacifist. He uses a vocabulary of subservience to denote concepts of anarchy. His spirit of compromise is epitomised in his much quoted dictum: 'It's not every Hungarian what can help being a Hungarian' (vol. 2, p. 142). That sentence is an elegant compromise, national tolerance founded on national intolerance. Švejk's relationship with Lukáš is a good relationship because he too is a compromiser, a Germanised Czech who is willing to speak Czech with his men. That is, from a liberal point of view, an ideal social situation of mutual respect. We remember Lukáš's thoughts about Švejk, thoughts which supply us with at least a hint of Hašek's interpretation of his hero: 'Well for heaven's sake I often speak exactly the same sort of rubbish as him. The only difference is that I use different words' (vol. 1, p. 171). This relationship, which, once or twice, Hašek sentimentalises, is contrasted to the usual social situation between the common soldier as victim and the officer as representative of a tyrannical state.

The care with which Hašek differentiates between the speech of common soldier and officer, and between the speech of the common soldier in the presence of an officer and amongst his fellows,[22] emphasises that social situation. Officers ill-treat and swear at their batmen, and the batmen swear at their officers behind their backs. Hašek shows these officers as representatives of a degenerate regime. They are corrupt, fiddle accounts, steal, cut down on their men's food to have more money for drink and whores. Sometimes Hašek's attacks are little more than grotesque defamation. The crassest example of that is

Captain Tayrle vomiting into the lap of a nymphomaniac countess (vol. 3, p. 172). One general's daughter had been a lesbian before the war and has now turned to manlier things, though the whole officers' mess dress up as women first so that she has her pleasure too (vol. 3, p. 171). Hašek's treatment of the field clergy and the Church is similarly anti-authoritarian. They are boozing fools. The padré Katz is the most grotesque of them all, but that is partly because he is the embodiment of that wartime literary type, the opportunist Jew. The puling, cowardly padré Martinec is strikingly similar to Werfel's cowardly padré in *Barbara*,[23] and Werfel was hardly anti-authoritarian. Anti-clericalism has, however, a fine tradition in Czech literature and Hašek does not go essentially further than the *Vormärz* satirist, Karel Havlíček (1821–56). The antisemitism of *Švejk* is inordinate, but so it is in Medek, and Medek was authoritarian.

The anti-authoritarianism of the content of *Švejk* is reflected in its conception. Before *Švejk* Hašek had been breaking rules in a minor way in the hundreds of short stories he had published, but these were rules of subject-matter, not of narrative technique. *Švejk in Captivity* was the run-up to the long jump of rule-breaking in *Švejk in the War*. In *Švejk in Captivity* he already breaks some of the rules, chiefly the one which states that a writer does not defame living men under their real names, but also the cardinal rule of pre-war Czech literature, that if one takes as one's hero a character who does not have the traditional traits of the Romantic and neo-Romantic hero, negative or positive, one makes fun of that hero. The good soldier Švejk is a parody of the good soldier. Švejk's (and to a less extent Marek's) irrepressible and apparently digressive[24] anecdotes are a parody of the explanatory device of flashbacks. They explain nothing. The non-action of the novel is a parody of conventional plot development. Even the dry narrative which links episodes contains elements of parody, e.g. in the background to the drumhead mass, the latrines, 'whose fragrance is a surrogate for the mystic fragrance of incense in Gothic cathedrals' (vol. 1, p. 134). The sordid social and military behaviour of the ruling classes is a parody of their polished behaviour in literature and in the eyes of the ruled. The fly-blown portrait of Franz Joseph is a parody of imperial magnificence. The essence of parody is realism, and the raising of the petty, even sordid, detail into prominence beyond the conventional objects. It is breaking the rules of conventional perception. The Great War had broken all the rules of the behavioural code; faithfully to represent that war in literature one had to break the rules of the literary code. It is that awareness which connects the works of Hašek and Kraus.

Karl Kraus (1874–1936)[25] was born in Jičín, the son of a rich Jewish paper manufacturer, but his experience as a Bohemian German was negligible since in 1877 he moved with his parents to Vienna. He spent a few semesters reading law in Vienna, but soon gave that up. At about that time he was converted to Roman Catholicism; in 1918, however, he left the Church, disillusioned, indeed disgusted. He began his artistic career by taking drama lessons, at which one of his fellow pupils was the producer Max Reinhardt (1873–1943), who later suffered considerably at Kraus's pen. Kraus made his stage début as Franz Moor in Schiller's *The Robbers*, but was apparently a flop. After that he became a freelance writer and journalist; he worked for a time on the liberal *Neue Freie Presse*, a newspaper which he was later to attack as one of the instigators of the War. Instead of being an actor he became a public lecturer and drama and poetry reciter, and in that role he was successful. Finally he founded his own Theatre of Poetry; he used to sit at a table on the stage and recite, especially Goethe and Shakespeare, without moving and without adapting his voice to distinguish characters. His audiences were fascinated. He was a perfectionist and expected the perfect from contemporary drama and literature, but by comparing them with such as Shakespeare and Goethe, he was always disappointed. His perfectionism was masochistic. Nevertheless he did 'discover' such significant writers as Else Lasker-Schüler (1876–1945), Georg Trakl (1887–1914), and Franz Werfel (1890–1945). In 1899 he founded his periodical, *Die Fackel*, of which 922 numbers were issued between then and 1936, and to which from 1911 onwards he was the sole contributor. *Die Fackel* was the platform for Kraus's well-nigh paranoic attacks on the degeneration of language. During the war he was for some unaccountable reason never arrested; he even continued giving recitals, some of them pretty audacious for the times. After the war he continued his attacks on contemporary social, scientific and artistic phenomena, including psychoanalysis. With the rise of Nazism Kraus was dismayed into virtual silence. His dying words were 'Pfui Teufel', which may be translated with that pre-Lady Chatterley three-letter word 'Ugh'.

Kraus's *The Last Days of Mankind* (1922)[26] is less conventional a drama than *Švejk* is a novel. It has a ten-scene prologue, five acts together comprising 209 scenes, and an epilogue. It has a dramatis personae of something over 500 characters. It contains serious poems, comic songs, soldiers' songs, philosophical musings, quite apart from dialogue and a wealth of documents. The action of the play, in Kraus's own words, consists of a picture of those 'unreal, unthinkable years, which can be perceived by no conscious sense, years to which no memory can have access, years spent in a bloody dream when figures from an operetta played out the tragedy of mankind' (I, p. 5). It is a 'technoromantic adventure' (II, p. 84) which begins with a newspaper seller bawling out the news of Sarajevo and ends with an apocalyptic vision, whose conclusion is the Voice of God broadcasting down from

Heaven the words of Franz Joseph on his declaration of war: 'I did not want to do it' (II, p. 308). It progresses from the grotesque horror of intellectual depravity which had begun with the war to the grotesque horror of physical depravity in which the war ended. Its ordered chaos mirrors the ordered chaos of the war. The settings range from Vienna cafés to the trenches, from the German Crown Prince's tennis court to churches, from staff headquarters to railway compartments. The action ranges from newspaper-reading to torture and death, from a father beating his hungry child with the flat of his bayonet to drunken officers in the mess complaining about the fearful noise coming from the battle their men are fighting, from German *hausfrauen* discussing the latest patriotic toys to 250 wounded soldiers being burnt alive in a dairy. The characters of *The Last Days* range from common soldiers, rowdies and prostitutes to privy councillors, generals and emperors, from babes and sucklings to dodderers and corpses, and disembodied voices. The heroes, the initiators of the action, are, in Erich Heller's apt words,

> troglodytes living in the skyscrapers of history, barbarians having at their disposal all the amenities and high explosives of technical progress, fishmongers acting the role of Nelsons, ammunition salesmen crossing Rubicons, and hired scribblers tapping out on their machines the heroic phrases of the bards.[27]

In short, its heroes, like its scenes, and like the punctiliously differentiated forms of speech employed, Viennese, Berlin dialect, newspaper jargon, propagandists' jargon, military jargon, German with a Hungarian accent, even Croatian and Czech, and even standard literary German, are shrapnel from the explosive destruction of mankind.

This destruction is watched over, commented on, analysed by Kraus as divine judge,[28] as a scathing but compassionate chorus, as a genial but elevated sceptic, in the figure of the Nagger. His popular, superficial counterpart is formed by the newsvendors who comment on the war from the official point of view. Like any true conservative the Nagger-Kraus is a fatalist. If mankind has been so stupid as to lower its values from those of men like Shakespeare, Goethe, Jean Paul, if they can adulate aesthetic snobs like Hofmannsthal rather than Trakl, if they can take a ponce like Rilke seriously and praise the verbal diarrhoea of such as Thomas Mann,[29] if they have so much respect for scientific and technological progress, they cannot be expected to do anything but lead themselves into such a catastrophe. A conservative is a fatalist and not a pessimist because he believes that it is at least possible that enough people will see the light to change things. That is why the Nagger has as his somewhat tepid collocutor, the Optimist, except in his first few appearances and then again once or twice in the course of the work.[30] This Optimist is one of the few speakers in *The Last Days* who does not demonstrate symptoms of either helpless passivity or degenerate idiocy. He may be taken in by many of the products of the Central Powers' propaganda machine, but he still has the capacity to interpret, albeit usually in a misguided fashion.

The (Anglophile) Nagger is anti-war (that does not mean pacifist) and anti-militarist. The Great War, as animal, behaved in the way it did because of the decadent situation which obtained when it broke out (I, p. 145); those who died in the war did not die for or on account of the fatherland, but quite naturally, given the state so-called civilisation was in when war broke out (II, p. 233). The decadent society of Austro–Hungary is epitomised by the cult of bibliophile editions (I, p. 151), the cult of books which are good to look at rather than good to read. Militarism serves only the Jewish-capitalist idea of the destruction of the world (I, p. 149). Militarism is simply the instrument of the daimon who wishes to see the destruction of Christian civilisation (II, p. 78). Like any good Austrian the Nagger is also anti-German. Instead of the nation of poets and thinkers (*Dichter und Denker*), the Germans are the nation of judges and hangmen (*Richter und Henker*), and their much-famed education system is nothing more than an ornament with which they decorate their vacuousness (I, p. 150).

Kraus is not a plain and simple anti-German chauvinist for, however much he was attracted by the values of the Austrian nobility, he loathed the Habsburgs – quite as much as Hašek in *Švejk in Captivity* and the other wartime stories and pamphlets. According to Kraus, Franz Joseph was completely gaga by the time the war came along (II, pp. 96–7). Never before in the history of the world had such a nincompoop, such a non-personality, such an infectious disease, imprinted so much with his lunatic insignia (II, p. 79). Franz Joseph was a beautifully bearded man who lacked nothing but personality (II, p. 81). The Austrian Chief of Staff, the Archduke Frederick, is a pathfinder in the era of glorious dumplings (II, p. 86). As far as Franz Joseph's successor, Charles, is concerned, Kraus does little beyond hinting at his wonderful life in the Brandýs garrison (II, p. 198), where he had once demonstrated his immense sense of humour by shooting out the eyes of a portrait of the blind Hussite leader, Žižka. Logically enough Kraus loathes pro-Habsburg patriotism as much as he loathes the Habsburgs. Most of his satire against such patriotism is embodied in the figure of The Patriot, who is always talking of the war as a war of Austrian and German self-defence. The essence of Austrian First World War patriotism is contained in the following exchange.

The Second Admirer of the *Reichspost*: What we need is a bloodbath! a bath of blood and steel!
The First Admirer: Have you been called up yet?

The Second: Come off it! I'm in a reserved occupation! What about you?

The First: Unfit for active service.

The Second: A sigh of relief is uttered by the populace! (I, p. 51)

The meaning of tragedy is reduced to a pretty nothing if, as Kraus says his drama is to be performed on Mars rather than Earth. *The Last Days* is certainly no tragedy if its heroes are men like the Admirers of the *Reichspost*. And yet what Austria and Kraus see as the tragedy of Austria *is* to be seen in men like the Admirers of the *Reichspost*.

The Last Days is a satirical tragedy. It is significant that, on the news of Sarajevo, it is a collection of drunkards who shout 'Dahn wi' the Serbs! Dahn with the bastards!' (I, p. 23), that a plebeian demonstrator shouts with the absolute understanding of the uncomprehending: 'Dahn with the Serbs! Dahn with 'em! Up with the Habsburgs! Up with 'em! Up with the Serbs!' (I, p. 41), and that a tub-thumping Viennese ululates: 'May the Serbian puppet kick the bucket' (I, p. 43). In other words patriotism is meaningless, a matter of learning a slogan or two. We may compare these scenes with the picture of the rheumatic Švejk being pushed in his bathchair by his aged servant and shouting 'Let's get at Belgrade! Let's get at Belgrade!' (vol. I, p. 62). Kraus's frequent satire on the supposed brotherhood of Germany and Austria (Germany was responsible for getting Austria out of its messy messes) is usually based on the propaganda slogans concerned with the Nibelungs or the notion that Germany and Austria were fighting shoulder to shoulder, e.g. in the following exchange between the German soldier, Wagenknecht, and an Austrian:

> Wagenknecht: Look out what you're doing. You're leaning on my shoulder!
>
> Sedlatschek: Ever so sorry – (I, p. 134)

Like a good Austrian Kraus is not too keen on this German superiority. He ridicules Franz Joseph by making him God after his death, but he laughs at Kaiser Wilhelm by making him God in his lifetime:

> First General: Your Majesty is no longer the instrument of God ...
>
> Wilhelm II (*puffing and snorting*): Wha's 'at – ?
>
> General: ... but God has become the instrument of Your Majesty!
>
> Wilhelm II (*beaming*): I see, I see. Tremendous![31]

All this is straightforward satire. A little less straightforward is Kraus's use of refrain-characters, people who occur several times in the course of the play, and with similar or the same phrases; not so much the two Jewish newspaper subscribers or the two autograph-hunting misses or even the multinominal pair, the Count Leopold Franz Rudolf Ernest

Vinzenz Innozenz Maria and the Baron Eduard Alois Josef Ottokar
Ignazius Eusebius Maria, as two Officers and Poldi Fesch (Dashing
Leo) who utter the same words at odd intervals through much of the
play, no matter what is happening in the war. They act as recurrent
reminders of the stupid unfeelingness of the younger members of the
ruling classes. (The older members of the ruling classes are all gaga.)
The first of the Officers is always popping up to say 'Hello, Nowotny.
Hello, Pokorny. Hello Powolny, ah, but you understand politics, don't
you? What do you say to this, eh?' The second makes his entries to
say 'I went on a hell of a binge yesterday. Have you seen Schönpflug's
new picture? It's absolutely stunning!' Poldi Fesch's refrain concerns
a time to be spent in the future or spent in the past on the dance floor
with Sascha Kolowrat. These refrains belong to the Absurd. Their
equivalents in *Švejk* are the good soldier's dictum 'No panic' ('To chce
klid') and his exagerated use of the military mark of respect 'Melde
gehorsamst' (in English usually simply: 'Sah!').

At first sight to compare the popular *Švejk* with the intellectual *Last
Days* appears a futile exercise and yet they are similar in their anti-
traditional conception. All one needs to do to turn *Švejk* into a drama
of the *Last Days* brand is to delete everything but the dialogue. All one
needs to do to turn *The Last Days* into a novel of the *Švejk* brand is to
insert some unobtrusive narrative between the scenes. Both works have
a chorus commenting on the War; Kraus has the Nagger; Hašek has
Švejk. Both the Nagger and Švejk are conservatives upholding what
they consider common human decency. In *Švejk* the good soldier is the
picaro; in *The Last Days* the reader-survivor is the *picaro*. Neither
Hašek outside Švejk and Marek nor Kraus outside the Nagger provides
us with anything but representative types. Both works are a collage of
pure invention, personal experience, and documents, though, to be sure,
documents are a good deal more in evidence in *The Last Days* than in
Švejk. Hašek and Kraus find the same aspects of wartime Austro-
Hungary obnoxious e.g.: the degenerate ruling classes, the imbecile staff
officers (and their sexual proclivities), the army chaplains, the *bour-
geoises* and noble hospital-visitors, the incompetent and unethical military doctors, newspapers, propaganda, the literary establishment. Both
are fascinated by the debasement of language. Both make fun of wartime slogans and of military words like *Superarbitration*; Kraus objects
also to words like *Lebensmittelkartenabmeldeschein* and *Grenzüber-
trittbewilligungsamt*. Both Hašek and Kraus choose the same phrase
from Franz Joseph's August 1914 Manifesto to his peoples to stress the
phrase's stupidity: 'I have considered everything carefully.'[32] Both, in
their attempt to show the absurdity of the war, show us absurd situations, which have nothing directly to do with the war. In *Švejk* we have,
for example, the M.O.'s visit, in the hospital chapter; it is satire on the

medical profession as a whole, as well as on the effectiveness of military hospitals:

> The M.O. Grünstein went from bed to bed, followed by a medical corps N.C.O. with a notebook.
> 'Macuna?'
> 'Sir!'
> 'Clyster and aspirin! – Pokorný?'
> 'Sir!'
> 'Stomach-pump and quinine – Kovařík?'
> 'Sir!'
> 'Clyster and aspirin! – Koťátko?'
> 'Sir!'
> 'Stomach-pump and quinine!'
> And so it went on. (vol. I, p. 71)

We may compare this scene with the following from *The Last Days*, a satire on the femininity of German women. The setting is a party in Hasenpoth, a Baltic gentleman addressing a Baltic lady. I am afraid I cannot render the Baltic pronunciation in English:

> Gentleman: Madam.
> Lady: What did you say?
> Gentleman: You're not dancing.
> Lady: No.
> Gentleman: Why?
> Lady: If I dance, I sweat. If I sweat, I stink. If I don't dance, I don't sweat, and I don't stink. (I, p. 274)

Both Hašek and Kraus enjoy the grotesque. On thinks of the sloshed schoolmaster lieutenant Dub with his whore when Švejk comes to disembrothel him. One thinks of Kraus's picture of two German businessmen of massive girth, Gog and Magog, in Switzerland: Gog, after a long session of war-sloganing with his friend, suddenly turns to his wife and says: 'Well now, Elsie? You're glad 'ubby didn't 'ave to go and fight for 'is country, eh?' 'Yes, my little Siegfried', answers Elsie (II, p. 221). And Kraus's chief of staff saying 'Boom, Boom' every time a cannon goes off in a war-documentary film is as grotesque, and depraved, as Hašek's high-ranking transvestites. Both *The Good Soldier Švejk and his Fortunes in the World War* and *The Last Days of Mankind* are funeral orations for the Habsburg Monarchy. Both Hašek and Kraus make their congregations laugh by flagrantly breaking the rule of funeral orations. Instead of saying nothing but good about the dead Monarchy, they say nothing but bad. The difference in method is that Hašek blatantly pinches the imperial bottom, where Kraus elegantly stamps on the imperial toes.

14 Dead Man Erect: F. T. Marinetti, *L'alcova d'acciaio*

Christopher Wagstaff

It is strange that so 'voluntary' a First World War as Italy's did not produce more war literature after the war, though less strange when it is remembered that much of Italy's war literature was written before the war began, by the Nationalists and the Futurists. When the fighting was over and the writing recommenced, much of the gilt had worn off the warrior myths. Novels, in the sense of fiction, were rare, and the diary or memoir predominated.[1]

From the technical point of view, the most sophisticated work was nevertheless a novel, Corrado Alvaro's *Vent'anni*, in which the author moves backwards and forwards in time, in and out of the minds of a number of protagonists whose parallel experiences are traced through the war. This technique allows the author to reflect and comment, through his characters, on what is narrated, an opportunity which he uses to make subtly argued, intellectual attacks on the interventionist myths. The other well-known novel is Borgese's *Rubè*, which can be characterised as technically Stendhalian, in that it follows an introverted hero into, through, and out of the war, which is seen as educational experience.

The raw diary is represented by Gadda's *Giornale di guerra e di prigionia*, which would not belong in this survey but for the importance of its author and for the fact that it can serve as a term of comparison for the memoir or re-worked diary. Of the large number of these, two stand out: Comisso's *Giorni di guerra* and Lussu's *Un anno sull'altipiano*. Unlike some well-known representatives of the genre (Monelli's *Le scarpe al sole*, Baldini's *Nostro purgatorio* and Frescura's *Diario di un imboscato*, for example) they eschew rhetoric and literary pretensions. They are exclusively first-person, eye-witness narratives, telling a simple – though selective – chronological tale. The facts speak for themselves, and tell quite different stories: Comisso's of a private, and later officer, whose innocent eye observes passively and enthusiastically a spectacle devoid of moral import, Lussu's of an officer smiling in outrage and horror at the homicidal incompetence of alcoholic superiors who send his men to certain and futile slaughter.

Marinetti received from the war little that he did not bring to it. The Futurist movement, founded by him in 1909 as an aesthetic avantgarde in literature, the visual arts, music, drama and the cinema, was from the moment of its foundation politically active. Marinetti propagated the ideas of industrial and technological development, imperial expansion, aggressive military and cultural nationalism, the heroic palingenesis of the individual and of the nation, distrust of socialism and contempt for the corruption and inefficiency of liberal democratic parliamentarianism.[2] These ideas, in various guises, had been the property of middle-class intellectuals in Italy since the 1890s, and they contributed to an ideology which saw in war the chance of achieving the goals to which they aspired. Behind Marinetti's version of the ideology lie Nietzsche, Darwin, Sorel, Bergson, Pareto, Morasso, Corradini and D'Annunzio.[3] In *L'alcova d'acciaio*[4] – his account of his experiences in the last few months of the war – this ideology emerges coherently and artistically complete, and stands as a clear cultural signpost pointing from the war to Fascism.

There are three aspects of the novel to be examined: memoir, propaganda and ideology, all merging together, but with the latter predominating, and subordinating the entire narrative to a vision of human existence that pre-existed the historical reality of the war.

The novel is its flimsiest at the level of memoir; Marinetti wishes to glorify his sensibility rather than communicate his experiences. He writes about his sexual conquests both at the front and while on leave, and about his participation in the defence against the Austrian assault at Asiago in 15 June 1918, the crossing of the Piave at the end of October, his helter-skelter advance in an armoured car through retreating and surrendering Austrian armies and his triumphal entry the following week in the vanguard of the Italian advance into villages like Vittorio Veneto, where he received a liberator's welcome from the female Italian populace.

Marinetti was a seasoned war correspondent,[5] but his dispatches had always said more about his 'futurist genius' than about the wars he was covering. *Alcova* is no exception. A comparison between this novel and Norman Gladden's memoir, *Across the Piave*[6] – which covers the same events up to the entry into Vittorio Veneto – shows us how little Marinetti is telling us. Gladden was a machine-gunner, and tells us how he shot, at what, in what situations. Marinetti, in the Asiago episode, was in charge of a mortar unit. He tells us nothing about mortaring activities, but he does carry on a lyrical elaboration of a poetic conceit, begun in a previous war narrative,[7] concerning machine guns and erotic women:

> Then we hear the furious dance and the ta-ta-ta-ta-*ta* – capricious, merciless, ironic and feminine – of the Saint-Étienne machine-gun, six yards off to the right, like an Andalusian woman spitting out passionate fire and red carnations from her balcony masked with foliage. (pp. 28–9)

He describes with aesthetic detachment and enthusiasm the Austrian bombardment. The reader needs another source to discover that it was a bombardment of terrifying and unprecedented magnitude. Nevertheless, Marinetti's elated band of an élite few individualists speeding through the abandoned Austrian lines, capturing prisoners without firing a shot – even capturing an entire corps of four thousand – probably describes what actually happened. What few details he allows to loom from the rhetorical fog tally with Gladden's account. It is, however, extraordinary that a man who had his hernia operated on so that he could join up in 1915, fought through the Alpine campaigns, was wounded and decorated in 1917, and returned to the fray to remain there to the end,[8] could come through such a war and in three hundred and eighty pages on the subject show almost no trace of having been touched by it, or of even having noticed what was actually going on.

Marinetti had always been a propagandist – for the Futurist movement, which meant, therefore, also for the war that the futurist ideal required. Moreover, Italy's commitment to the war was peculiarly ambiguous. Italian industry needed the war;[9] certain political groups saw it as necessary and good; but many in Italy did not want the war, and the ordinary Italian soldier had to be coerced and cajoled to remain at the front. The Italian defeat at Caporetto in October 1917 was blamed on the adverse effects of 'defeatism' and its propaganda on the troops. In response the Italian government launched a huge propaganda campaign,[10] which is reflected in *Alcova*.

Desertion was widespread and harshly punished.[11] Marinetti does not suppress the matter; he transforms it. An officer tells him about two Italian deserters he has shot: one wanted only to punish his wife for infidelity, and the other to kill his father for sleeping with his fiancée. The officer concludes: 'With deserters like that we are bound to win the war' (p. 22). The force that drives men to war (which, as we shall see, is sexual) also motivates them to fight a 'war' on the home front against sexual rivals. The appalling reality of self-mutilation and desertion is transformed into warrior propaganda. This is a consequence of Marinetti's techniques of characterisation. He has only one way of portraying characters in his writings: the moral portrait. Women are voluptuous and capricious, men virile and robust. Any visual adjective is merely a peg on which to hang the moral quality. Morality is a matter of psychology, however: and psychology is a matter of drives. A character either manifests these drives (which are really only one drive: sexual agression) or else is frustrated. There is a third category, of people who do not belong in the same 'species' as Marinetti, and are pacifists, neutralists, traditionalists, cowards, rational, Germanic or old. A deserter must either be suffocated beneath the weight of the past or else he is driven to desert by his drive. Since he is part of the glorious Italian front line, he belongs in the latter category.

While recovering in hospital from wounds in 1917, Marinetti wrote a short treatise to raise the morale of the troops called *Come si seducono le donne* ('How to Seduce Women'), in which there is a chapter exhorting women to respond to the superior sexual attractions of mutilated men.[12] In *Alcova*, wounds are 'flesh yearning to become metal' (p. 85), and beautiful women are excited by the wounded:

> Just a few yards off, between two rose bushes, a beautiful virgin threw open her thighs to the ferocious desire of a mountain infantry-man who had lost both arms and was literally eating her face with kisses and stamping his love between her breasts with repeated blows of his chest. (pp. 94–5)

If you want young men to get themselves blown apart, it makes sense, in Marinetti's psychological system, to suggest that it makes women desire to be laid by them. It makes sense in 1917, but less so in 1921, unless Marinetti is attempting to justify a war whose value was being questioned.

Italy needed a victory to justify the war, and Vittorio Veneto was to be that victory. The fact that the advance was a hasty decision to assure bargaining power at Versailles, that any real fighting to get across the Piave was as much Allied as Italian, and the fact that the Austrian army disintegrated in mutiny before the Italians could get to it were an embarrassment to the government, which suppressed the facts.[13] Marinetti, however, does not suppress them; he transforms them, rhetorically. In his narrative, the fact that he arrives after the fighting is over, and the fact that the Austrians have mutinied and fled, or simply surrendered without resistance, are perfectly plain. He gives as a reason for this the indomitable will to victory of the heroic Italians: 'We bear on our faces the crushing defiant arrogance of victory and our eyes are invincible projectors of forces' (p. 314). For Marinetti, this is an *explanation*.

In the very coherence and completeness of Marinetti's ideology lies the denial of the reality of the war, and indeed the very intensity of his visionary aspirations produces an almost totally rhetorical representation of human existence. In order to take control of reality, which he has to do if he is to make of it a language for his ideology, Marinetti renders abstract the real, concrete world and concrete the world of his own subjective feelings. Marinetti is hungry and describes his dream: 'My hunger dreamed of a supremely elegant tablecloth, an infinite silken flight of soft, fluctuating, pearly reflections'. (p. 346). The mighty Austrian bombardment of 15 June 1918 evaporates into Decadent aestheticism as a shell explodes: 'The soft, nonchalant sloth of its smoke, rising, becoming dishevelled and gracefully twining round an early star' (p. 20). 'Isms', in the plural, abound. Marinetti is full of 'optimisms', Italian soldiers are full of 'heroisms', women of 'ironies', the letters soldiers receive are 'too many postal sentimentalities *(sentimentalismi)* on the eve of a decisive battle' (p. 23). Conceits are taken to extraordinary lengths (pp. 285–6, 312, 327, 331 ff.). The whole novel is to a certain extent a conceit on the analogy of the will dominating reality and being invincible like machines: 'I feel the material of my heart become transformed into metal, into an optimism of steel' (p. 200). But by now we are in the realm of making concrete the abstract. In chapter XXVII his feelings of joy, of invincibility at victory are expressed by describing in vivid prose the eleven erupting volcanoes which are their 'concrete' expression. Marinetti, in 1912, told poets to glorify 'matter' in their poetry, and to destroy their own ego.[14] What this often meant, in Marinetti's case, was to glorify his own ego as though it were matter, so that by 1913 he is defining 'the sole concern of the narrator, to convey all the vibrations of his ego.'[15]

Marinetti is not just using ordinary language in a rhetorical manner. Reality becomes language and language becomes 'pure' rhetoric, so that the real world becomes part of a basically musical instrument of self-expression. The stylisation is at times that of grand opera, and the novel must be read as a kind of modulated bellow (if not read that way, it soon becomes intolerably monotonous). Towards the end a motorcyclist announces:

'– Our troops have entered Trieste and Trento!'
A savage fury shakes me. I hurl myself forward, grab him by his arm and hold him still. He rebels and nearly falls. I nearly fall with him and his motorcycle.
'– If you are lying I shall roast your brains!' I scream at him. 'Tell me! Explain to me! Swear to me! The news, that it's true, that it's sure!'
'– I swear it, the general himself told me so three times!'
'– Swear it!'
'– I swear it!'
'– On your mother!'
'– On my mother!'
'– Aaaah! aaaaah!'
I squeeze with both hands my heart which swells, swells, dilates

and splits its walls which are now those enormous mountains, while my gaping mouth drinks in with voluptuous triumph . . .' etc. (pp. 323–4)

The first line of this passage in the original Italian (*I nostri sono entrati a Trieste e a Trento!*) is an hendecasyllable, and other metrical lines abound both in this passage and all through the novel. A number of features of this passage (repetition, elaboration, antiphony etc.) are typical of the Italian verse tradition. All this the work of Italy's most passionate denouncer of traditional metre and creator of 'words in freedom'!

The threat to roast the messenger's brains belongs in an artistic tradition which is not the one we associate with the twentieth-century novel. The 'lived' story that Marinetti is telling us is not really 'lived', for much of what is told is a rhetorical structure designed to induce a certain response in the reader. If it is read out loud, declaimed as it was no doubt composed (Marinetti generally dictated, and he first became known as a reciter of poetry), its powerful histrionic nature is immediately effective. The effect is part of the ideology:

> I want this book to dance, dance, dance, alive and throbbing with joyful rhythm in the reader's hands. I want its dance, mad with love and limitless heroism, to transform the reader's hands into the agile hands of the juggler. He too will shoot out of his armchair and standing erect will strain to increase his height on the tips of his toes like a ballet-dancer in uplifting intoxication which will drive him to compete in reckless acrobacy with the savage rhythm of my book. He will be intoxicated at seeing it on high almost balancing on the sudden jet of joy which will spurt from his heart. He will wait with open arms for it to fall fall at last.
>
> But let's be clear, I am talking about the reader of genius, a friend to every spiritual courage! With brutal ferocity my book will hurtle down on to the nose of the sour little cowardly bespectacled lover of the past, trembling behind his lenses like a microbe under the microscope. It will detach itself from him to hurl itself at him again and to slap him. (pp. 16–17)

The book is an *action*, and it is carried out on the reader: to narcotise him or to assault him. It is written on a monotone, in which 'inebriation', 'madness', 'joy' are one set of key words and the other set is summed up by the word *spavaldo*, meaning 'arrogant and defiant'. Various blends of these two motifs are the obbligato theme of the novel (e.g. the novel's opening sentence, and pp. 63, 78, 318).

The reader is to respond with precisely the feelings that Marinetti attributes to himself in the novel. Reason and rationality are anathema in this activist world. Marinetti must communicate his state of mind intuitively, through a rhetoric of contagion.

The *arditi* (crack assault troops, later the backbone of the Fascist squads) are portrayed as being without minds: 'A confusion of bare arms can be seen pumping like pistons and pouring like taps bottles of wine and glasses of beer amid a fantasmagoric flickering of blue lights and grotesque shadows' (p. 53). Their non-humanness is conveyed not only by the way they are mechanised, but also by the way in which their surroundings are made unreal, so that the activity of these *arditi* is deprived of any sense or purpose. Marinetti is not despising the common soldiery; he associates himself with this anti-rationality:

> I wander around all night with the *arditi* setting off and multiplying the singing, intoxicated not with wine but with the transfiguring alcohol which all the philosophers dream of breaking down and destroying in their cold and meticulous stills and which is called patriotism. (p. 55)

The novel carries a number of attacks on the general staff who want to run the war with logic: 'War . . . is the one thing in the world which does not admit of habit. You have to make your play. Whoever wins wins, whoever loses loses, and that's the end of it!' (p. 180). The narcotic frenzy of vitalism, mechanical metaphors applied to men, sporting metaphors applied to carnage, are rhetoric, not war. Marinetti, in his manifestos, has used military metaphors to describe literary polemic. In this novel he produces a simile in which he compares military aggression with literary polemic: Austrians surrender 'like idiotic professors in love with the past who, feeling our futurist boots in their behinds, reluctantly give up their old dictionaries of Austria's worn-out glory' (p. 320). If war is a way of talking about literature and literature is a way of talking about war then perhaps neither is quite what it seems, and what is important is the rhetorical exploitation of the agression common to both.

If the *arditi* are machines, other troops are 'like cogs in the great machine of battle' (pp. 40–1). The workers in the port of Genoa are dehumanised, while the machines are humanised. Barges are 'unloaded by microscopic little men who swiftly carry on their heads baskets of coal running on the elastic swaying of hung planks. To and fro of the little men between the barges and tall heaps of coal scattered with glinting lights. The sweating torsos glisten too' (p. 67). On the other hand, 'a firm solidarity of will in war swells the biceps of the cranes who swivel proudly on their joined feet to be admired as good patriots by all the attentive houses in the amphitheatre-port' (p. 67). The war is an expression of the will of the cranes, whom the men serve and fuel. Men are industrial fodder.

Marinetti's war is the earthly paradise of the machine; it is futurist war, aesthetic spectacle and experience, the total work of modern art. Rather than the individual feeling himself submerged in monotony or a passive target for shrapnel, a feeling expressed by many witnesses, for Marinetti 'forces predisposed everything in favour of our typically swift and personal victory' (p. 104). Regressive dehumanisation of man – irrationality, mechanisation – is a positive factor for Marinetti, it is progress, wherein the machine is measure of man. Already in 1910 he was predicting the future 'electric war';[16] in *Alcova* he explodes with enthusiasm at the possibilities:

> In the war of the future ... there will be small armies of 100 thousand experienced and picked men, in dynamic action before the nation which will give all its labour to producing for them. ... There will also be ghost-planes laden with bombs and pilotless, guided from a distance by command planes. Pilotless ghost-planes which will explode with their bombs, guided even from the ground with an electrical panel of push-buttons. We shall have aerial missiles. One day we shall have electric war. (p. 175)

This prediction leads to a fantastic vision of even more technologically advanced hardware, operated by men who are described in lyrical terms as 'tamers of primordial forces' (p. 176). When written, this was part of the Futurist Utopia, and that it has, in certain details, been achieved does not make Marinetti's projection any less rhetorical, or political: we shall have occasion to return to 'the nation which will give all its labour to producing for them'. The war that Marinetti describes is also one in which the individual realises his will to dominate: hurtling through the enemy's abandoned lines and fending off women in his armoured car, he is 'dominator of the heart-motor totally obedient to me' (p. 79).

The only mention of trenches in the novel comes in a speech Marinetti makes to Genoese women who are seeing troops off to the front from the station: 'barrack and depot life is so stifling with stupidity and cowardice that it turns the trench into paradise' (p. 102). When, in the scene in which the women give themselves to the war-wounded, one of the virgins, pausing from voluptuous intimacy with a metal thigh, says to Marinetti: 'You know I am a good patriot, but I don't understand, I can't admit, try as I might, the necessity for this eternal, brutal carnage', he reacts quickly: 'I shut my friend's mouth with a long kiss' (p. 89). He then makes her listen to a speech in which he says that war and life are synonymous, and goes on:

> In the distant origins of humanity we see dogged peoples offering bloody corpses to their Gods. Then a Hebrew God also hungry for

human flesh. The earth in its envelope of atmospheres contains forces of domination, extremely intricate and difficult to decipher, which we define with inadequate words such as: spring, youth, heroism, will to ascendancy of races, revolution, scientific curiosity, thrust of progress, civilisation, record. All these undoubtedly telluric Forces adore human blood, in other words, struggle, our need to destroy one another. (p. 90)

The crude social and biological Darwinism, echoes of the *Golden Bough* and of Nietzsche, fused with the ideals and fetishes of competitive free enterprise, are here explicitly used to defend the ideology of war as a *natural* expression of vitality. So fundamental is this ideology of violent struggle to the novel that Marinetti has allowed doubt to be voiced by a character just so that he can make his point antagonistically, by sexually and intellectually dominating the woman.

With the removal of inhibitions, natural, instinctive man is released, his 'forces' greater than those of reason. Many in Europe thought the war a necessary regressive step to prepare for a better world. For Marinetti regression *was* that better world. Being a poet, he needed images for this regenerate natural man, and he took from his Decadent heritage the analogy of sex. *L'alcova d'acciaio* is *all* sex: there is not a cloud, not a hill, not a machine that is not described in sexual terms. The 'steel alcove' is his armoured car, ready for the divine, naked female body of Italy; it is a woman too, whom he dominates by controlling. The rhetoric falls apart when the female armoured car, dominated by Marinetti, is described as dominating in turn the female road with 'lesbian virility' (p. 80). Sex too is just a language.

One of the many ladies Marinetti lays has made a vow to give herself to the first Italian soldier who liberates her from the Austrians. She is not in love. Nor is Marinetti: 'I did not feel love for Graziella, but an overwhelming frenzy of spirit and nerves full of tenderness' (p. 267). She has fought off an Austrian's attempted rape, and yearns to be washed clean. Marinetti: 'I made ready for the most marvellous erotic pleasures with every delicacy and also a strange and brutal drive together with an amazing artistic enthusiasm compounded of stylistic preciosities and musical cadences.' 'I was a mad creator and a crazed sculptor. I was beyond every human or divine social law' (p. 267). 'Endless night, intoxicated with sublimity. Night beyond space and time' (p. 266). His copulation is an alienated lay, the discharge of an instinct, which in its turn is a rhetorical distillate of Darwinian and Nietzschean domination and a mythical transcendence: beyond space and time, and every human or divine social law.

The image Marinetti has chosen to convey natural man's drive, his instinct, is an aggressive sexual drive. But since natural man is an heroic *individual,* his sex act has to be free of emotion, it has to be humanly alienated. Women are elegant, capricious, small-breasted to differentiate them from the ties associated with females – maternity, family, marriage: one quick lay and away. In 1910 Marinetti wrote: 'We are convinced that love – sentimentality and eroticism – is the least natural thing in the world. The only thing that is natural and important is coitus...'[17] In *Alcova* he says that love would destroy 'the ultimate aggressive activity of coitus' (p. 90). The language sex speaks in *Alcova* is the language of the mystical ideology of natural man, who exists on a higher sphere than rational, peaceful, loving man.

The Italian soil, which Marinetti in his armoured car liberates, is described as parts of the nubile body of a woman: the thighs, the breasts, etc. Victory having been achieved, Marinetti finally entertains 'Italy' in his 'steel alcove':

> The great virile thrust of this motor of mine which is at once heart, penis, inspirational genius and artistic will, enters you, causing a violent pleasure for you, for me, I feel it! I am the super-potent futurist genius-penis of your race, your favourite male who, in penetrating you, gives you back the refecundating vibration (p. 281)

There is nothing behind this image; Marinetti is a rutting machine who gives his partner 'refecundating vibration'. A rhetorical penis ejaculating rhetoric. Whereas other women are alienated sex-objects, Italy is the female principle: 'My Italy, delicious earth-woman, mother-lover, sister-daughter, mistress of every progress and perfection, polyamorous-incestuous, holy-infernal-divine!' (p. 283). Marinetti has drawn the human emotions away from women and projected them towards a mythical apotheosis of the *patria.* But the religious drive that impels the patriot is still aggressive and sexual: 'A deep, very spiritual, religious love! ... And at the same time a sensual love, all bites, kisses, scratches and violent caresses!' (p. 284).

Alcova is perhaps the best example of Marinetti's putting into effect two statements from the original 1909 Futurist Manifesto: 'There is no beauty except in struggle. No work of art that is not of an aggressive nature can be a masterpiece'; and: 'We want to glorify war – the world's only hygiene – militarism, patriotism, the destructive act of the anarchists, beautiful ideas for which one dies and contempt for woman.'[18]

'War, the world's only hygiene' became one of Marinetti's favourite slogans. The word 'hygiene' suggests a sort of purging; and the slogan is often accompanied by a condemnation of sexual love. The purging that Marinetti undergoes in his sexual encounters in *Alcova* is also an exorcism; it is exorcising death. 'At a bend in the road appears a wagon clumsily reared up on top of three smashed carts. It seems to want to assault them and impregnate them with a final thrust of its bull-like loins. A revolting stink. Beneath it the carcasses of three oxen are putrefying' (p. 367). That final thrust of its bull-like loins is an affirmation of life in death. Machine-man, 'dead' in human terms, but with that mechanical rutting drive, is alive and indestructible within Marinetti's terms of reference, since all activity is a product of that one drive. Since in other respects he is a machine, he is therefore already 'dead', so he need never fear death: he is immortal.

In an industrial age, in which each man must compete alone for personal gain and self-affirmation, by identifying with the machine each man defends himself against annihilation. In the rut, he enters death's abode, defies death, transcends time and space and affirms the primeval indestructibility of his drive; he is the hero of a myth. If love, or any human tie, calms his aggression, it destroys his drive, his life, his heroism. Hence Marinetti's 'solution to the problem of love' is the brothel, and is described in these terms: 'Mechanisation of love. I can feel the house vibrate with an uninterrupted, mechanical piston-like pumping of violent instincts stripped of all civilisation' (p. 14).

Marinetti began his literary career as a Decadent poet, seeing in the barbarism of the industrial age, which trampled over traditional cultural values, the possibility of rejuvenation. Marinetti insisted that, to survive, culture had to embrace the menacing barbarism, and produce a mass culture of the machine age, dominated by a new élite of artists – the futurists. Rather than bewail the passing of human values Marinetti would have men purge themselves of them. Men would undergo the 'hygiene' of war and emerge purified of everything except their elemental drive. The reward that awaited such heroes was a state of mind: 'intoxication', 'arrogant defiance', 'joy'; the condition of one who does not fear death.

When once the reader reflects that the machines to which men are urged to surrender their humanity are owned by somebody, and earn somebody a profit (the machines of war as much as any others), then the implications of Marinetti's ideology become clear. Marinetti's war novel is significant because it expresses what the industrial age requires from culture: a vision of existence in which the machine does not submerge the individual, but rather offers him release from the very inhibitions with which previous culture had suppressed his drive. For this reason, the ideological perspective that Marinetti imposes on the war, while concealing the superficial realities of suffering, monotony, dirt and disease, reveals the deeper reality of the social and economic forces that brought it about.

Strategies of Survival:
David Jones, *In Parenthesis,* and
Robert Graves, *Goodbye To All That*

Diane DeBell

> The two experiences – to live in action and to live in
> meditation – are forever incompatible.
>
> Herbert Read
The Contrary Experience

In Parenthesis and *Goodbye To All That* were published long after the close of the Second World War. Different as they are, both communicate the struggle inherent in simultaneously accommodating the ravages of a brutal physical experience and transforming that experience into an acceptable and accurate literary perception. Both writers suffered emotional breakdown as a consequence of active service in the trenches, Robert Graves in bouts of neurasthenia (better known today as combat fatigue), and David Jones in two nervous breakdowns later in life. The task of writing about that experience becomes, for both of them, a means of making personal sense of it, and the time gap between the experience and its literary presentation appears in both cases to have facilitated the act of contemplation. Edmund Blunden and Herbert Read have referred to the burden of retrospective analysis.

> A scare was burnt into the mind that was to endure to the end of life.[1]

> You will be going over the ground again . . . until that hour when agony's clawed face softens into the smilingness of a young spring day; . . .[2]

All of Jones's later writings as well as many of his paintings are haunted by the war, whereas Graves appears to have set aside the war, more or less, with the writing of this autobiographical work. There is a fundamental difference in personality between the two which substantially governs the manner of seeing past experience and the creative form that memory takes. More like the Edmund Blunden of *Undertones of War* than like Graves, Jones approaches his subject obliquely. Graves, more like the Herbert Read of *In Retreat*, confronts that experience directly and at times boisterously. There is a deeper pain in *In Parenthesis* but a wider range of impinging experience in *Goodbye To All That*. Graves provides the raw material, the greater variety of issues, but also a less intensely obsessive struggle with accomodating the human imagination to the specific experience of trench warfare.

Both writers served in the Royal Welch Fusiliers (the regiment too of Siegfried Sassoon), Graves as an infantry officer, Jones as a foot soldier. The one was removed by status, the other by aesthetic response from the communal experience of soldiering. Despite a struggle to perceive the mass consequences of war, both writers implicitly aspire to an élitist position of sensibility that will make detachment from the horror possible. Graves achieves this by living through the war as an officer, while Jones does so in the form and detail of his art.

In his Prologue to the 1957 revised edition, Graves says,

> I partly wrote, partly dictated, this book . . . during a complicated domestic crisis . . . It was my bitter leave-taking of England where I had recently broken a good many conventions; . . .[3]

The consequent autobiography incorporates a rebellious tone in keeping with this statement and it reads as an attempt to free himself from his past – that of the public school boy, infantry officer, and husband. Graves is saying goodbye to a Victorian childhood tempered by Swinburne and a genteel education, yet his book does not entirely convince the reader of his detachment and escape either from the war or from his English governing class past. At most those two are temporarily explained and then dismissed.

The original 1929 edition opens and closes in a somewhat more poignant and less distanced manner.

> . . . an opportunity for a formal good-bye to you and to you and to you and to me and to all that; forgetfulness, because once all this has been settled in my mind and written down and published it need never be thought about again . . .
> This is a story of what I was, not what I am.[4]

In the Preface to *In Parenthesis*, David Jones says,

> This writing is called 'In Parenthesis' because I have written it in a kind of space between – I don't know between quite what – but as you turn aside to do something; and because for us amateur soldiers . . . the war itself was a parenthesis – . . . and also because our curious type of existence here is altogether in parenthesis.[5]

In a sense, Jones is dismissing his work as a 'war book' altogether.

He also adds 'it happens to be concerned with war. I should prefer it to be about a good kind of peace . . .' (xii–xiii). That it is about war is an accident, claims Jones. It might have been about any one of a number of specifically historical and personal events. In this way, the war operates as a metaphor for human experience that is restricted in time and intensified. It could be articulated as a metaphor for the burden of the sensitive imagination.

Paul Fussell[6] refers to the privacies and secrecies of the sensitive individual which mark the literature in England of the Great War. It is a connection with Romanticism that emerges in much of the English writing about the war experience and accentuates the separation of the individual from communal experience – a separation that could be read as a specific political failure of the English intelligentsia. The war was fought on foreign soil and there was an unbridgeable experiential gap between the front and home. Though a powerful sense of comradeship developed among the men in the trenches, it was not sustained once the fighting was over and it was mildly frustrated during the war by the continuation of class differences which were consequent upon traditional service hierarchies. The rapid disappearance after the war of a sense of community among veterans must have intensified the difficulty of integrating one's own sense of order and sanity with the memory of disorientation and chaos.

In neither of these works did that wartime unity of feeling become a basis for political analysis or a desire for wider ideological change. Jones's conversion to Catholicism, of course, provided a spiritual base for a continued sense of community; nevertheless, it also provided for a withdrawal and growing isolation from the emerging technological culture in which he lived. Graves, in an analogous way, separated himself physically from England thus bringing about a permanent separation from his intellectual and cultural contemporaries. 'I retired to a mountain village in Majorca where I hoped to avoid the more shocking sights and sounds of pluto-democratic civilization.'[7]

Both of these works are private documents and are conditioned by a tradition of romantic conservatism and a history of solitary suffering. Appropriately, the sacrificial image recurs throughout both the poetry and the prose of English war writing.

> My men, my modern Christs,
> Your bloody agony confronts the world.[8]

And in a quieter vein, Edmund Blunden describes himself at the close of his work as 'a harmless young shepherd in a soldier's coat.'[9] The image of soldierly sacrifice is one that anticipates the growing helplessness of English political and intellectual life in the twentieth century. Paul Fussell extends the essentially Romantic perception involved to include the more explicitly Romantic poetry in England of the Second World War, and Karl Miller broadens that perception of the war poet even further to include an attitude towards experience itself rather than towards an explicitly historical event. In referring to Wilfred Owen, for example, he points to 'the sensitive individual [who] sat apart in order to feel what it was like to be a romantic person, with fits of melancholy.'[10] So, precisely, did Graves choose to spend his periods of leave in solitary walking holidays in North Wales while Jones lived much of his life as a partial recluse either in one of Eric Gill's communities, on the south coast with his parents, or in a nursing home in Harrow. Both men aspired to detach themselves from the war experience. In the manner of their writing and in its content, they struggled to avoid acknowledging the full horror of it.

With the possible exception of Ford Madox Ford's tetralogy *Parade's End*, the best English writing from the Great War is individually isolate, tremulously sensitive, and largely restricted to aesthetic response rather than to an analysis of action and event.[11] Jones's *In Parenthesis* is probably the most private piece of English writing to emerge from that war, and one of the most linguistically and culturally obscure. Its structure is lyrical and its literary-cultural frame of reference is wide and idiosyncratic. *Goodbye To All That* is private in a very different sense. It is necessarily limited by its autobiographical form to the perceptions and experiences of the writer himself but it also retains a framework of traditional values – not by way of explicit defence but rather in Graves's use of behavioural patterns that affirm rather than challenge the social structure which is also responsible for waging the war. This seeming paradox between Graves's rejection of any justification for war and his ability to operate successfully as an infantry officer within it, is characterised by Bergonzi's reference to him as an 'embodiment of the "stiff upper-lip" attitude without its customary inflexibility of mind.'[12]

Goodbye To All That is a wonderful cache of anecdotal information. It relies upon a dramatic presentation of material accompanied by very little added comment, with rapid transitions occurring from one event to another. It is a method by which horror can be accommodated if not fully penetrated. For example, in the following passage Graves encounters his first dead man and speaks about it to two other officers.

> Going towards company headquarters to wake the officers I saw a man lying on his face in a machine-gun shelter . . .
>   I asked: 'What's wrong? Why has he taken his boot and sock off?'

'Look for yourself, sir!'
I shook the sleeper by the arm and noticed suddenly the hole in the back of his head. He had taken off the boot and sock to pull the trigger of his rifle with one toe; the muzzle was in his mouth. . . . Then he (one of the officers) said to the other: 'While I remember, Callaghan, don't forget to write to his next-of-kin . . . I'm not going to report it as suicide.'
At stand-to, rum and tea were served out. (pp. 88–9)

And the passage continues with a discussion of an entirely new subject. The shock of the experience is never mentioned except as it emerges naturally in the dead-pan record of the event. Graves refers to this manner of recording the experience as 'history' (p. 79). Yet it is neither history nor a fully personalised or fictionalised account. Its power lies in its planned drama and its abrupt dismissal of the event.

The raw material of *In Parenthesis*, unmediated by myth and exaggerated for satiric effect, lies in this work. The rudimentary outlines of Jones's work become clearer through a reading of the Graves autobiography. Looking at the two together calls into question the line dividing personal experience from a consciously fictionalised account of personal experience – that is, of treating historiography within a fictionalised or quasi-fictionalised mode of remembering.

Goodbye To All That is perhaps the most valuable source in English for the individual and collective experience of trench warfare. However, it is difficult to validate the presumed factual content because it is a personal account and an emotionally charged one. Despite its compression and its seeming understatement, it thrives on a fascination with the shocking isolated event. Fussell has called it a 'fiction-memoir' (p. 220) and bases his analysis of the work on a metaphor of theatre in which 'the [usual] scene is a conventional almost ritual confrontation between character types representative of widely disparate classes who are presented externally by their physical presence and their dialogue' (p. 211).

The work also demonstrates implicitly the difficulty of finding an adequately honest voice for the war experience during the war itself due to the contrast between home sentiment, which was solemn and sentimental, and the rapidly changing perceptions of the men at the front as their responses to the reality of trench warfare recorded its waste and uselessness. The only psychological posture that seemed to suffice effectively was one which depended on the strength of personal pride, and the desire to support one's comrades. Only the immediate task at hand could be accommodated emotionally, as the following conversation with Sassoon indicates.

We decided not to make any public protest against war. Siegfried said that we must 'keep up the good reputation of the poets' – as men of courage, he meant. Our best place would be back in France, away from the more shameless madness of home-service. (p. 192)

The conversation reveals the war poet's isolation and an implicit despair of his ability and/or opportunity for communicating the reality of the war. Graves disapproved of Sassoon's later public protest against the war and was partly responsible for having him hospitalised, thereby averting court martial. Graves's decision appears to have been connected with his sense of responsibility for his men, which emerges in his writing as the consequential burden of the officer's superior knowledge. One notes the growing professional confidence of the young Graves as the autobiography progresses. According to his own account, he was temporarily in command of the battalion by 1917 and on one occasion argued successfully against the Staff's desire to take a German salient. He is often merciless in exposing the mindlessness of General Staff decisions. But clearly his impulse to do the job well countered what pressure he might have felt to use his position and his imagination to subvert the forces of which he disapproved. In 'P.S. To *Goodbye To All That*', published in 1930, Graves reveals his self-consciousness and ambivalence about both the autobiography and his own attitudes toward modern warfare. In a lengthy justification he both removes himself from an association with any specific political response and envisages (both facetiously and seriously) an alternative to modern war which would satisfy what he believes to be man's need to engage in armed conflict. It would be a 'war that falls somewhere between a football match with large numbers of players on each side and an eighteenth-century battle.'[13]

In Parenthesis is formally and intellectually a very different kind of work and one that warrants a much more extensive analysis than is possible here.[14] I will give it more attention than the Graves work because it is a more complex and inaccessible piece of writing. Essentially, it is the work of a delicate and shy creative intelligence as it attempts to assimilate the consequences of radical and distasteful change. Jones sees the war as a brutal model of the new technological world which is utterly unpleasant to him despite his genuine desire to find signs of value within the created objects of that world. In his critical writings, Jones affirms a commitment to contemplation and craftsmanship, reflecting a line of thinking that reaches back to William Morris, and which, in a late nineteenth-century manner, cultivates a medieval spirit of intellectual and practical piety. The material world is connected to the idea of the sacred. And one's natal place is a matter of the numinous. Continuity for the individual derives from his conscious or unconscious experience of the geographic, historical, and linguistic conjunctions which designate his specific cultural roots. The individual is 'saved' as it were by his integration into a specifiable tradition – which in turn provides a community experience and a rooted identity. Jones conjectures that it is mass culture and its consequent mobility that erodes human dignity. And so he creates out of the landscape and the language of his own home (Southern England and Wales) a mythopoeic reassertion of the importance of origins in opposition to an industralised urban society. We see the consequences of this in *In Parenthesis* in the natural mingling of the men of Britain (Welsh, Cockney, English, and so on) as evidenced in their speech (Shakespeare's *Henry V* provides Jones with a useful analogue here); in the numinous treatment of landscape detail; and in the rapid accommodation the men make to their alien and squalid homes in the trenches, recreating a natural community in the bowels of the earth. The growing mechanisation of the war is a tangible and inescapable reminder of the way in which modern man's made objects have ceased to correspond to his humanity.

The manner by which Jones attempts to reactivate the cultural traditions of his people and to give contemporary meaning to their past is by building up through association, allusion, and the accretion of recurrent images a fabric that becomes richer as one gradually grasps the many-layered references. It is here that the notes to his text become important. They explicate that tradition which is seen to be vanishing and which is, in any case, privately idiosyncratic, and they are an integral part of the act of commemoration to which the text is dedicated. The operative word here is 'anamnesis'. It is a term used by the Catholic Priest in the Mass and it signifies that the poet like the Priest is a conservator and a rememberer.[15] The poet/priest identification is a familiar one in the modern tradition which focuses on Joyce.

To this end, *In Parenthesis* uses a variety of literary forms and mythic themes without binding itself exclusively to any one. The text is associated with poems of commemoration, with elegies and laments, with literary boasts, oral epics, biblical narratives, and particularly, the Roman Mass. It exploits myths of regeneration, of ritual sacrifice, of female protection, and of fertility and waste. It is a synthetic mode of narration, eclectic in its choice of forms and its use of language. Bernard Bergonzi refers to it as 're-mythologising,' and places it correctly in a context of experimental works relying on myth which include *The Waste Land* and *Ulysses* (p. 198).

At its simplest, the narrative consists of a plot that records the fictional movement of No. 7 Platoon, of B Company, 55th Battalion, The Royal Welch Fusiliers, from its training base in England across the Channel and into the trenches. The account builds up in tension to the attack on Mametz Wood in which most of the Company were killed. The single exception is Private Ball who is only wounded. None of the figures in the account are more than voices in the poem. Their characterisation matters only in that they record the variety of personalities (Mr Jenkins, Sergeant Snell, Corporal Quilter, Lance-Corporal Aneirin Lewis, and Private John Ball) and several modes of shifting consciousness. There is a slight identification of Private Ball with the author but the work is not autobiographical in any explicit sense.

The various literary and mythic elements used in *In Parenthesis* essentially play two roles, one in terms of value and the other in terms of structure. In the first case, they lend dignity to the sordid spectacle of trench warfare by associating it with experiences that have acquired wider cultural value. Jones sees the foot soldier as a universal and recurrent image of the passive and suffering hero and he seeks to render the ugliness of the experience palatable by establishing as far as possible continuities with earlier human experience rather than focusing on the apparent discontinuities.

Characteristic of his generation, a world existed in David Jones's imagination that was obliterated by the First World War. It was a destruction that bore cultural as well as personal consequences. And *In Parenthesis* is a poet's attempt to render a sensuous apprehension of that obliteration. The soldiers whom Jones commemorates ('appointed scape-beasts come to the waste-lands') (p. 70) were trapped in a meaningless self-destruction that allowed no opportunity for large or satisfying gestures,

> and when the chemical thick air dispels you see briefly
> and with great clearness what kind of show this is. (p. 164)

But if Private Ball could see excalibur in a twisted piece of steel post (p. 50) or if, for Lance-Corporal Aneirin Lewis, 'Troy still burned, and sleeping kings return, and wild men might yet stir from Mawddwy secrecies', then that appalling experience of 1914–18 might in some way be accommodated. Perhaps, even 'for all the fear in it', the poet's imagination might 'lend some grace' (p. 27) to it. It might be possible to bring the profane into the realm of the sacred by refashioning it in the work of art.

The possibility that mythic and literary associations can lend value and dignity to the soldier's ratlike existence depends upon an implicit trust in the efficacy of ritual. That is to say, Jones would claim that men are dependent upon the accidents of their birth and culture for the values to which they give allegiance and for the patterns that govern their behaviour. When a man becomes a foot soldier, he trusts in the communal values that have placed him in the trench. When the poet realises that an order of command has the power to prompt a man to walk upright to his probable death, then he has come upon a revelation about the power of the logos; and this power is a confirmation of the soldier's need for, and response to, ritual. Such behaviour also suggests to the poet that the language of command has the power to assert itself against whatever might be referred to as instinctual behaviour and thus, for Jones, holds something sacred. And the movement of those men to their deaths in compliance with the word of command is prepared for with care from the first pages of *In Parenthesis*. Language for Jones (whether of military command, of the Mass, the poet, or the soldier) is a symbolic system similar in its formal power to the myths he uses and analyses in the work, and it is resonant with shared human experience as it attests to the comradeship of the men.

The core of the cultural tradition Jones calls upon is British-Celtic-Imperial Roman and his understanding of art is sympathetic to the thinking of Catholic aestheticians such as Eric Gill and Jacques Maritain. The centrality of the Mass and its very fine integration through language and images into the Welsh material derived from and associated with the sixth-century poem *Y Gododdin*[16] provides a useful model for the way in which Jones uses a number of disparate texts in the work. In an essay published in 1957, he reveals the way in which these two materials are joined in his imagination.

> The poetry of the 'first-bards' was concerned with a recalling and appraisement of the heroes in lyric form . . . Certainly this is the end to which the art of our liturgy proceeds. Perhaps the Mass prayer *Unde et memores* . . . may illustrate what I am with difficulty trying to say. Aneirin's poem *Y Gododdin* does make a kind of anamnesis of the personnel of a troop of heavily armed, mounted warriors . . .[17]

In the Preface to *In Parenthesis* Jones says that he wishes the reader to play the part of Welsh Queen. By tradition, the poet must sing to her first in honour of God and then of the Battle of Camlann, 'the song of treachery and of the undoing of all things' (xiii). The Mass and the ancient heroic elegy operate as models for these two tasks in Jones's imagination.

There are a number of reasons why *Y Gododdin* figures so prominently in *In Parenthesis*. For one, Jones is recounting a battle in which he was himself one of few survivors, as was the poet Aneirin. And, by selecting the role of bard who records his people's history and preserves their achievements and losses, he is able to appear to distance himself from his work and simultaneously to indicate his position as witness and participant in the events taking place.

> The geste says this and the man who was on the field . . .
> and who wrote this book . . . the man who does not know
> this has not understood anything. (p. 187)

This procedure allows the poet to control material that is not only
a part of his own experience but the source of extremely painful
memories. It provides a model for narration that he can retain throughout the work yet it is a flexible enough model not to impose restrictions
on him. The bard has traditionally been allowed to order his material
with great freedom – using many voices or one, celebrating or lament-
ing, stringing together events in an episodic manner or telling one
complicated story. And here, as Jones says is often the case for the Celt,
the poet celebrates defeat.

Anthony Cronan says that Aneirin's poem 'is clearly a political poem,
that tries to mitigate the futility of the exploit (and the more general
defeatism of the times) by stressing its heroic glory. That was what the
poet was for; not indeed to deny the failure . . . but to make it tolerable
to men's imaginations.'[18] And in the Preface to *In Parenthesis*, Jones
says 'We search how we may see formal goodness in a life singularly
inimical, hateful to us' (xiii).

The account of the earlier battle also suggests betrayal by those in
command and emphasises the youth, beauty, and trust of the men killed
in the battle, 'The many men so beautiful' (epigraph to Part 1).
Historians date *Y Gododdin* at about A.D. 500 – what Jones calls a
'young time' for Old Welsh. It was also the time in which Arthur is
thought to have lived and lends itself, for that reason, to the use of
Malory in the work. Jones sees the sixth and seventh centuries as a
pivotal period in the history of Britain because it determined the present
cultural and linguistic make-up of the Islands. The period is important
because of its implications about a dying past, its portents for the
future, and its analogous relationship to 1916 or that period about the
time of the war which 'modernists' tend to call a 'turning-point'.

> So did we in 1916 sense a change . . . We feel a
> rubicon has been passed . . . (ix and xiv)

It is by now a cliché to speak of the war as a 'turning-point' for the
modern world. Nevertheless, it recurs in the literature in such a re-
petitious way as to make the idea take on an imaginative validity that
must be recognised as affecting all later thinking about the war and so,
if for that reason alone, it must be considered 'true'.

It is clear enough that *Y Gododdin* was a poem of commemoration
and celebration, despite its grim subject-matter, just as the Mass
includes sacrifice and redemption and thereby, celebration and joy.
Relying upon the arguments contained in the writings of Fr M.

de la Taille, S.J. (*Mysterium Fidei*, 1919) and the interpretation of that work published in English by Rev. M. C. D'Arcy, S.J. (*Mass and the Redemption*, 1926), Jones perceives the Catholic Mass to be an affirmation of the joyousness of Redemption rather than a meditation (principally) upon the continual suffering of Christ. The perspective rests with Christ as Glorious Victim – not merely as Victim. It is within this emotional perspective that Jones uses the Mass in *In Parenthesis*, but it also functions structurally through a cycle of sacrifice. Ritual sacrifice operates in stages: the oblation (which may occur before or after the immolation;[19] the immolation; and the mactation. In Fr de la Taille's theological treatise, the events of the Christian Passion are defined in such a way as to perceive the Last Supper as the oblation which binds Christ to the immolation on Calvary. In this way the Passion includes both the Supper and Calvary in one continuous sacrificial act, its beginning marked by Judas's treason. Jones uses this model in *In Parenthesis*. Images of shared food in the manner of a shared supper recur from the time that the soldiers are in France – that is, have been removed from their own land (which removal implies their betrayal into sacrifice). This timing appears to be an oblique reference to the understanding that betrayal has already occurred, presumably by the somewhat anonymous chain of command and governmental structure that has led the victims into France. It is also relevant that movements across the Channel both before and after the journey are associated with the transportation of animals. The men sleep in horse-stalls, they entrain in cattle trucks. In the last pages of Part 7 the remaining few who are alive bunch like sheep (associational with the actual animals of bloody sacrifice and the symbolic sheep of the Christian Church) to move through a single open space along the German lines.

The metaphor of the Mass as ritual sacrifice is threaded through the narrative from the very beginning. On p. 4 the words of command for calling the troops together preparatory to movement are referred to as: 'The liturgy of a regiment departing has been sung.' Presuming that the betrayal occurred by the beginning of Part 2, the several episodes involving shared food begin to occur. 'The distribution of eked-out bacon' (p. 16) is an early moment. Once in the trenches, the first morning's sharing takes on the dimensions of ritual. The act of Communion itself is called up in 'Each one turns silently, carrying with careful fingers his own daily bread' (p. 74) and in:

> Bring meats proper to great lords in harness and: I say Calthrop, have a bite of this perfectly good chocolate you can eat the stuff with your beaver up, this Jackerie knows quite well that organising brains must be adequately nourished
> But O Dear God and suffering Jesus

why dont they bring water from a well
rooty and bully for a man on live
and mollifying oil poured in
and hands to bind with gentleness.
    Fetch those quickly
whose linened bodies leaning over
with anti-toxic airs
would change your pillow-slip –
for the best part of them.
And potent words muttered, and
an anaesthetist's over-dose for gaped viscera. (p. 173)

Several rituals and several registers of language come together in this passage: the Communion of shared symbolic food; the burial rite; the medical care and binding of wounds common to a hospital; and the last rites before death. They are held together by language that is essentially demotic but which includes diction from each of the rituals involved. And the passage demonstrates the combination of slang and liturgical language which characterises Jones's writing and about which he writes in the Preface,

> Private X's tirade of oaths means no more than 'I do not like this Vale of Tears'; whereas Flossie's 'O bother!' would waste a country-side had she an efficacious formula. I say more: the 'Bugger! Bugger!' of a man detailed had often about it the 'Fiat! Fiat!' of the Saints. (p. xii)

The Mass is repeatedly enlarged in the work by its association with rites of sacrifice that prefigure the Passion as well as the various pagan rites of sacrifice available to Jones through the contemporary studies of anthropology that particularly influenced him (for example, Frazer's *The Golden Bough*).

The second stage of sacrifice, following the oblation of Holy Thursday in the Last Supper is the point at which the narrative has been focused since the beginning. We witness the deaths of all of No. 7 platoon of B Company with the one exception, Private Ball.

In Part 7 the men die in the attack on the German lines. Jones records the deaths in a commemorative manner – emphasising not just the horror of violent death but also the immediate incomprehensibility of the events that accompany it.

> Talacryn doesn't take it like Wastebottom, he leaps up & says he's dead, a-slither down the pale face – his limbs a-girandole at the bottom of the nullah,
> but the mechanism slackens, unfed

and he is quite still
which leaves five paces between you and the next live one to
the left. (p. 158)

The movement of Part 7 presses forward to the images of regeneration
and renewal spun by the Queen of the Woods as she weaves her flowers
and garlands for the dead men. It is in this portion of the narrative that
the deaths are redeemed. It is an image consonant with various pagan
rituals of springtime as well as with the joy of the Christian Easter, and
with the English tradition of pastoral.

> The Queen of the Woods has cut bright boughs of various flowering.
> These knew her influential eyes. Her awarding hands can pluck for
> each their fragile prize. (See pp. 185–6.)

Images of oblation are invoked after the deaths as well as before, the
most notable one when the blood of the German soldier spatters
Private Ball,

> you scramble forward and pretend not to see,
> but ruby drops from young beech sprigs –
> are bright your hands and face. (p. 169)

The Biblical sources for the sprinkling of the blood of the victim *after*
the killing are Leviticus in the Old Testament (which devotes its attention to the laws of ritual) and Exodus, xxiv, 8 (in which Moses sprinkles
the blood of the oxen on the people in ratification of the Old Covenant).
Rituals of sacrifice recur in the Old Testament and are the background
against which the Passion plays its drama. Jones incorporates both the
prefigurations of Old Testament sacrificial allusions and the specific
events of Christ's sacrifice in the events of Part 7. For example, the
moment of hesitation in the Garden,

> you can't believe the Cup wont pass from
> or they wont make a better show
> in the garden. (p. 158)

At this moment Private Ball is both fully aware of and unable to comprehend the immediacy and meaning of the events in progress. And he
echoes Christ's thrice repeated,

> O my Father, if it be possible, let this cup pass from me: nevertheless
> not as I will, but as thou wilt.[20]

.   .   .

It is in this moment of hesitation, says Fr de la Taille, that we witness evidence of the bond between the Last Supper offering and the consequently inevitable death on Good Friday. Once Christ had offered himself as victim, he was bound to go through with that death much as the soldier once committed to the movement of battle could not turn back.

16 The Very Plain Song of It: Frederic Manning, *Her Privates We*

C. N. Smith

The quality of *Her Privates We* was recognised widely when it was first offered to the public at large in 1930, and though it never enjoyed the huge sales of such works as *All Quiet on the Western Front* and *The Spanish Farm* it has been reprinted several times.[1] Its place among the more significant novels attempting to come to terms with the horrors of experience on the Western Front in the First World War is now assured. In much of its detail it is realistic and honest, and this is a precondition of success in this sort of war fiction. But Manning goes beyond the squalor and the horror and sees the richness of human life in appalling circumstances. His focus is on Bourne – that remarkably complex, intellectual private – and the small group of soldiers with whom he is associated. But just as Manning knows better than to reduce this human diversity to average or typical figures, so too he appreciates that a convincing and fair evocation of so great a conflict must take into account the nature of the military formations in which the men serve. There are, in fact, few war novels written from the angle of the private soldier which are more scrupulous in their attitude to commanders at every level, though Manning is certainly no apologist for a hidebound officer caste.

Even more remarkable is the carefully thought-out response to war itself. Manning makes a distinction – a valuable one – between the individual's response to the grave dangers of battle and the rather different way men react to the multiple pressures of army life when the battalion is withdrawn from the front line. In both situations Manning finds positive values. He is not a militarist or an enthusiastic soldier; he does not come, as Jünger does in his *Storm of Steel*, to prize conflict as a unique, tonic experience. But in *Her Privates We* there is a complex portrait of the infantrymen's lot in the First World War which goes some way to explain how they managed to endure while, as R. H. Mottram put it, the Great Powers maintained 'during years, a population as large as that of London, on an area as large as that of Wales, for the sole purpose of wholesale slaughter by machinery' (Preface to

Sixty-four, Ninety-four). With so much First World War fiction conveying a deep loathing for war and all things military, it is no wonder that Manning's more dispassionate weighing of positives and negatives should have been welcomed as something valuable.[2]

'By the time he had picked himself up again the rest of the party had vanished . . . the world seemed extraordinarily empty of men, though he knew the ground was alive with them' (p. 1). These words from the opening of *Her Privates We* convey the essence of Manning's appreciation of the experience of extreme danger. The novel begins with an abortive attack and, after quite a long period for rest and refit following that initial mauling, ends with Bourne killed and the group of his chums broken up, at the start of a new offensive. Though safety is never more than relative when the battalion is pulled back, the risks that are daily run are different in nature from those in the front line. Placing the first battle scene at the very start of the book makes an immediate impact, and the device of Bourne's nightmare is indicative of Manning's method: the deliberate pause for reflection is as characteristic of this novel as the graphic account of events, either major or minor. The lengthy preparations for the next big push permit a gradual increase in tension and foreboding before the final attack. In this way Manning keeps to the fore the basic fact which every infantryman had to accept: one day he would have to quit whatever uncomfortable shelter the trenches afforded and, in response to orders from superiors in whom he did not feel unlimited confidence, go over the top. For commanders, the infantry are tactical units – brigades, battalions, companies – and the operational order that the men were not to pause to help wounded comrades is indicative of their conviction that human emotion was best discounted. The staff had made suitable arrangements for the treatment of casualties and having made this concession to humanitarianism felt free to order the men to stifle their instinctive desire to linger to do what they could for their chums (p. 161). But in *Her Privates We* there is not only a protest against such attitudes. In fact it is significant that the protest is voiced, not by Bourne, but by Weeper Smart.

Through Bourne's actions in the two assaults Manning offers an analysis of that resurgence of individuality, that heightened awareness of the self which results when men are thrust into extreme peril even in large masses. The events themselves might have no obvious significance, and Manning does not endeavour to set them into a context of history or invoke grand concepts of political causality to rescue them from absurdity. What discussion there is of the wider issues takes place behind the lines (pp. 165–73) and is apparently forgotten when the danger is greatest. Yet, doing as he must, acting as his military training dictates, Bourne has accepted the role that has been thrust upon him. 'It had seemed impossible to relate that petty, commonplace, unheroic figure, in ill-fitting khaki and a helmet like the barber's basin with which Don Quixote made shift on his adventures, to the moral and spiritual conflict, almost superhuman in its agony, within him' (p. 11). Bourne's heroism is not conventional fire-eating any more than it is the gay insouciance of so many soldiers in propaganda novels to which Weeper Smart's glum realism is a riposte. But in the portrayal of acute self-awareness, with a little momentary exhilaration to carry a man through initial apprehensiveness, there is an interpretation of the experience of battle, not only in the First World War, but in any other, which contrasts strikingly with talk of a doomed generation going to die as cattle.

The sense of heightened individuality, though real, is fleeting. The appearance of a subaltern or of the Company Sergeant-Major is enough to begin the process of re-integrating Bourne. Shem is discovered resting in a dug-out, and the difficulty Bourne has in communicating with him at first is indicative of the strains to which their human relationships have been subjected (p. 5). The soldiers are called out, make their way uncertainly along the trenches, an officer – not named yet, which is significant – gives his orders in a voice 'cracked and not quite under control' (p. 5). But gradually the soldiers become a group – a unit, as army parlance, for once selecting the *mot juste*, would call it. As they come up to the tents a shell falls, but now it hardly disturbs them. Captain Malet calls them to attention, as the camp details look on 'tactfully aloof; for there is a gulf between men just returned from action, and those who have not been in a show, as unbridgeable as between the sober and the drunk' (p. 6). But the collective will that holds the group together is still relatively weak. Manning adroitly doubles the dispersal of the group and the dissolving of sense of oneness as the men dismiss with Bourne's dream that night. In this way Manning indicates that though the men apparently return to normal rapidly the change is in fact slow, and this helps to emphasise the magnitude of the experience they have been through.

Soldiering does not, however, consist solely – or even mainly – of taking part in great battles, a point often stressed by military historians who argue that First World War fiction tends to falsify front line experience by making heavy fighting an almost daily occurrence.[3] Placing battle scenes at the beginning and end of the novel gives due stress to the supreme test. But the remainder of *Her Privates We* explores the related, but significantly different topic of army life. As Bourne is detailed off for work in the orderly room and then, after rejoining his chums, detached for a spell of training as a signaller, opportunities are created for depicting a number of aspects of the work of a battalion. It might be felt that Manning has made things a little too easy for himself by giving Bourne a quite exceptional capacity for getting on well with a personage so elevated in the military hierarchy as an R.S.M. without souring his relationship with his chums or incurring the suspicions of the N.C.O.s. But, this implausibility apart, *Her Privates We* provides a remarkably comprehensive reflection of the life of a battalion on active service. This is done without recourse to the techniques of the 'group' novel, as exemplified by C. S. Forester's accomplished Second World War propaganda novel *The Ship*, and without turning Bourne into a mere observer or making him go through a gamut of experiences like a picaresque hero.

In the depiction of army life there is a strong element of criticism, though it is stretching a point to interpret the title of *Her Privates We* as an explicit attack on the supposed survival of Victorian attitudes in the forces.[4] The whole episode of Bourne's period as an extra clerk in the orderly room is an expression of the common soldier's distaste for those who regulate his existence without fully sharing in the risks, and it is notable that Bourne feels as strongly about the injustices suffered by the junior officers at the adjutant's hand as about the absurd errors that imperil the privates. Exasperation at the army's inability to cope with the situation comes across in a whole series of incidents. For instance, after men needlessly lose their lives when parading outside the orderly room, the devious and disingenuous way those in charge shuffle off responsibility is described with scathing irony. When Scottish troops are caught in a similar situation as they queue up for rations the implication that the army as a whole is steadfastly unwilling to learn from experience hardly needs stating. Two other incidents skirt farce, though the laughter is always bitter. The chain of command principle is admirably ridiculed in the matter of Bourne's damaged steel helmet (pp. 101–102), while the episode when an irate Frenchwoman halts the advance of the brigade on manoeuvres additionally makes a deeply felt ironic comment on the whole business of rehearsals before a big show (pp. 181–5). Sober military historians may well protest that the attitudes expressed in such episodes are less than fair. But it is hardly to be wondered at if soldiers snatching a little rest after a mauling and before being thrown into battle once again failed to appreciate the administrative achievement, great though it was, that kept them supplied and the military policies which, even if not for the time being conspicuously successful, at least staved off disaster through months of warfare on an unprecedented scale.

Yet *Her Privates We* is not by any means a diatribe against the army, despite Manning's strictures. Indeed, he even permits Bourne to make a somewhat improbably eloquent speech in defence of the High Command (p. 171). None of the inadequacies of headquarters can escape scornful mention from the soldiers. But Bourne insists it is only fair to give the general a chance: 'he's not thinking of you or of me or of any individual man, or of any particular battalion or division. Men, to him, are only part of the material he has got to work with . . . It's not fair to think he's inhuman.' Bourne's whole appreciation of the system is summed up in his realisation that it is the task of H.Q. to plan and that 'once we go over the top it's the colonel's and the company commander's job. Once we meet a Hun it's our job.' Among the officers and N.C.O.s with whom he comes into contact, some – the new colonel of the battalian, for instance, and Captain Malet – are singled out for almost starry-eyed adulation. As for the troops' attitude to their superiors, it is summed up when, after no end of apparently futile preparations for the next big push, culminating in the bizarre business about wearing greatcoats *en banderole* which would have had the effect of virtually making it impossible for them to move their arms, they are ordered to have leather bars nailed across the soles of their boots: 'it was characteristic that the men did not grumble at this latest order, as they saw at once its utility, and the precaution seemed to give them some confidence' (p. 222).

If *Her Privates We* must be judged somewhat deficient in its portrayal of the rigid hierarchy of a battalion on active service, and particularly in the depiction of relations between corporals, sergeants and C.S.M.s and R.S.M.s, where matters of status assume great importance, this is offset by the sympathetic portrayal of the private soldiers. Asked about the motives that led them to volunteer, Bourne's chums are somewhat embarrassed. The phrases of high-flown patriotism do not come to their lips, and treaty obligations never meant much to these artisans and farm workers, while a spell on the Continent has not increased Martlow's love of the Belgians (pp. 164–72). The call of duty could hardly be given a less prepossessing expression than Weeper Smart's glum account of the pressures that finally compelled him to take a step he never ceases to profess to regret, and on Bourne's decision to join up we are left to draw our own conclusions. But these questions all refer to the past, to a period before the army and the war imposed a new perspective. A little information is provided about the past of some of the major characters, though not all, for it is the exigencies of the moment that really matter. When we learn about somebody's background here it is most often a means to emphasise what he is cut off from. Among Bourne and his chums something new is developing. It is not, as he insists, friendship, for conditions are too unstable and disparities too great (pp. 87–8). Regimental pride, by which the Regular Army set such store, hardly seems to count though the Battalion plainly has some awareness of corporate existence. More important psychologically is the sense of mutual responsibility that gradually forms between Bourne and his chums. The group is disparate, and changes a little in the course of the novel, with Weeper Smart joining it quite late on and

Shem disappearing just before the end. Humphreys approaches its fringe, but receives no welcome: his exclusion, simply as a matter of course, and not as a consequence of any thought out plan, emphasises the solidarity of the group. Already nearly complete when the narrative begins, so that the reassertion of its pull can convey Bourne's return from the loneliness of going over the top, its dissolution provides an aesthetically satisfactory conclusion to a novel which, since its focus is on individuals, not on nations, could not convincingly end any other way. Manning stresses the aleatory turning of events, and it is not just a desire to avoid conventional heroics that leads him to portray Bourne's death as the immediate result of quite commonplace decisions in an insignificant skirmish. Yet the implication is plain. Weeper's decision to volunteer for the patrol, his 'Ah'll not leave thee' (p. 273), is the last expression of the group's cohesion. It counts for a lot. But Bourne knows that in dying men are alone. 'It was finished' (p. 274), and the words echo another sacrifice.

Thinking over Bourne's death, Tozer reflects that he was 'a queer chap' (p. 274). Older, better educated, from a different social class, Bourne certainly contrasts with his chums, and the difference is emphasised by the technique of interpreting most events through his reactions, as well as using his experiences as the basis for the narrative. The introduction of Weeper Smart, that highly sensitive, if uncouth character, half-way through the novel has, however, the effect of offsetting any impression that Bourne alone appreciates the full import of circumstances, just as the episodes with the deserter Miller are a counterpoint to the acceptance of duty. It has been assumed by critics from the outset that there is a lot of Manning in Bourne. *Her Privates We* was first published anonymously, and the work is ascribed on the title page to 'Private 19022'.[5] But since this was Manning's regimental number and since Bourne is named after the Lincolnshire town in which his creator lived after the war, it would seem Manning wished to veil, not to conceal for ever, the authorship of the novel. Evidence about his military career is fragmentary. Enlisting in the King's Shropshire Light Infantry early in the War Manning had already failed an officers' training course before being drafted to the Seventh Battalion at the front, whereas Bourne's self-knowledge has spared him the embarrassment of a false start (p. 99). After a spell in France, Manning again tried for a commission. As a subaltern in Ireland he had a wretched time of it, however, and had left the army before the Armistice. The thought of needing to give into pressure and apply for a commission haunts Bourne throughout *Her Privates We*, but Manning's experiences as an officer are reflected only indirectly – and with significant sympathy – in the orderly room scenes, where we see the pressures under which junior commanders had to work. It is known too that Manning was in poor health throughout his time in France, and in a letter written while he was at training camp in South Wales he remarks that he has decided not to drink at all because he knows he will not be able to take it. The selfsame letter contains a graphic account of wild boozing which is plainly the basis of the anecdote narrated in Chapter III. But whereas Manning had been very much the outside observer, Bourne has become a major figure and a prodigious drinker. This relatively small point typifies the reinterpretation of personal experience.

In fact, though there is no doubt that *Her Privates We* has a basis in reality, though the operations of the 7th K.S.L.I. form the background to the novel,[6] though, despite the author's assurance that the characters are fictitious, old soldiers of the Battalion claimed to be able to recognise some of them,[7] Bourne is only a partial self-portrait of Manning – and a somewhat idealised one at that. Bourne's origins, like those of the other soldiers, are never fully explained. In part this is for artistic reasons, as a means of portraying the strange relationships with all their intimacies and reservations that constitute comradeship, rather than friendship. But plainly Manning did not wish to use his novel for a public discussion of his own decision to join the army and the problems he must have faced in the ranks of an English county regiment. The son of a prominent New South Wales public figure, he had been sent to England where he had to be privately educated on account of the delicacy of his health. In the years immediately before the war he had begun to make a reputation as a writer, with volumes of rather too carefully polished verse to his credit and *Scenes and Portraits* in prose after the manner of Renan, whilst his *Eidola* of 1917 offer a variety of war poetry that appears anaemic in tone and idiom beside *Her Privates We*. It is only by piecing together the evidence that the reader becomes aware that Bourne, like his creator, is an Australian, but the fact, like the reference to his being of a different religion (p. 58), is not developed. Bourne's impatience with any insistence on needless class-distinctions (see especially pp. 208–12) is sometimes supposed to reflect his origins, but the point is not stressed by Manning. When Australians are mentioned, no opportunity is created for Bourne to show his own personality fully; rather, tribute is paid to a national archetype with which he – like Manning – is temperamentally incapable of conforming.

There is, of course, no reason whatever why a novelist should not develop personal experience as he wishes provided the derivative is convincing, and Sassoon's observation that Sherston is a simplified version of his open-air self, uncomplicated by the particular problems besetting authors applies to much First World War fiction.[8] It is, however, only at the cost of certain implausibilities that Manning refashions his material. Through the figure of Bourne and his chums he conveys admirably his interpretation of the nature of battle, but in the depiction of army life the relationships of his hero with other privates as well as with his superiors are made too blithe, while the matter of sexual deprivation is treated with such delicacy that it resembles a daydream (pp. 127–30). Bourne is an exceptional figure with privileges and idiosyncrasies, and the more clear-sighted of his chums recognise that it is inevitable that he will be obliged to try for a commission. Significantly Manning, who says little about the initial formation of the group, does not explore the psychological strains to which Bourne would have been subjected had his superiors' plans for him come to fruition. Death spares him that problem.

Written and published when the war novel boom was at its height, *Her Privates We* invites and merits attention in the first place as a depiction of experience at the front and as an interpretation of the impact of war and army life on individuals. Comparisons between Manning and Bourne add a dimension, making the novel a fascinating human document which is perhaps more revealing than its author appreciated. Attention has already been drawn to the narrative skill which, by avoiding both the over-ingenious mechanism of a well-made plot and the temptations of trying to present a grand historical sweep from Mons to the Armistice or a full account of Manning's military career, concentrates on essentials and indeed in itself conveys something of the private soldier's sense of being deeply involved in matters which personally he cannot fully comprehend. One side of Bourne's character is reflected, though only obliquely, in the field of allusion created by the Shakespearean quotations that give the work its title and serve as epigraphs for the chapters. Though perhaps less out of key than Bourne's sudden recall of a Latin tag (p. 61), contrivance is, however, rather too obvious, and the irony, like that of the grim paraphrase of a line from Gray's *Elegy* (p. 64), is heavy-handed. Such artifice, like the somewhat routine references to moonlit nights, does not show Manning at his best as a literary artist. He has, however, two great gifts of which the Wardour Street preciosity of his pre-war writings had given little hint. Occasionally he slips, as when he speaks of 'that thin wood known as three-ply' (p. 137) and puts supercilious inverted commas round 'chips' (p. 68) or when he overworks the subjunctive and the pronoun 'one'. But the use of precise terminology to create an impression of actuality is a feature of a novel which breathes reality without becoming heavy with detail or relaxing its psychological grip through pausing for needless description. Even more impressive is the command of dialogue styles. The group of Bourne and his chums comes into contact with many other characters, some playing a considerable part in the novel, others, like god-like Agamemnon at the exercises (p. 182) making only a brief, but vivid appearance. With a few words of dialogue, again and again Manning creates a vivid impression. He can capture the more elegant idiom of the commanders to a nicety, but his greatest triumph is the differentiation of the privates by their manner of speech. The original version of the novel, privately printed under the title *The Middle Parts of Fortune*, had been less inhibited in its use of four-letter words than *Her Privates We*. But little is lost by bowdlerisation, except that Bourne is less clearly differentiated from his chums when they have to make do with the conventional euphemisms. The cussing, however, combines with a sprinkling of soldiers' Anglo-Indian words and a regular use of regional dialect to produce the indispensable medium for the expression of the human interaction, especially when drink loosens everybody's tongue and lets each man cast aside momentarily some of his reserve.

Her Privates We is a complex work, expressing primarily through the deep character of Bourne responses to the War more subtly differentiated than are found in much First World War fiction. Inconsistencies and loose ends do exist, and it would be special pleading to account for all of them as expressions of the relationships which, under the conditions prevailing, could never become complete. Nonetheless, even after another World War and half a century it is not difficult to see what qualities in Bourne and in *Her Privates We* led Eric Partridge, himself an old soldier, to claim that the book was 'uncontradictably the best English war novel'.[9]

17   Richard Aldington and *Death of a Hero* — or Life of an Anti-hero?

John Morris

> He was living in a sort of double nightmare – the nightmare of the War and the nightmare of his own life. Each seemed inextricably interwoven. His personal life became intolerable because of the War, and the War became intolerable because of his own life.[1]

For much of his life Richard Aldington (1892–1962) felt his country had forgotten him. Significantly, perhaps, 'authorities' disagree on where he was born and where he died.[2] Nor is it entirely clear why he should have argued with, and become angry with, so many former associates like Pound and Eliot with whom in his youth he worked as Imagist poet and editor. Certainly he came to feel a sense of betrayal by the British literary 'Establishment' which – after the Great War 'had been declared against him personally' – included the entire social spectrum: Government, church, class, family, the arts. For Aldington the war, in which he was gassed and shell-shocked, brought home unforgettably, as Burma did for Orwell, a sense of the hypocrisy upon which nation, Empire and class depended.

Death of a Hero (1929), written in France while *All Quiet on the Western Front* was being prepared for publication, has all the hallmarks of expatriate brooding: obsession, pride and a hurt excess of Englishness. Aldington's war novel is therefore not particularly about war: it is about betrayal, crystallised for him by his own experience and set down as the life and death of his 'hero' George Winterbourne. Though Aldington's (and Winterbourne's) experiences may be taken to represent the betrayal of a generation of young men some of whom – Sassoon, Graves, Remarque – recounted similar betrayals, the social and temporal gulf isolating Aldington was peculiarly his own and felt with extraordinary intensity. Henry Miller, who met Aldington only once, spoke of him thus:

> *A good human being,* I thought to myself. More like some fine breed of dog than a literary creature. Something in his eyes which spelled sadness, but the sadness of the animal which knows not why it is sad. Or, as if at some time or other he had experienced a profound betrayal.[3]

I began with comment upon Aldington's personal qualities because like many modern novelists he was an 'egotistical' writer.[4] The bitterness, anger and passion which characterise his work have been regarded by some critics as defects that typify both creator and what he created, and yet the fierce sarcasm directed against the 'Establishment' in *Death of a Hero* has been *admired* by others as the novel's chief glory. *The Colonel's Daughter* (1931) and *All Men are Enemies* (1933) exhibit similar qualities, indeed the former – a militantly cynical picture of English village society, especially of the shabby-genteel, post-war, ex-army, officer class – is remorseless in its dismissal of the very idea that most of these 'grotesques' could be motivated by emotions other than envy, greed or lust.

In fact, Aldington tended to create stock characters, often from people known to him personally. The reader may well feel rather cheated when characters are transferred from novel to novel with only a new name to distinguish them. Such a technique suggests a lack of imaginative power and an approach which treats novel-writing like spare-part surgery. In both *Death of a Hero* and *All Men are Enemies*, the maidservant takes the young hero 'down home' to Kentish hop-picking country; the influential, butterfly-collecting, scholarly, figure of Antony's father in *All Men are Enemies* had appeared as Mr Hamble in *Death of a Hero* while Dudley Pollack is in essence recreated as Henry Scrope in *All Men are Enemies*. Were such short cuts in the process of characterisation justified, however, in the creation of 'grotesques'? Was this a legitimate satirical device to show how those who thus betrayed their own humanity were the link between social hypocrisy and war – that only in this way could he 'kick the grotesque Aunt Sallies of England into the limbo they deserve'?[5] But are all of Aldington's characters (except the Aldingtonesque hero) stereotypes? In *Death of a Hero* can the narrator really be distinguished from Aldington, or either of them from Winterbourne? Do any characters develop enough to suggest an inner life of their own? To what extent did Aldington – especially in *Death of a Hero* – sacrifice the novel (with its traditional use of character as a means of enlarging the reader's experience) to the angry exposition of ideas and feelings? Would his characters be more appropriate to a fable than a novel? These questions cannot be ignored because, quite simply, two-thirds of *Death of a Hero* portray the social tragi-comedy of the hero's development into the young man who volunteers in 1915 and is sent on active service in the winter of 1916.

First published in September 1929 *Death of a Hero* was an immediate best-seller, making Aldington an internationally known writer for the first time. Written at great speed (partly in the company of his friends

Frieda and D. H. Lawrence on the Mediterranean island of Port Cros)
Aldington, with his characteristic honesty, produced a novel which in
Britain could be published only in an abridged form – the soldiers' use
of four-letter words, for example, being found 'objectionable'. The
novel is divided into three main parts: *vivace, andante cantabile* and
adagio – the third alone portraying combat conditions. There are also
a Prologue and an Epilogue. The Prologue, 'Mort d'un Eröe', is
marked *allegretto*; and the Epilogue is a tragic dirge in verse spoken by
a broken survivor of the war in which the hero, George Winterbourne,
committed suicide by walking voluntarily and unnecessarily into a bar-
rage of machine-gun fire. The musical notation thus suggests a symphonic progression, though the Prologue might have been better
marked *scherzo*.[6] Perhaps I should 'come clean' at this point by saying
that, in my opinion, Part III of the novel is the best of Aldington's prose
I have read and that as war literature it deserves the epithet 'great'.
While the other parts of the novel are frequently memorable they suffer
too often from imperfections of characterisation and uncertainties of
style for their form to contain a (presumably) justified bitterness and
anger directed against the 'cant', 'humbug' and hypocrisy of what
Aldington called the 'Kiplingesque or kicked-backside-of-the-Empire
principle' (p. 227).

Published critical approaches to the novel have tended to be sparse,
infrequent and either strongly 'for' or 'against' as if they had a case to
be dismissed rapidly one way or the other. Walter Allen's *Tradition
and Dream* (1964), for example, a deservedly respected 'critical survey
of British and American fiction from the 1920s to the present day'
makes one tiny but explosive reference, describing *Death of a Hero* as
'a formless novel, incoherent and hysterical, reading as though written
in the white heat of battle itself'.[7] It is, of course, ironically true that
other critics have *praised* the novel for somewhat similar reasons.
Maxim Gorky called it 'an utterly harsh, angry book' and added that
he 'would never have thought that the English could produce a book
like it'.[8] Lawrence Durrell has described it as 'the best war-novel of the
epoch'.[9] In fact 'Britain's best war-novel' is a label frequently attached
to it, but without further explanation or elucidation. A much better, if
still brief, treatment of *Death of a Hero* is to be found in *Prose Writers
of World War I* by M. S. Greicus, who puts his finger on what is surely
the major starting-point for any analysis and assessment:

> hysterical evocations are at once a virtue and a major flaw in the
> novel. The work captures the mood of his generation, its sentimen-
> tality, its *naïveté*, its disarming expectation of justice. It is also guilty
> of every charge levelled against 'war books'. Its subject-matter com-
> bines the sensationalism of 'modern sex' with the horror of war,

through a narrator who holds all of modern civilisation in contempt.[10]

Generally, however, assessments have been unbalanced and prejudiced because critics have concentrated either on the flaws all too apparent in Parts I and II and found the novel *as a whole* wanting; or upon the merits of honesty, realism and passion (very relevant to Part III), and from these claimed majestic qualities for the entire novel. In a very real sense a dichotomy between the writer and what he produced is highlighted both by the novel itself and by its critical reception. It is significant that the most unstinted praise has tended to come from friends of Aldington while some savage and dismissive attacks seem to have emanated from the enemy camp of those whom Aldington offended and from whom he became estranged.

All critics agree, nevertheless, that whatever merits or demerits they may contain, the Prologue and Parts I and II of the novel are angry and bitter. Why should they have been so? Who is the target for these emotions? Here again Greicus expresses an important basic attitude revealed in the novel:

> *Death of a Hero* must be seen in the tradition of rebellion that had begun with Samuel Butler's *The Way of All Flesh* (1903). Aldington equated the war with the stupidities of antiquated Victorian values. His story involves the discovery that the intelligentsia, who were behind the movement against these values, were themselves as corrupt as the morality they opposed. He saw his generation caught in the middle at a time when public attitudes were shifting toward the new values.[11]

Greicus could have gone further and claimed that Aldington, like the Prince of Denmark, rants and raves at a comprehensive rottenness (as he sees it) infecting an entire Empire. The 'Kiplingesque or kicked-backside-of-the-Empire principle' preached (for Aldington) dishonestly and hypocritically that only discipline, self-denial and physical toughness mattered, while at the same time perpetuating a society which allowed self-indulgence and mental and physical lethargy to those made rich by the exploitation of overseas possessions. It was not the exploitation so much as the hypocrisy that so angered Aldington. Thus in his view the 'humbug' and 'cant' which corrupted public and private life contributed directly to the self-imposed death of a man ironically termed 'hero' who died no longer capable of belief in, or respect for, the society and the loved ones for whom in theory he had fought. His betrayal by society predetermined his final self-betrayal on the battlefield. Such, it seems to me, is the thesis behind Parts I and II and thus they cannot, in terms of the full novel, be judged in total separation from what they are supposed to achieve by preparing the ground for Part III.

The peculiarly idiosyncratic note of loathing and contempt which at times almost screams at you from the page has been, of course, strongly censured. But the note confirms Aldington's characteristically personal sense of affront at what social betrayal did to George Winterbourne (and countless others like him). The 'hero', like Aldington himself, is totally misunderstood as a boy at home and at boarding-school *because of* his merits: it is his sensitivity and sensuality which condemn him in the eyes of people in authority over him who either ignore, or dishonestly hide, those qualities in themselves because Victorian convention demanded that the Middle Class should not recognise publicly and socially such dangerous attributes. And so the Prologue shows an exaggerated and 'grotesque' picture of what the sham has produced: his mother has become an ageing fornicatress (whose son's death, communicated by War Office telegram, acts as sexual stimulant!) while his father has turned into a pathetic, mindless convert to Roman Catholicism whose regimen of self-denial is the negative substitute for a necessarily guilt-laden life. But it is those who should have known better, the intellectuals and those of his generation (especially the female members), for whom Aldington reserves his most complete contempt because they turned out to be a fifth column fighting for the enemy in the war against social hypocrisy. Like Aldington, Winterbourne finds a place in the avant-garde artistic life of London, scratching an existence by writing reviews. Yet those people, with whom the young Winterbourne needs to associate if he is to make a successful career, are seen as a group of fatuous *poseurs* with arrogant and naive assumptions as to their importance in the world of the Arts. Here again such figures by their very names suggest 'grotesque' characterisation: Upjohn (the inventor of 'Suprematism' and, later, 'Concavism'), Shobbe, Bobbe and Tubbe. Yet some, if not all, of these are clearly caricatures of actual associates with or for whom Aldington had worked. Most of them are met by the reader initially at a 'banal party'. Bobbe, who 'exercised his malevolence . . . by trading upon his working-class origin' and spoke of the need for 'a genuine out-reaching of the inward unconscious Male-life to the dark Womb-life in Woman' (pp. 124–7), is clearly a caricature of Lawrence – D. H., not T. E., of course. Waldo Tubbe similarly satirises T. S. Eliot, though here Aldington comes close to hitting below the belt:

> Mr Waldo Tubbe . . . of the United States . . . was an exceedingly ardent and patriotic British Tory, standing for Royalism in Art, Authority in Politics, and Classicism in Religion. Unfortunately, there was no dormant peerage in the family; otherwise he would

certainly have spent all his modest patrimony in endeavouring to become Lord Tubbe. Since he was an unshakeable Anglo-Catholic there were no hopes of a Papal Countship. . . . Consequently, all [he] could do in that line was to hint at his aristocratic English ancestry, to use his (possibly authentic) coat-of-arms on his cutlery, stationery, toilet articles, and book-plates, and know only the 'best' people. (pp. 110–11)

Sometimes the caricature seems spiteful:

[George] did indeed feel repelled by most of the gathering, particularly by persons like Mr Robert Jeames, the Poets' Friend, who made anthologies of all the worst authors, wore a monocle and spats, and lisped through a wet tooth. (p. 126)

Is this not uncomfortably close to Harold Monro, who in fact showed unprecedented disinterestedness in helping young writers and nearly bankrupted himself by providing free quarters for poor poets? What could possibly justify such (apparent) hatred? Does the following offer an explanation?

Upon the charity of these . . . gentlemen our hero chiefly . . . subsisted, skating indeed upon very thin ice in his relations with them, and expending treasures of diplomacy and dissimulation which might have been employed in the service of his Country. It subsequently transpired . . . that his Country did not want his brains but his blood. (p. 111)

The reader may well wonder whether it was the potential bloodshed or the actual charity which hurt the writer.

There are similar passages of invective directed against women: their hypocrisy, their lack of logic (especially as it concerns 'Free Love' since a menstrual false alarm traps George into marriage) but above all in their downright fickleness and faithlessness towards men. Returning on leave from the front, George notes at Victoria Station that 'Here and there a woman threw her arms about the neck of a soldier in a close embrace which at least at that moment was sincere.' (pp. 339–40)

Like the intellectuals, young women are regarded as betrayers defecting to the old hypocritical ways despite pretence of new thinking and new approaches to life. Yet it could well be argued that Aldington undermined his case by making so many of his characters into 'grotesques' or stereotypes or at best gross caricatures. Even in the case of Elizabeth (the wife), Fanny (the mistress) or George Winterbourne himself (a less angry *persona* of Aldington) the novelist seems to have been attracted to the creation of types. Indeed no sooner have George and Elizabeth met, at the 'banal party' than Aldington asks the reader to 'consider them for a moment, please, rather as types than individuals'. One might be excused for supposing the moment to be a very long one. When George returns from the front on leave he is again cornered by Upjohn and Tubbe who ask the infantryman ridiculous questions like 'Are you still writing for periodicals?' and 'how did you spend your leisure in France – still reading and painting?' Elizabeth has taken up with a stereotyped Cambridge intellectual called Reggie Burnside and when George has dinner with this group all he wants to do is get drunk and thus avoid noticing them (pp. 341–5). But again one must ask whether the writer's dislike and contempt themselves determine the need for grotesques and stereotypes (because as such they are not worth liking) or whether such a technique serves a useful satirical purpose.

Such doubts and reservations are of primary importance, for there can be no question that emotionally and intellectually the terrible aftermath of the 'cant' which Aldington observed is the motivation and indeed the very core of *Death of a Hero*:

> If you want to judge a man, a cause, a nation, ask: Do they Cant? If the War had been an honest affair for any participant, it would not have needed this preposterous bolstering up of Cant. The only honest people – if they existed – were those who said: 'This is foul brutality, but we respect and admire brutality, and admit we are brutes; in fact, we are proud of being brutes.' All right, then we know. 'War is hell.' It is, General Sherman, it is, a bloody, brutal hell. Thanks for your honesty. You, at least, were an honourable murderer.
>
> It was the regime of Cant *before* the War which made the Cant *during* the War so damnably possible and easy. (p. 222)

Here the two main elements of the novel are fused: the social and the military. But would it not have been more valid and thus more successful if the social element had been (and been intended to be) as convincing and realistic as the military? And is there not a danger that George Winterbourne's death will seem less tragic than pathetic because it affected, by the definition of Aldington's characterisation, no one of any significance whatsoever?

Part III, which is almost entirely devoted to George Winterbourne's military experiences – first as a private and from 1917 as a lieutenant, in the Royal Infantry – is immediately more impressive. With a sense of relief the reader feels that at last he is getting to the real substance of the novel. The choice and economy of words suggest from the very beginning a sense of purpose and urgency which contrasts noticeably with the exaggeration and emotionalism of much that has gone before and which at times seemed as much self-indulgent as angry. Now, however, the discipline of recording actual events honestly and realistically imposes a new order and cogency:

> 'Draft! – Draft! 'Tenshun!'
> Two hundred and forty heels met smartly in one collective snap at the same time that the rifles were sharply brought to the sides. The draft stood to attention, gazing fixedly to the front. A man unconsciously turned his head slightly in trying to catch a glimpse of the approaching officers out of the corner of his eye.
> 'Stand still, that man! Look to your front, can't you?'
> Silence, except for the moaning wind and the crunch of gravel under the officers' boots. (pp. 232–3)

Of course the hypocrisies and dishonesties in British society which Aldington had derided are present in the army too. But the new young Officer Class are portrayed as purposeful, hard-working and above all honest, not only to their men but to themselves. The men, Winterbourne's fellow rankers for much of Part III, are (as perhaps their speech was intended to suggest) not only down-to-earth but prepared to accept that their fate, however terrible, was to be shared. In other words the ties and rewards of comradeship – real, and essential for survival, – are substituted in George Winterbourne's life for the false liaisons and career-orientated relationships left behind in London. Aldington paints vividly, and in a sense touchingly, the association that develops into regard and friendship between Winterbourne and Lt Evans, for whom he acts as runner. Although Evans is portrayed by the familiar 'typing' of Aldington's characterisation he emerges as someone whom Winterbourne would have derided in London yet admires and, more importantly, needs in the trenches of Northern France:

> Evans was the usual English public-school boy, amazingly ignorant, amazingly inhibited, and yet 'decent' and good-humoured. He had a strength of character which enabled him to carry out what he had been taught was his duty to do. He accepted and obeyed every English middle-class prejudice and taboo. What the English middle-classes thought and did was right, and what anybody else thought and did was wrong. He was contemptuous of all foreigners. (p. 285)

Not a promising basis for friendship with an avant-garde artist; and yet Evans becomes more loved and worthy of love to Winterbourne than the subject of any 'beautiful friendship' imaginable in Soho, Chelsea or Hampstead: 'He was exasperatingly stupid, but he was honest, he was kindly, he was conscientious, he could obey orders and command obedience in others, he took pains to look after his men' (p. 286).

Here at last perhaps we approach a situation which may with justification be called tragic, for Winterbourne and others like him, because the new military 'society' was ephemeral – for more reasons than the obvious one. The long-term effects of continual subjection to shell-fire produced 'war neurosis' which affected not only personality but the very bases of human behaviour: moving, talking, thinking. One undoubted achievement of *Death of a Hero* is the terrible precision with which Aldington records in George Winterbourne's life and death the remorseless extinction on the battlefield of a hitherto developing psyche of unusual sensitivity.

I have claimed that Part III of *Death of a Hero* is the most impressive of the novel. Nowhere is this clearer than in the way in which Aldington relates the social abuses portrayed in Parts I and II to the advent of the war portrayed in Part III. 'Under canvas at the Boulogne rest camp' Winterbourn ponders the paradox and the absurdity of the 'War to End Wars'. Were not German soldiers also men and did he not admire *for their manhood* the English soldiers with whom he travelled? If, as was clearly the case, they did not allow themselves to be forced by war or propaganda into a hatred of their fellow men of either side then surely English and Germans alike 'had saved . . . from a gigantic wreck . . . manhood and comradeship, their essential integrity as men, their essential brotherhood as men'. Then who was the real enemy? Again Aldington repeats his attack on the hypocrisy and humbug of those in authority (the enemies of ordinary men) though now the attack is directed against an international enemy. And then the author takes one further despairing step (anticipated in a poem like Matthew Arnold's 'Dover Beach') and asks whether the humane virtues could or should survive at all:

> But O God! O God! is that all? To be born against your will, to feel
> that life might in its brief passing be so lovely and so divine, and
> yet to have nothing but opposition and betrayal and hatred and
> death forced upon you! To be born for the slaughter like a calf or a
> pig! To be violently cast back into nothing – for what? My God! for
> what? Is there nothing but despair and death? Is life vain, beauty
> vain, love vain, hope vain, happiness vain? (p. 259)

Such naked emotion has point and justification against a background of European betrayal and it is not until Aldington has communicated its perception on such a vast scale in the desperate mind of Winterbourne that its savagery and crudeness can become acceptable or justifiable. It is a vision of an international collusion of those who rule to destroy by total war all that is humane.

Yet Aldington is at his most convincing as a war novelist when he writes about combat itself *as* combat and not as the aftermath of 'cant'. The major writers of the Great War (and the major painters too) all captured that strange symphonic beauty created by some hellish paradox out of the horror of that War. Wilfred Owen's 'Anthem for Doomed Youth' and 'Strange Meeting' and Paul Nash's 'We are making a New World' are echoed in the following magnificent passage:

> The whole thing was indescribable – a terrific spectacle, a stupendous symphony of sound. The devil-artist who had staged it was a master, in comparison with whom all other artists of the sublime and terrible were babies. The roar of the guns was beyond clamour – it was an immense rhythmic harmony, a super-jazz of tremendous drums, a ride of the Walkyrie played by three thousand cannons. The intense rattle of the machine-guns played a minor motif of terror. It was too dark to see the attacking troops, but Winterbourne thought with agony how every one of those dreadful vibrations of sound meant death or mutilation. (p. 321)

Such writing (the former Imagist can be heard here) is much more than description: it is aesthetic and moral judgement. It is too a brilliant elucidation of the significance of artistic movements like Futurism and Cubism as modes of interpreting such unprecedented phenomena as total war. The passage also highlights another admirable quality: a peculiarly sensual and sensitive realism when Aldington describes a gas attack, the effects of exhaustion, the sounds of shells which vary as they differ according to size and power, the entire audio-visual-sensual language of the Great War is communicated as effortlessly as that of natural beauty when he describes the beauty of the countryside. Relish of sensual beauty or ugliness is combined with precise observation in both cases. He writes as an entomologist who loves butterflies and hates lice.

Though Aldington failed for much of the novel, in my estimation at least, fully to demonstrate the connection between the hypocrisy of peace and the hypocrisy of war, because his characterisation lacked depth and perception, he nevertheless gave to his war novel a quality that might answer a frequently voiced criticism of war literature: that its subject-matter and its significance are necessarily too restricted. For in the destruction of George Winterbourne in the autumn offensive of 1918 we see the destruction of a lover of life whose final acts were in seeing life in the landscape of death, finding a society in the chance gatherings of shocked men and experiencing true love in compassion for those already doomed. The anti-hero becomes hero in this society albeit a demented and ephemeral one.

If there is tragedy in this novel it exists not because the hero could never return home but because he had no home – no permanent person or place off or on the battlefield – for which to stay and fight.

18 The Denuded Place: War and Form in *Parade's End* and *U.S.A.*

Malcolm Bradbury

It seems important to say that many of the novels written about the First World War did more than report it, debunk it, or expose its horror or inhumanity; they also, often, took it as an apocalypse, a crisis moment in the history of civilisation and culture. And, because literary forms are themselves socio-cultural creations, imbued with the meanings and structures of a civilisation, its codes of morality and its modes of language, they took it as a crisis for artistic form itself – a challenge to the texture of morality, character and realism that had helped make up the substance of the traditional novel.

For this reason, many critics have seen the war as the great turning-point into modern form, the apocalypse that leads the way into Modernism. The matter is not that simple; many of the features of style and form we associate with post-war fiction had emerged much earlier, when the novel changed under pressure from the symbiotic and dangerous mixtures of naturalism and symbolism that dominated the 1890s. The modern novel existed before the modern war, and we may rightly sense an element of prophecy in the fact; the styles of naturalism and indifference war seemed to require in its modern form pre-date the event.[1] However, the war undoubtedly changed style, and it helped ratify modernism. It enforced the naturalist insights; it also intensified the sense of historical disorder and irony that many experimental writers had begun to probe. The war, in fact, became a turning-point in the implicit historiography of modern fiction; that is to say, many novelists wrote it into their novels as a sufficient explanation for modern style, for the spatialisation of form, the jump from the diurnal to the symbolist world, as well as for their newer, harder techniques of expression, their rapid cutting, their mechanisation of human figures, their indifferent urbanisation of the landscape.[2]

Pre-war modernism, then, tended to modernise form as such; later modernism, after the war, tended to see the new disjunction in history too, and modernised life, man, history as well. And of the great transition into the modern place, modern time, modern indifference, modern hardness, the war was the ultimate symbol. It expressed itself, again and again, as violation, intrusion, wound, the source of psychic anxiety, generational instability, and of the mechanistic inhumanity that prevails in, say, D. H. Lawrence's *Lady Chatterley's Lover* (1928) – a novel dominated by the 'false, inhuman bruise of the war'. Historiography, traditional realism, were dislocated; new styles of life and styles of art were compulsory. The preoccupation of the 1920s with a disjunct history, Joyce's 'nightmare from which I am trying to awake,' whereby the world becomes discrete fragments, redeemed only by symbolic form, is a primary version of this. The 1920s became preoccupied with the anti-epic, the discontinuous construct which associates the parts of a culture without being able to attach them. Epic is associated with war itself, and the war epic became, by the later twenties, a great but also an ironic enterprise. There *were* realistic versions, like Mottram's *Spanish Farm*; but realism itself seemed dislocated, and various forms of experimental structure appeared in this later period, the period of considered war novels rather than war reporting or war impressions. I want here to look at two such 'experimental' epic sequences, one by an English writer, one by an American, both by writers with modernist credentials, though their versions of the new form are very different.

The two sequences, both of them dynastic works about war *and* peace, and therefore historical versions of the change that war made, not alone in society, individual psychology and cultural hope, but also in aesthetics, are Ford Madox Ford's four-volume *Parade's End*, consisting of *Some Do Not* . . . (1924), *No More Parades* (1925), *A Man Could Stand Up* (1926) and (sometimes dropped) *Last Post* (1928); and John Dos Passos's three volume *U.S.A.*, consisting of *The 42nd Parallel* (1930), *Nineteen Nineteen* (1932) and *The Big Money* (1936). The contrasts between the works are considerable; Ford was a writer well versed in modern fictional forms before he wrote of war, Dos Passos was effectively made a writer *in* the war; Ford's sequence is very much of the 1920s, when history seemed disordered, Dos Passos of the 1930s, when politics seemed a possible solution. Ford's aesthetic devotion was to 'impressionism', a creed of 'rendering' in fiction he traced back to Flaubert and saw restored in the work of his friends Stephen Crane, Conrad, and James; Dos Passos's tradition went back to American naturalism, crossed with aestheticism, and his commitment was to a form of 'expressionism', which he saw as a radical mode, and associated with writers like Biely in Russia and with film-makers like Eisenstein. Politically they were at different ends of the spectrum; Ford was a liberal-conservative, ambiguous about post-war democracy, while Dos Passos was well left, and his standpoint was a complex mixture of democratic Marxism and populism (it would later turn to conservatism). Both, then, took their large tasks in different ways, working out of different traditions; both influenced the novel-tradition in each of their countries. But both were writing about the way war crossed traditions of social possibility and expectation, and assumed a consequential disintegration of forms. And their tasks – of writing a modern historical novel at a time when the novel-form had become ambiguous about history, of finding a mode to express war as an outcome of and effect upon modern historical and public life – therefore had an essential similarity; that is why I set them together.

Parade's End is the culmination of Ford Madox Ford's achievement, rivalled only by his novel of 1915, *The Good Soldier*,[3] not directly about the war. But it came late in a long, mixed career;[4] Ford – then Ford Madox Hueffer – had been writing since the turn of the century. An exemplary Edwardian novelist, he had steadily oscillated between the claims of liberal realism and experimentalism. He collaborated with Conrad, wrote historical novels, like *The Fifth Queen*, and novels of contemporary political and social life (*The Inheritors, A Call*, etc.): novels in different ways devoted to the 'Condition of England' question central to the fiction of the day, and to its predominant theme, of the movement from the older, caring world to the new world of mechanism, atomism, indifference. Like Forster, in *Howards End* (1910), Ford was preoccupied with the ideal polity, the connected society, unifying reason with emotion, commerce with art. But his conservative-liberal politics and his avant-garde tastes were hard to reconcile; art, he felt, transcended issues, required an ultimate technical expertise, a Flaubertian perfection of form, which set the writer outside and beyond purposes, political commitments. In 1908 he tried to reconcile his interests in *The English Review*, the journal he edited; it was a valiant effort to merge the old-fashioned socio-political 'great review' with the modern 'little magazine'. But in the following years, perhaps because of increasing social tension and international stress, the avant-garde movement peaked in London. Ford moved excitedly with this, seeing a new experimental age. He intensified his commitment to 'impressionism'; he wrote *The Good Soldier*, just before the war; part of it appeared in the Vorticist magazine ominously called *Blast*. *The Good Soldier* intersects his social and aesthetic concerns. On the one hand, he sees society redeemed from its present crass materialism by the acceptance of social responsibility and duty; on the other, he sees it lost by virtue of the fact that society withholds and represses, especially in the sexual realm. From that ironic contrast, Heuffer gained a technical position, a detachment, the possibility of a rendered vision; the novel would be a 'hard', 'flawless' object of the modern Vorticist type, like 'a polished helmet', and it would interseam the causal, progressive, realistic novel, which sustained society in its substance and significance, with an oblique, fragmentary method of association and juxtaposition, which would question it.

Like many writers in England just before the war, then, Hueffer was experiencing a growing social disillusion coupled with a deepening interest in modernist technique. The war was to drive that process much further. In 1915, Hueffer published two propaganda books on behalf of the war effort.[5] They attack German imperialist materialism, the threat of the new nation-state; they also attack the emergence of the same processes of materialism and statism in England. Ford confessed his own old-fashioned ideals, and realised the war was a general threat to them. Nonetheless, though over military age, he got a commission in the Welch Regiment, and served for a time on the Western Front, an experience that produced in him a 'profound moral change'. Certainly he came back from the war with a vastly greater suspicion of vested interests and materialist forces, a strong identification with the men at the front, and a deep conviction that England was sinking back into negativism, commercialism, and anti-art. It was now that he changed his name from Hueffer to Ford, and, after various attempts at post-war pamphleteering, left London for Paris. This was partly because he felt London was betraying the effort of the war, partly because of personal and financial problems that made it unlikely he could live by writing at home; also in part because he had conceived an allegiance to the post-war international republic of letters, of which Paris now seemed the Anglo-American centre. There he joined the modernist expatriates, edited *transatlantic review*, associated with Pound, Stein, Joyce and Hemingway, and began *Parade's End*. An habitual, if not always an accurate, memoirist, he records much of this story in his novel-memoir *It Was the Nightingale*.[6] His justifications for the sequence are partly modernist-aesthetic – he wanted to write a great cosmopolitan work – and partly socio-historical: 'I wanted the Novelist in fact to appear in his really proud position as historian of his own time.' He saw himself as taking up the vacancy left by the death of Proust, as the creator of the 'ponderous novel'; yet the subject of the novel would be 'the public events of the decade' and 'the world as it culminated in the war'. It would be a work of 'rendering', but also a novel with a purpose: 'I sinned against my gods to the extent of saying that I was going . . . to write a work that should have for its purpose the obviating of all future wars.'[7]

Ford wished, then, to write a book about large social tendencies and forces, and considered using the method whereby 'all the characters should be great masses of people – or interests.' In this notion, he came close to the method of Dos Passos's *U.S.A.*, which sustains its massiveness by following the story of many characters, some fictional, some historical, and certain systems of interest through an historical process. But Ford felt this method was not for him; it was too large, and also risked inhumanity, the turning of men into statistics; and, wanting a greater humanism, he resolved to focus his sequence around one central character who experiences the tribulations of peace *and* war. He also noted that observation of active warfare had led him to 'a singular conclusion', that what preyed most on the minds of non-professional soldiers were not the horrors – 'you either endure them or you do not' – but 'what was happening at home'. In particular, what was happening at home was a massive change in mores, in the dispositions of political and class power, and in men–women relationships. This, of course, is Dos Passos's concern too; but Ford's resolved method is not to amass a large society behind the events of war, rather to a create a central character who has a place in peace and war, and is capable both of suffering and critically observing change: a character based, in fact, on an old, dead friend, Arthur Marwood, a Yorkshire Tory. His central character, then, would be a man torn both in public and private life by the pressure of the times, 'a poor fellow whose body is tied in one place, but whose mind and personality brood eternally over another distant locality'. To give his hero the right kind of intersection with history and with public life, he would be an officer and a gentleman, but, more, a member of the Ruling Classes – a landowner with Westminster connections. In all this, then, Ford went in the classic direction of the realist historical novel, the Lukáczian prescription, the novel about the representative historical agent who carries the forces of the time with him, who is the man of history. And in this, one might say, Ford is opting for a very English possibility, the novel of social and historical life in which individuals can clearly represent their class, can function as a primary social focus.

However, Christopher Tietjens is more than the embodiment of his class; he is, indeed, at odds with it. For Tietjens is also 'the last Tory', the 'Christian gentleman', he witness to the chivalric view of life, a man whose roots go down into English society and life; but who is already lost and suffering amid the new dispositions of power, the new sexual mores, the new habits and standards of Georgian England. Tietjens' world has, indeed, already newly disappeared before the War starts; he has already become absurd in his chivalry, his code of honour, monogamy and chastity. From the start a certain comic absurdity attaches to him; he is a mealsack elephant. His enduring values are already part-displaced; misfortunes accumulate around his ideas and ideals, around his house, Groby, around his attempts to establish his standards in life. He is in fact a comic character, and *Parade's End* is indeed a certain sort of war comedy, in a species that was to reappear in fresh form in the parallel English trilogy for the Second World War,

Evelyn Waugh's *Sword of Honour*. Like Waugh's Guy Crouchback, Tietjens retains ancient, hereditary notions of chivalry; he quests for just causes and true wars. He is a man of 'clear Eighteenth-Century mind,' passionate yet constrained, agonised yet expressionless, living out the contradictions of the old code to their last possible conclusion, hoping to take 'the last train to the old Heaven'.[8] He is a romantic figure caught at the point of extinction, a man of parades in a new world in which, socially as well as militarily, there are no more parades. And like Guy (or Don Quixote) he is thrust into a world of chaotic and lowered history. So, comically, he has to be taken along the path of disillusionment; the bleak and terrible events of the war are that path, and he follows it, with elephantine blundering, to base reality. At the same time his ideals function as an essential criticism of that lowered world, and subtract political significance from most of the events that take place. His war thus starts long before the outbreak of hostilities, in the strange, chivalric marriage he makes to a deceitful wife, pregnant by another man, and in his growing, but chaste, emotional relationship with the new woman, Valentine Wannop.

W. H. Auden once noted that the sequence 'makes it quite clear that World War I was a retribution visited upon Western Europe for the sins and omissions of its ruling class, for which not only they, but also the innocent conscripted millions on both sides, must suffer'.[9] It is true that Ford is much concerned in these novels with the debasement of the ruling class, the selfish corruptions and false motives, 'the swine in the corridors' of Whitehall, the bungled political issue of the Single Command, with the horror and boredom of the battlefield. Yet *Parade's End* is not primarily a sequence about the system, nor about the horrors of trench warfare and bombardment. Ford saw the battlefield as part of a larger experience, as a place always intruded on by 'money, women, testamentary bothers'; hence the social war and the sex war move to the lines, with Tietjens' bitch-wife Sylvia and the malicious General Campion, who wants her as his mistress and who misuses Tietjens in his pursuit, always in the background. War is thus always connected in the book with political and social events, but those events are themselves part of the larger victimisation of Tietjens and his ancient values. It is Tietjens' purgatory, a version of the great, pressing machine of modern life. And through it Tietjens is pressed into adaptation. He suffers, is buried, wounded, persecuted, forced into action and heroism, split away from the past. If he recognises the flaws in his own class, and the demanding democracy of the front, he is also insistently deprived of his more chivalric hopes; it is a gross, modern, material, selfish war. The war in fact deprives him of many of the social meanings that have made him the potential hero of the story in the first place; he loses his old values, his old heaven, his world of parades and moral prohibitions.

But he gains his new woman and a new life, becoming, ironically, an antique dealer in the new, paradeless world: 'The war had made a man of him! It had coarsened him and hardened him . . . It had made him reach a point at which he could no longer stand unbearable things.' The world too has changed accordingly:

> Feudalism was finished; its last vestiges were gone. It held no place for him. He was going – he was damn well going! – to make a place in it for . . . A man could now stand up on a hill, so he and she could surely get into some hole together![10]

But the point is that Ford does not tell this as a simple fable of moral growth; indeed so detached in his method, so ironically placed his narrator, that the book can be, and has been, read in several ways: as a tragedy of Tietjens' accumulated suffering, or a comedy of his emergence into a new life, as a conservative assault on the decline of English society, its cold, bureaucratic mechanism exposed by the war, or a celebration of the greater democracy and justice of the post-war world.[11] The peculiarity of the tone arises in part because Ford is always trying to merge a coherent structure, a historical fable, with an impressionistic technique; the technique qualifies the structure. The problem of relating an intense impressionism with a 'hidden long logic' is one Ford must have known from Crane's *Red Badge of Courage*, that ambiguous novel set on another battlefield, in the American Civil War. But Crane was above all concerned with the consciousness of his central character; hence his impressionism. Ford's is a less interior technique; he uses impressionism for private and public purposes at the same time, to relate inward motions of consciousness with compounded exterior circumstances. Moreover Ford was dealing not with a brief set of incidents but a long historical span, embodying a logic and an evolution, indeed an extended Spenglerian cycle from feudalism to modern class war and materialist democracy. His task was more broadly spread; he was using impressionist modes not to suggest the freedom or independence or even the mechanisation of consciousness, but the motion of mind amid historical coercions; men are subject to historical facts and historical change. Likewise the war itself is a reality prior to any aesthetic intervention in it. What the novelist is responsible for creating is therefore not the facts, which are historically predetermined objects of representation, but the 'treatment'. Thus far Ford himself saw impressionism as a heightened realism, a mode of dealing with the reality of life; his war is not, like Crane's, a metaphor. But he also saw it as a technique for coping with the perceptual chaos of the times, with the novelist's incapacity to intervene; it was a mode of detachment and irony. And it was also a way of representing the subjective motions of consciousness moving not only parallel with, but atemporally against, the significant motion of history, the insistent realities of war. In any case, those realities were in part a dislocation *of* reality; as he said in *It Was the Nightingale*, war damaged confidence in substance: 'it had been revealed to you that beneath Ordered Life itself was stretched, the merest film with, beneath it, the abysses of Chaos.'[12]

Thus, if one part of Ford's effort went into substantiating the historical novel as a form for dealing with the times, another part went into taking it away again. The first book, *Some Do Not* . . . , begins on a prose of apparent solidity, realistic weight:

> The two young men – they were of the English public official class – sat in the perfectly appointed railway carriage. The leather straps to the windows were of virgin newness; the mirrors beneath the new luggage racks immaculate as if they had reflected very little; the bulging upholstery in its luxuriant regulated curves was scarlet and yellow in an intricate, minute dragon pattern, the design of a geometrician in Cologne. The compartment smelt faintly, hygienically of admirable varnish; the train ran as smoothly – Tietjens remembered thinking – as British gilt-edged securities . . .[13]

This is England in 1912, given with weighty realism. But it is of course a very hard-edge realism, which does not so much humanise as render things stark and abstract. The train has a glossy brittle newness; the two young men are at a temporal distance; the language, like the upholstery, has an abstract foreign geometry. Ford is opening up an aloof space between the material and the novelist, an indirect, angular form of presentation, and it is into this space that technique comes. History and form alike will tell against this solid world; the desubstantiation of this reality will be manifested both by the novelist and the war. Using the method he calls *progression d'effet*, Ford accumulates, by juxtaposition, a sequence that establishes this world of 1912 as one of already breaking principles, muddled history, colliding forces. Harsh machinery intersects with organic life; subjective consciousness struggles with public responsibility; sexual instincts subvert moral codes. In this increasingly chaotic world Tietjens attempts to stabilise life by asserting the need for principle, 'a skeleton map of a country';[14] but his mind wanders, the knacker's cart comes round the corner, and – in using a larger structural irony he will make into a basic device of the sequence – Ford shifts the action in time directly to 1917, to a war-wounded Tietjens, socially absurd, publicly unpopular, lost in the chaos he has attempted to control. Impressionism thus becomes a technique for dematerialising the solid world, partly in order to extend its historical significance, relating one part of life to another, partly in order to move the action inward into consciousness and allow for its anguish and disordered movement, the movement that itself mirrors a decomposing world.

It is this double motion that allows Ford to make impressionism into an effective technique for coping with the war, for creating a significant historiography. It allowed Ford to merge realism with technical modernism, treating a disjunctive history but granting it historical significance. In *No More Parades*, the next volume, the impressionistic mode can dominate as a method for representing the contingency and fragmentation of the battlefield itself, the chaos of conduct, the loss of rule and order, the massing of perceptual and mental chaos. Historical solidity and substance are shattered.

Now, in the next volume, *A Man Could Stand Up*, which passes between the battlefield and the Armistice, between the consciousness of Tietjens and that of Valentine Wannop, a painful, disorderly new coherence can start to emerge. With *The Last Post*, Ford faced his most difficult problem, that of dealing with a post-war world in which both chaos and a new economy of order exist. The technique is fragmentary, as is Tietjens' past and the present form of his social being; but, as with *Lady Chatterley*, the book gestures toward the need for a new life and a new language amid the ruins. Ford settles for a modernist technique with vague organic overtones, a tentative and ironic resolution. It was an answer he seems to have been uneasy with himself; he proposed on occasion dropping the book from the sequence.[15] In fact it has stylistic validity, and enforces the ironic meaning of the whole; what it lacks is the urgent strength the war sections gave to Ford's entire technique. It is indeed the war part of the novel that makes it Ford's most triumphant work, an extraordinary probe into a culture, wherein the double inheritance of technique he carried with him – part realistic, part modernistic – fuses itself into a historical meaning. In his fable of Tietjens entering a lowered history, a world of reduced substance and solidity, Ford led the way for many subsequent English novelists who found the world of the twenties and thirties, or indeed the sixties and seventies, capable of acquiring meaning only if treated with something of Ford's comic and modernistic indifference.

If Ford Madox Ford was able to find the ideal style for a world bisected and changed by war in modes that came through to him in part from earlier, pre-war modernism, John Dos Passos, a young man just out of Harvard when the war started, took a slower and longer path. The modernist tradition in fiction had made its impact in England well before it did in America, where naturalism persisted long in the native line. Indeed the modernist excitements seemed to arrive there from Europe just around the moment when Europe became the battlefield to which American attention had to turn. Thus the entry of America into the war roughly coincided with the emergence of a remarkable new generation of American writers who would come to dominate the twenties and thirties; and most of this new and experimental generation in fact experienced the war and Europe simultaneously. And, just as most of the naturalist writers of the 1890s in America seem to have clustered as reporters at the battle of San Juan Hill (the imperial battle with which, in fact, *U.S.A.* begins), hungry for 'reality', so this fresh generation, already disposed to throw off American innocence and isolation, found the brute, but more ambiguous, reality *they* were seeking, the entry into sophistication and awareness they desired, by coming into the European conflict, as combatants or civilian support. The private ambulance brigades in particular functioned as field-seminars in literature and reality, alike devoted to the assimilation of experience and the production of text; the Norton-Harjes brigade, in which Dos Passos served, also contained Robert Hillyer, John Howard Lawson and E. E. Cummings.[16] Dos Passos, who (like Cummings) got into difficulties after writing a letter to a Spanish friend in a pacifist-revolutionary vein, shared the divided emotions of many of his genera-tion. American progressive opinion was itself split: for Americans, entry into war was a political choice. Thus the war could be seen as Wilson's moral crusade in defence of civilisation and democracy; it could also be seen as the great betrayal, an entry into European cor-ruptions, a Morgan-financed struggle to protect capital and stave off revolution. It seemed the latter to Dos Passos; hence it was in the para-doxical role of a pacifist hungry for experience that he went to the battlefields. The paradoxes continued; indeed his confusion then shaped his long-term attitude to war and his continuing obsession with it as the key fact, the fulcrum, of modern American history.

Dos Passos had left Harvard as an aesthete hungry for experience, but, influenced by Emma Goldman, he had begun to acquire anarchist sentiments and a deep suspicion of the American commercial structure. Nonetheless, he urged his father to let him serve, and, when refused, moved to Madrid to be on the fringe of things. On his father's death, he joined Norton-Harjes, telling his friends he had not 'gone militarist' but 'merely wanted to see a little of the war personally' and face 'the senseless agony of destruction'. In letters, diaries, poems and the novel he was now collaboratively writing with Hillyer, he condemned 'the mountain of lies', the 'merry parade that is stifling in brutishness all the fair things of the world', while asserting his pleasure in his own involvement. He saw the war as 'suicidal madness', an act of self-brutalisation, but also as the ultimate experience, demanding immer-sion and expression: 'I want to be able to express, later – all of this – all the tragedy and hideous excitement of it. I have seen so little I must experience more of it, & more. The grey crooked fingers of the dead, the

dark look of dirty mangled bodies . . .' He saw the war as a crime of
the capitalist and nationalist systems, demanding a revolution, like the
Russian; he also saw it as a personal initiation, a movement beyond the
old lies, the hard, false shells into which experience had been falsely
coded, into real experience of life, into comradeship, emotional frank-
ness, sexual freedom, a life beyond the confinements of old America.
On the one hand, the war was the ultimate destruction of language,
overwhelmed as it was by the senseless 'gibber' put out by politicians,
by governmental lies, by the 'shells of truths putrid and false' which
infected the air; on the other hand it was urgent facts and sensations
demanding expression, crying for shape and form. On one side, war was
the false, feudal past of civilisation oppressing the open present, sub-
jecting the young to the old; on the other, it was an expression of
modern man's materialism, brutalism and violence, crushing and
violating the timeless civilisation of the past. The war was the modern
naturalistic flux of sensation, the act of subjection to process; it was
also the threat to liberalism and democracy. Dos Passos was, indeed,
massively split – and above all between an aesthetic response to war,
which condemned all brutalism and the massive offence against 'all
the finest things of art and mind', and a political response to it, as a
direct manifestation of the old power system, the dominant machine
which men might cast off by turning war into revolution. It was this
massive range of mixed feelings, portraying the war both as opportunity and betrayal, which generated the contradictions and uncertainties of his characters in *U.S.A.*[17]

The same mixture of feelings fed the evolution of his style when,
having come to see the war as both a subjective and as an historical
crisis, he began, over many years and several novels, to search for the
right forms and tones, and the right historiography, for rendering and
placing the experience. This writing began at the front: *One Man's
Initiation* (*1917*)[18] is a segment of a much larger project begun then. It
is an immediate book, like Barbusse's; and, as its title suggests, it is an
individualised, subjectivised version of the war, centred around a single,
sensitive soldier, Martin Howe, with origins like Dos Passos's own, who
sees the war predominantly as a violation of his sense of form and cultural value. The themes that were to grow in importance in Dos Passos's
later versions as he tries to leave this guilty aestheticism behind – the
mountain of lies issued by the government, the brutal effect of the
army machine, the fascination with the movement towards popular
revolution across Europe which became evident in the wartime period
– are there in the book, but they have only observational value; their
presence is impressionistic, held within the framework of Howe's own
awareness. That Dos Passos wanted to take a broader, a more historical,
a more explanatory view of the war is evident from his next war novel,

Three Soldiers (1921); as its title suggests, the aesthetic-bourgeois response now seemed not enough, and Dos Passos sought to expand the
angle of vision, the range of process. Thus the three soldiers represent
different social types, broader aspects of the culture; and now the
dominant subject becomes the oppressive machine of modern life, above
all the military machine, crushing individualism. As is argued elsewhere
in the present volume, *Three Soldiers*, powerful as it is, moves only so
far away from the subjective, aesthetic mode.[19] Dos Passos cannot quite
assert an historical significance for his story; the war becomes simply
an 'unbearable agony', a choice between self-abnegation or desertion;
stylistically, however, the rhythmic mechanisation of life becomes
itself a part of Dos Passos's own modern style. Dos Passos was moving
toward a more collectivist technique, one in which individual characters
become constituents of a common process, become expressive aspects of
modern life. It was, of course, a harder style that itself seemed to suppress some of the individuality Dos Passos valued in his sensitive heroes;
in this respect he seems to be moving away from himself, and from the
papers that blow around Andrews' room at the end of *Three Soldiers*.
The new, harder, more expressionistic and collective style becomes
realised in *Manhattan Transfer* (1925), a remarkable novel focused,
now, not on war but on that other key metaphor of naturalist and
expressionist writing – the modern city, plural, contingent, at once culture and anti-culture. In shifting in this direction, Dos Passos moved
toward facing the contemporary problems of post-naturalist writing,
that of merging a vision of the city as a determining, destructive mass
with the city as a focus of energy, the collective eros. The modern city,
at once Waste Land and modernist wonderland, at once dislocation
and connection, was a key preoccupation of the twenties. Influenced by
Biely, Eisenstein, Griffith, by the synchronic renderings of the plural
city attempted in the urban novel and the collage, image-association
techniques exploited in modern film, Dos Passos suspends himself
between the versions, making the city a dark but mechanical womb,
giving and suppressing life. But it is finally the destructive city of
mechanism and bland destructiveness that predominates; the characters become the impersonal environment; the technique co-operates,
but sustains its own implicit critique.

Manhattan Transfer uses the spatial and synchronic techniques so
popular in the 1920s, techniques which portray a dislocated history,
seen as cyclic or purposeless or irrelevant, and make aesthetic responses
not just an aspect of individual awareness but an aspect of superimposed
form. But with the thirties history and politics came back in again very
explicitly for intellectuals; and with *U.S.A.* Dos Passos sought, over
three massive volumes, to use his spatial techniques in an historical
continuum, and to treat history as a process. *U.S.A.*[20] is indeed a very

thirties history, read backwards into American life to cover the evolution of the society from 1900 – the time of Dos Passos's own coming to consciousness, the life-span of his generation, the start of a century thought peculiarly American (the book begins with a collage of celebration, the greeting of new times by noise, labour and the churches, and by Senator Beveridge's assertion: 'The twentieth century will be American . . . The regeneration of the world, physical as well as moral, has begun . . .') – through to the late 1920s, seen from the thirties radical standpoint as the nadir, the discredited decade, dominated by commercialism and materialism, the suppression of radicals, culminating in the execution of Sacco and Vanzetti and the rising bull-market absurdities that heralded economic crash. It is therefore in its chosen shape a negative history, a process of disintegration. Dos Passos attempts the task with the large modernistic apparatus he had begun to evolve in *Manhattan Transfer*, using pluralised methods of narration, large ranges of characters, intersections between documentary matter and naturalistic fictional materials; the problem was to make this into an historical schema. The result is, as the broad title proposes, a massively epical enterprise in the modernist mode, the relevant materials spreading over a massive geographical span, a long historical curve, and a notional concern not only with the internal but the international life of the United States – seen on the one hand as the evolving life of a people, on the other as an ever-expanding political system turning from power into superpower, and from a simple to a complex capitalism.

To explore this, Dos Passos evolved an extraordinary technical compound. There are four basic structural levels – the narrative history of his fictional characters; the factual biographies of real public figures; the 'Newsreel' collage of documentary, period matter, of headlines and reports; and the 'Camera Eye', a stream-of-consciousness flow identified with the individual history of the novelist himself. The technical levels each have their own implicit historiography; the individual stories, which sometimes run parallel, sometimes intersect, some of them lasting for the whole sequence, some of them dropping from sight, make up a compound narrative of disappointment and failure; the portraits of 'historical' individuals make up a radical hagiography of heroes (Big Bill Heywood, La Follette, Veblen, Bourne, Lloyd Wright, radicals and dreamers) and villains (Wilson, Morgan, Insull, politicians and capitalists); the Newsreels, mixing headlines and editorials, songs and speeches, are a sometimes contingent, sometimes ironic collage; the Camera Eye sequence follows a helpless narrator, the inertly subjective story of a figure hungry for speech and clarity, but finding little more than impressions to register until the Sacco-Vanzetti case provokes him to explicit verbal outrage.[21] Meanwhile the structure of the book mimes

and oscillates between two possibilities: the collectivist and expressionist epic, and the modernist anti-epic – where the sum of the parts represents not a collective meaning but a loss of meaning. The book begins
on a collective hope, expressed through the young man in the prologue
who walks through the emptying urban streets, seeing the disjunctive
lives, but finds himself greedy for speech, ambitious to master contradictions in the Whitmanesque spirit:

> U.S.A. is the world's greatest rivervalley fringed with mountains and
> hills, U.S.A. is a set of bigmouthed officials with too many bank-
> accounts. . . . But mostly U.S.A. is the speech of the people. (p. vii)

But by the end language cannot emerge from the growth and progress
of the nation; it can only be an assertion against process ('America our
nation has been beaten by strangers who have turned our language
inside out . . .', 'We have only words against'). The multiplications and
divisions of consciousness are the cumulative process of the book and,
though the techniques themselves persist, they appear in the course of
the sequence to change in their function – to move from being the
means of a collective, to the means of a contingent, historiography. The
change is made possible because behind the four main narrative levels
there is an implied further historical process, of growing mechanisation,
dehumanisation, the suppression of aesthetic hopes and radical im-
pulses, the defeat of organic possibilities, the underlying functioning,
therefore, of primary economic laws. It is this that generates the
internal shifting of the text as it develops through the three volumes,
turning juxtapositions into ironies, the connection of individuals into
disconnection, the celebration of the land into a sense of man's isolation
from all its possible meanings.

Across all this the war intersects, closing the first volume, dominating
the second, leading into the third; it is the turning-point of American
historical experience and the point of shift in the dominant tone. *The
42nd Parallel*, covering the years from 1900 to the American entry, is
broad in geographical scope, moves rhythmically toward a rising progressive impulse and an international challenge to the dominant system,
and then moves the action slowly over the Wilsonian period toward
Europe; this book ends with Charley's enforced silence as his ship
approaches wartime France. The same broken communications dominate *Nineteen Nineteen*, set largely in Europe, around the war and
then the Versailles Peace Conference, which gives the volume its title.
The characters move on to the sealanes, the battlefields, into the ambulance corps or the civilian service or the staffwork on the peace plan.
Dos Passos treats the fighting and the threat of death, but, as with Ford,
his war is fought at the endless intersection of the public and the
private. It is the sense of mortality, but also 'the plot of the big

interests'; it is the chance for new sexual encounters, but also the feeling of debased animality and corruption. The headlines deceive; the facts appall. The big powers conspire; the revolutionary rhythm grows again after the events in Russia. But such is Dos Passos's tone of ironic naturalism that the bursts of aesthetic contemplation or social hope sink back into the historical contingency; the characters in *U.S.A.* do not simply experience history, they are suffused in it, and the diurnal movement of time defeats idealism or understanding. 'What I say is all bets are off . . .', says the American sailor who hails Dick Savage in the middle of the war, '. . . every man go to hell in his own way . . .' And in the fictional mode of indifference and inertia that predominates in the text, every man does: 'Singing out savagely, "To hell wid 'em I say," the sailor threw the bottle against the head of the stone lion. The Genoese lion went on staring ahead with glassy doglike eyes.'[22] The inertia of history is not the absence of history; the Peace Conference brings the theme to culmination. Dick Savage conducts an elaborate lovelife at the centre of the story; behind it, Wilson's Ten Points, the product of an idealism already corrupted from within and without, collapse as a policy, the consortium of interests reconspires, the Red Scare begins, and the onward path to commercialism and capitalism is set. *The Big Money*, set in the twenties, follows the rest of the path, towards a society economically cohesive, socially divisive, personally self-destructive.

In creating *U.S.A.*, Dos Passos, like Ford, like Lawrence, and like many of the American writers of that 'transitional generation' who began writing in the 1920s, reaches out toward an organic ideal. For English writers this had been the socially substantial past, with romantic and rural overtones. For many American writers it was much the same; the green breast of America, before industrialism, though crossed with the Whitmanesque, collective spirit, the ideal of cohesive democracy, the immigrant hope. The mythology is implicit in Dos Passos's book too, in the contrast between the pre-war and the post-war world; it is interfused with radical, if not quite Marxist, imperatives. Dos Passos sustains, throughout the book, against the idea of history as process, the idealism hidden in the people somewhere, the timeless history of the continent, the unexplored landscape beneath 'history the billiondollar speedup'. This is history as myth, the myth of collectivity; he cannot, however, deliver it. This is partly because he has indeed abstractified history and process: it is a force at odds with individual life, individual being, generated abstractly by others or by economic law itself; but it is also seen, in the naturalistic way, as that into which individual life sinks. Ford Madox Ford's characters may suffer from history; but, because history is also the lives of individuals, is a cultural momentum for which they assume some responsibility, they also act in it and suffer for as well as from it. But in the end Dos Passos's characters do not, unless, that is, they are suffering radicals at odds with it or capitalists in conspiracy with it, like Morgan or Wilson or Hearst. For history is a force-field which denies self-realisation. In a famous essay, Jean-Paul Sartre noted that Dos Passos's characters have no existential centre; they function collectively; individual experiences settle in or leave them without their having any say in the matter; they therefore acquire an automatic aspect, glimpsing occasional alternatives to their condition but sinking back again into the contingencies of life, the movements of larger tendencies they cannot master. As Sartre notes, this is an authentic modern style, part of the negation of self that gives modern men not lives but destinies.[23] As for subjective life in *U.S.A.*, that is displaced on to the 'Camera Eye', where it is a function of the author only, and operates as a flow of consciousness shifting loosely through vague collages of impression and judgement. This is part of the naturalist inheritance in American fiction, the line that links Dos Passos to Dreiser, for example, though Dreiser assumes that, while his characters are mechanical reflectors of experience, sunk into the material and historical world, the world repays their energy and assimilates it. But where Dreiser uses naturalism energetically Dos Passos uses it ironically; the momentum of individuals should not yield, but does, insignificance, randomness, oblique withdrawals from potential meaning, sacrifice to entropic rhythms.

Ford saw the war as a movement away from historical realism, a desubstantiation of life which would be mimed in a modern style. Dos Passos, as a radical idealist, postulates a realism of collective wholeness somewhere in the future, an organic potential that appears to have a social place though it is really out of time. His novel too uses much of the substance of realism in order to reveal why *U.S.A.* is not in fact a realist work. It was written in the 1930s, when social realism was coming back, particularly for writers with Dos Passos's far-left sympathies. But Dos Passos sustains a modernist mode, and he does this because *U.S.A.* is not intended as the exterior history of a crisis, but the expressive *form* of a continuing crisis of his own aesthetics, one that would take him out of radicalism again. It is a book about the severance of ideals and history, about the gap between any ideal construction of words and the greed, fear, sexual need and social hypocrisy which are the structure of a life in time. Like *Parade's End*, it ironises history even as it seeks to give it meaning; it is a form that despairs of form as a story of significant life. The dehumanising techniques of the modern novel are sometimes taken on trust, as a formal elegance, a mannerism. But they are in fact a form of modern historicism, an exploration of the novel as an instrument for meaningful narration. Both *Parade's End* and *U.S.A.* finally explore them as such, suggesting the historical evolution that compels the style and in the course of the sequence intensifies it, brings it to the centre. And, despite the differences of political assumption, despite the different versions of history and culture underlying the books, the historical and the technical turning-point is manifestly the same: the intrusion, into history, reality, and our notion of man, of the war for which Americans found the right name: the World War.

Notes

I INTRODUCTION

1. Currently available surveys include: B. H. Liddell Hart, *A History of the World War 1914–1918* (London: Faber, 1934, repr. 1970); C. R. M. F. Cruttwell, *A History of the Great War* (Oxford: Clarendon Press, 1934, repr. 1961); Marc Ferro, *La Grande Guerre 1914–1918* (Paris: Gallimard, 1969), trans. N. Stone as *The Great War 1914–1918* (London: Routledge & Kegan Paul, 1973); A. J. P. Taylor, *The First World War: An Illustrated History* (London: Hamish Hamilton, 1963; also in Penguin Books, 1966, 1974); J. C. King (ed.), *The First World War* (New York, etc.: Harper & Row, 1972); Norman Stone, *The Eastern Front, 1914–1917* (London: Hodder, 1975). An illustrated presentation of front-line fighting is Michael Houlihan, *World War 1: Trench Warfare* (London: Ward Lock, 1974); for maps and tables see Martin Gilbert, *First World War Atlas* (London: Weidenfeld & Nicolson, 1970).

2. Thus for instance Barbusse's *Under Fire* was (reluctantly) allowed to appear in France in 1916; the English translation appeared in 1917; Franz Pfemfert was able to publish the collection *Die Aktionslyrik* (Berlin-Wilmersdorf: Verlag der Wochenzeitschrift Die Aktion, 1916), Siegfried Sassoon published his famous 'Finished with the War: A Soldier's Declaration' in the *Bradford Pioneer*, 27 July 1917.

3. 'Why Britain went to War', *The War Illustrated* 1, no. 1 (22 August 1914) 2–3. This and other essays appeared in book form soon after, in *The War that will end War* (London: Palmer, 1914).

4. 'Dieser Krieg ist nicht das Ende, sondern der Auftakt der Gewalt', in *Der Kampf als inneres Erlebnis* (Berlin: Mittler, 1925) p. 76.

5. William Haggard, *The Hard Sell* (London: Cassell, 1965, repr. Penguin Books, 1968) p. 76. In June 1918 Dos Passos called the war a 'party' in which 'Europe is so merrily suiciding': see T. Ludington (ed.), *The Fourteenth Chronicle: Letters and Diaries of John Dos Passos* (Boston: Gambit, 1973) p. 190.

6. These aspects are put in historical perspective by Marc Ferro, *The Great War*, Part 1. See also Malcolm Bradbury's essay, Chapter 18 of this volume, and the studies by Bergonzi, I. F. Clarke, Gibson, and Schröter listed in the Bibliography below.

7. As cautiously summarised by Taylor, *The First World War*, 1974 ed., p. 285. For pre-war conditions see Ferro, *The Great War*, Part 1.

8. *The Great War and Modern Memory* (New York and London: Oxford UP, 1975), esp. Chapter IX: 'Persistence and Memory'.

9. There are some publications in East Germany, for instance a Ph.D. thesis by H. J. Bernhard on Jünger, Remarque and Zweig (Rostock, 1959). In West Germany the field has been all but abandoned to sociology and political history (see the studies by Geissler and Sontheimer in the Bibliography); possibly its highly compromised over-activity in the thirties still mutes criticism.

10. See in this connection, for instance, Melvyn J. Friedman, 'Three Experiences of the War: A Triptych'; and J. K. Johnstone, 'World War I and the

Novels of Virginia Woolf' in George A. Panichas (ed.), *Promise of Greatness* (London: Cassell, 1968) pp. 541–55 and 528–40.

11. Thus Julius Bab wrote quarterly reviews of the war poetry for *Das Literarische Echo* (Berlin), collected in book form as *Die deutsche Kriegslyrik 1914–1918* (Stettin: Norddeutscher Verlag, 1920); see also Paul Adam, *La Littérature et la guerre* (Paris: Crès, 1916) and V. A. T. Lloyd, 'War in Fiction', *Fortnightly Magazine* 110 (November 1918), 764–71. An early general compilation of all kinds of works is F. W. T. Lange and W. T. Berry, *Books on the Great War*, 4 vols (London: Grafton & Co., 1915–16).

12. Among the earliest are T. Sturge Moore, *Some Soldier Poets* (London: Grant Richards, 1919); Albert Schinz, *French Literature of the Great War* (New York and London: Appleton & Co., 1920) and Siegfried Wegeleben, *Das Felderlebnis* (Berlin: Furche, 1921).

13. The most comprehensive is probably Jean Vic, *La Littérature de guerre*, 5 vols (Paris: Les Presses Françaises, 1918–24).

14. Philipp Wittkopp (ed.), *Kriegsbriefe gefallener Studenten* (Munich, 1928) seems to have had the widest circulation; it was published in translation as *German Students' War Letters* (New York, 1929) and a selection from it appeared as *Lettres d'étudiants allemands tués à la guerre (1914–1918)* . . . (Paris, 1932).

15. See for instance the comments by Edmund Blunden in *Undertones of War* (London: Richard Cobden-Sanderson, 1928; repr. Collins, 1965) p. 5; Eric Partridge, 'The War Comes into its Own', *The Window* I, no 1 (January 1930) 72–3; Herbert Read, 'The Failure of War Books', in *A Coat of Many Colours* (London: Routledge & Kegan Paul, 1945, rev. ed. 1957) p. 73.

16. Hermann Grimrath, *Der Weltkrieg im französischen Roman* (Berlin: Junker & Dünnhaupt, 1935), otherwise very limited and unreliable, gives a useful chronological breakdown from 1915 to 1931 (pp. 135–41).

17. See for this point Maurice Rieuneau, *Guerre et révolution dans le roman français de 1919 à 1939* (Paris: Klincksieck, 1974) p. 13. It is interesting to note in comparison that in Britain at the time compilations were made under different auspices: Sir George Prothero, *Analytical List of Books concerning the Great War* (London: Foreign Office, 1923); the Birmingham Library's Collection of War Poetry Catalogues (1921) and the British Museum War Subject Index (1922).

18. Eric Partridge does however go beyond that and gives a brief panorama; see Bibliography.

19. Thus around 1930 Aldington's, Jünger's, Zweig's and Remarque's books were available in French translations. Barbusse and Dorgelès had already been translated into English much earlier; and Jünger's and Remarque's books were both translated in 1929. Still keeping only to books discussed in this volume, Aldington, Mottram, Graves, Dorgelès, Barbusse and Giono appeared in German.

20. See the recent studies by John Williams, *The Home Fronts: Britain, France and Germany 1914–1918* (London: Constable, 1972) and Arthur Marwick, *War and Social Change in the Twentieth Century: A Comparative Study of Britain, France, Germany, Russia and the United States* (London: Macmillan, 1974); Marwick's earlier *The Deluge: British Society and the First World War* (London: Bodley Head, 1965); Gerald D. Feldman, *Army, Industry and Labor in Germany 1914–1918* (Princeton, New Jersey: Princeton UP, 1966); Gabriel Perreux, *La Vie quotidienne des civils en France pendant la grande guerre* (Paris: Hachette, 1966) and the volume *Vie et Mort des Français* by Ducasse et al. (see Bibliography below). A very early specialised study is Harold D. Lasswell, *Propaganda Technique in the World War* (London: Kegan Paul; New York: Knopf, 1923); many others have followed.

21. Not counting an impossibly biased survey of fiction by the Nazi critic Günther Lutz, 'Europas Kriegserlebnis: Ein Überblick über das ausserdeutsche Schrifttum', *Dichtung und Volkstum* (formerly *Euphorion*) 39 (1938) 133–68.

22. Notably Eugene Löhrke, ed., *Armageddon: The World War in Literature* (New York: Jonathan Cape and Harrison Smith, 1930) and the Open University volume *War and the Creative Arts*, ed. John Ferguson (London: Macmillan, 1972).

23. *Poetry and the First World War* (Oxford: Blackwell, 1961; the Taylorian Lecture); for Dédéyan's book, see Bibliography below.

24. See Rieuneau, *Guerre et révolution*, esp. pp. 3–4, 9; also the general treatment in George Lukácz, *Der historische Roman* (Berlin: Aufbau, 1955) and *Probleme des Realismus* (Berlin: Aufbau, 1955), which also offers a solution to the problem of representativeness of the writer discussed below, pp. 5–6. Lukácz is available as *The Historical Novel*, trans. H. and S. Mitchell (London: Merlin Press, 1962).

25. A. C. Ward formulates the point succinctly. 'We are prevented from knowing that truth [the truth about the war] because none of us is dispassionate about the War.' See his discerning chapter, 'The Unhappy Warriors', in *The Nineteen-Twenties: Literature and Ideas in the Post-War Decade* (London: Methuen, 1930) p. 140.

26. 'War Books', *The Criterion* ix, no. 36 (April 1930) 409.

27. In *Témoins* (Paris: Les Étincelles, 1929) and *Du Témoignage* (Paris: Gallimard, 1930).

28. This incident is described in Barbusse's *Les Enchaînements* (Paris: Flammarion, 1925); cf. Cru, *Témoins*, p. 563. Cru may well be right; the point is that he never stops to doubt whether he is or not.

29. The critical study to which this line of argument in most later contributions can be traced is Hermann Pongs, 'Krieg als Volksschicksal im deutschen Schrifttum', *Dichtung und Volkstum* 35 (1934) 40–86 and 182–219, also published in book form (Stuttgart, 1934).

30. *The Lie about the War* (London: Faber, 1930), esp. pp. 46–7. In 1970 Corelli Barnett asserted that war literature had indeed contributed to disaster by serving 'as powerful ammunition for pacifists and appeasers of Hitler in the 1930s'. See 'A Military Historian's View of the Literature of the Great War', *Essays by Divers Hands* xxxvi (1970) 5–6.

31. Quoted by Cooperman, *World War I and the American Novel* (Baltimore: Johns Hopkins Press, 1967) p. 198. For the debate and its ramifications in the States see Chapter vi of the above, to which I am indebted for this point.

32. This argument was also brought up from a historian's point of view by Corelli Barnett in *Essays by Divers Hands* xxxvi (1970) 7–11.

33. Thus for instance Eric Partridge in *The Window* i, no. 2 (April 1930) states that Manning's book 'obviously is not, and it obviously could not have been, written by an ordinary private' (p. 77). In *The Window* i, no. 1 (January 1930), however, he had accepted Ludwig Renn's *Krieg* (1928, trans. as *War*, New York: Dodd, Mead & Co., 1929) as the straightforward autobiography of a private rising to N.C.O. The book was in fact written by an aristocratic Saxon career officer.

34. *Old Soldiers Never Die*, with an introduction by Robert Graves (London: Faber, 1933, repr. 1970). *Der Glaube an Deutschland*, with an introduction by Adolf Hitler (Munich: Eher, 1931). This book soon became the 'officially' sanctioned paradigm of what a war book should be like in Germany.

35. *Poilu mon frère* (Grenoble: F. Eymond, 1930) p. 92.

36. See especially the essays by Christopher Wagstaff on Marinetti and by Peter Stern on Jünger in this volume. In general, it is true to say that if

Herbert Read was right when he argued, looking back, that war fiction painting a 'realistic' picture of the war and its horrors was in fact ministering to a 'hidden lust' for 'vicarious suffering and violence' in the reader (*A Coat of Many Colours*, p. 74), the authors who did not reject the war and those who glorified it bear as much or more of the burden than Read himself and other anti-war writers.

37. J. K. Bostock, *Some Well-Known German War Novels 1914–1930* (Oxford: Blackwell, 1931) p. 12. Parallels are without number. A very stark recent example is Charles Carrington (as Charles Edmonds, author of *A Subaltern's War*, 1930), *Soldier from the Wars Returning* (London: Hutchinson, 1965; repr. Arrow Books, 1970) pp. 292–3.

38. 'Commentaries on the War: Some Meanings' in Panichas (ed.), *Promise of Greatness*, p. 485.

39. Such as John Brophy (ed.), *The Soldier's War* (London: Dent, 1920); André Ducasse (ed.), *La Guerre racontée par les combattants*, 2 vols (Paris: Flammarion, 1930); C. B. Purdom (ed.), *Everyman at War: Sixty Personal Narratives of the War* (London: Dent, 1930); Ernst Jünger (ed.), *Das Antlitz des Weltkrieges*, 2 vols (Berlin: Neufeld & Henius, 1930–1); Guy Chapman (ed.), *Vain Glory* (London: Cassell, 1937).

40. *The Truth of Poetry* (London: Weidenfeld & Nicolson, 1969; repr. Penguin Books, 1972) p. 164, cf. p. 192. In the middle thirties the climate was already changing (which Read seems to forget); thus the British Museum Catalogue lists as a periodical: *War Stories: Fighting Thrills on Land, Sea, and in the Air* (London, 1935 onwards). The Spanish Civil War, however, was probably the turning-point and stands at the beginning of the development Hamburger has in mind. On this subject see Frederick R. Benson, *Writers in Arms: The Literary Impact of the Spanish Civil War* (London: London UP; New York: New York UP, 1967–8).

41. Listed in the Bibliography below.

42. In Panichas (ed.), *Promise of Greatness*, p. 482.

43. See Dédéyan, *Une Guerre dans le mal des hommes*, and Hoffman, *The Mortal No* (details in the Bibliography). Both generalise from too narrow a textual base.

44. Such as H. G. Wells, *Mr. Britling Sees It Through* (London: Cassell, 1916), Paul Géraldy, *La Guerre, madame . . .* (Paris: Crès, 1916), Ernst Gläser, *Jahrgang 1902* (Potsdam: Kiepenheuer, 1928; trans. Willa and Edwin Muir, London: Secker, 1929).

45. See Diane DeBell's essay in this volume; for the problem generally, Roy Pascal, *Design and Truth in Autobiography* (London: Routledge & Kegan Paul, 1960), esp. Chapters I and XII.

46. See the essays by Brian Rowley and Christopher Smith in this volume. For Manning see also my 'The Structure of Frederic Manning's War Novel *Her Privates We*', *Australian Literary Studies* 6, no. 4 (October 1974) 404–17.

47. See Malcolm Bradbury's essay in this volume and Rieuneau, *Guerre et révolution*, Chapter III, pp. 417–509, from which this term is taken.

48. Started in the late twenties, *Les Hommes de bonne volonté* appeared between 1932 and 1946. Currently available in the four-volume edition by Flammarion (Paris, 1958). Books XV and XVI, on Verdun, were translated by Gerard Hopkins (London: Souvenir Press, 1962; repr. Mayflower Books, 1973).

49. *August 1914* (1969), trans. Michael Glenny (London: Bodley Head, 1972; repr. Penguin Books, 1974).

50. Manning, *Her Privates We* (London: Peter Davies, 1930; 2nd ed. 1964, repr. 1970) p. 201.

CHAPTER 2

1. Ralph Hale Mottram (1883–1971), *The Spanish Farm Trilogy* (London: Chatto and Windus, 1927). All quotations are from this edition.
2. The Hawthornden Prize, 1924.
3. Bernard Bergonzi, *Heroes' Twilight* (London: Constable, 1965) p. 175. Bergonzi gives very little space to Mottram; so does M. S. Greicus, *Prose Writers of World War I* (London: Longmans, 1973) pp. 26–30. There is no thorough study as yet. I understand that David Clough (University College of Wales, Aberystwyth) is working on Mottram.
4. *Autobiography with a Difference* (London: Robert Hale, 1938).
5. *Ten Years Ago* (London: Chatto and Windus, 1928).
6. R. H. Mottram, John Easton and Eric Partridge, *Three Personal Records of the War* (London: Scholartis Press, 1929) p. 129. See also Mottram's later autobiographical work *The Twentieth Century: A Personal Record* (London: Hutchinson, 1969), Chapter 3, 'The "Great" War, as they called it', pp. 32–69.
7. Wilfred Owen, *The Poems*, ed. Edmund Blunden (London: Chatto and Windus, 1963) p. 116 – l.29.
8. 'Reality in War Literature', in: *The Linhay on the Downs* (London: Faber and Faber, 1934, repr. 1944) p. 232.
9. Bergonzi, *Heroes' Twilight*, p. 173.
10. W. E. Bates in his foreword to Mottram's *Ten Years Ago*.
11. Ernest Miller Hemingway (1899–1961), *A Farewell to Arms* (London: Jonathan Cape, 1929). All quotations are from the 1952 re-issue. There is also a paperback edition (Harmondsworth: Penguin Books, 1972).
12. Reprinted in *The Essential Hemingway* (London: Jonathan Cape, 1947, repr. 1961) pp. 293–5.
13. See Philip Young, *Ernest Hemingway* (New York: Rinehart, 1952), a study much to be recommended. See also John W. Aldridge, *After the Lost Generation*, 2nd ed. (New York: Vision Books, 1959) Chapter III, pp. 23–58; John Atkins, *The Art of Ernest Hemingway: His Work and Personality* (London: Peter Nevill, 1952); Carlos Baker, *Hemingway: The Writer as Artist*, 3rd ed. (Princeton UP, 1963); G. A. Astre, *Hemingway par lui-même* (Paris: Editions du Seuil, 1959 – richly illustrated, an engaging general introduction); for the present context specifically: Helmut Liedloff, 'Two War Novels: A Critical Comparison', *RLC 42* (1968) 390–406.
14. *Tradition and Dream* (Harmondsworth: Penguin Books, 1965) p. 119. Some contemporary historians agreed with this view.
15. This appeared first in Chapter 12 of *Death in the Afternoon* (New York: Scribners, 1932, last repr. London: Jonathan Cape, 1963) pp. 129–39. It was later included as a separate story in *The Fifth Column, and the First Forty-Nine Stories* (New York: Scribner's, 1938).
16. Which Hemingway included in the collection of war stories edited by him, *Men at War* (New York: Crown, 1942).
17. 'Mussolini: Biggest Bluff in Europe', 27 January 1923; see also 'Notes on the Next War', *Esquire*, September 1935, both repr. in *By-Line: Ernest Hemingway* (London: Collins, 1968).
18. 'In Memory of W. B. Yeats' (1939) II, l.5: 'For poetry makes nothing happen ...'. Auden included this poem in *W. H. Auden: Selected by the Author* (Harmondsworth: Penguin Books, 1958) pp. 66–7.

CHAPTER 3

1. John Dos Passos (1896–1970), son of a New York lawyer, was born in Chicago. He attended private schools until he entered university. He graduated from Harvard in 1916, went to Spain where he studied architecture. In 1917 he returned to the United States and volunteered for the Norton-Harjes ambulance unit in France. He also served in Italy briefly during 1918 on Red Cross ambulance duty, but enlisted in the U.S. Medical Corps as a private the same year and served until 1919.

2. Malcolm Cowley, 'John Dos Passos: The Poet and the World', *New Republic* LXX (27 April 1932) 303.

3. William March, *Company K* (New York, 1933); Thomas Boyd, *Through the Wheat* (New York, 1923).

4. See 'The Dynamo and the Virgin' in *The Education of Henry Adams* (Boston: Houghton Mifflin, 1918) pp. 379–91.

5. *Three Soldiers* (New York: Doran, 1921) p. 28. Subsequent references to *Three Soldiers* will be from this edition. A good current reprint of the novel is the Houghton Mifflin Sentry edition (no. 40) in soft covers.

6. For a full discussion of the nature and impact of the military environment, see Stanley Cooperman, *World War I and the American Novel* (Baltimore, 1967).

7. A notable example of cinema propaganda was Commodore J. Stuart Blackton's 'The Battle Cry of Peace'. The film starring Norma Talmadge and Charles Richman, was based on Hudson Maxim's *Defenseless America* (1915), a high-pitched demand for expansion of American armaments. Maxim himself was the brother of a major arms manufacturer who had been supplying enormous quantities of guns, especially machine guns, to the Kaiser.

8. In 'Shakespeare's Anti-Hero', *Shakespeare Studies* 1 (1966) 33–63. Dos Passos' protagonist, caught up in corruption from which he cannot escape and to which he cannot accommodate, has final recourse to a futile but willed act of negation.

9. See Malcolm Bradbury's essay at the end of this volume (pp. 193–209) and: John H. Wren, *John Dos Passos* (New York: Twayne, 1961); John D. Brantley, *The Fiction of John Dos Passos* (Amsterdam and Paris: Mouton, 1968); Melvin Landsberg, *Dos Passos' Path to U.S.A.: A Political Biography* (Boulder: Colorado Assoc. UP, 1972); Allen Belkind (ed.), *Dos Passos, The Critics, and the Writer's Intention* (Carbondale: Southern Illinois UP, 1971); Andrew Hook (ed.), *Dos Passos: A Collection of Critical Essays* (Englewood Cliffs, New Jersey: Prentice-Hall, 1974).

CHAPTER 4

1. All textual references in this essay are to E. E. Cummings, *The Enormous Room* (London: Jonathan Cape, 1928) which has a valuable introduction by Robert Graves.

2. D. E. Smith. 'The Enormous Room and The Pilgrim's Progress' in N. Friedman (ed.), *E. E. Cummings: A Collection of Critical Essays* (Englewood Cliffs: Prentice-Hall, 1972).

3 Examples may be found in F. W. Dupee and George Stade (eds), *Selected Letters of E. E. Cummings* (London: André Deutsch, 1972).

4. E. E. Cummings, *six nonlectures* (Cambridge, Mass.: Harvard UP, 1953, repr. 1972) p. 53.

5. See K. Widmer, 'Timeless Prose', *Twentieth Century Literature* 4 (April–July 1958) pp. 3–8.
6. M. Gaull, 'Language and Identity: A Study of E. E. Cummings's *The Enormous Room*', *American Quarterly* 19 (winter 1967) 645–62.
7. Ibid., p. 662.
8. Malcolm Cowley, 'Cummings: One Man Alone', *Yale Review* 62 (March 1973) 337.
9. P. 157. See 'O gouvernement français . . . meat of their hearts'.

CHAPTER 5

1. The first edition was published by Flammarion. An English translation by W. Fitzwalter Wray appeared in 1917 (London: Dent; since 1926 an Everyman volume, last repr. 1965). No full-length study of Barbusse exists in English. See however the chapter in Frank Field, *Three French Writers and the Great War* (Cambridge UP, 1975) pp. 38–78 which was published after the completion of this essay. In French, the most useful works are a special number of *Europe* (nos. 119–20, 1955) and parts of Pierre-Henri Simon, *L'Esprit et l'Histoire* (Paris: Armand Colin, 1954), For a Communist view see Jacques Duclos and Jacques Fréville, *Henri Barbusse* (Paris: Editions Sociales, 1946).
2. See the account in Vladimir Brett, *Henri Barbusse: sa marche vers la clarté, son mouvement Clarté* (Prague: Editions de l'Académie Tchéchoslovaque des Sciences, 1963) pp. 104–9 and the very fully documented one in Annette Vidal, *Henri Barbusse: Soldat de la Paix* (Paris: Les Éditeurs Français Réunis, 1953) pp. 63–9.
3. See e.g. J. N. Cru, *Témoins* (Paris: Les Étincelles, 1929) pp. 555–65.
4. *Le Feu, suivi du Carnet de guerre* (Paris: Flammarion, 1965) p. 302. All quotations and textual references are to this edition. The translations are my own.
5. *Le Feu*, pp. 126–7, 172, 184, 186.
6. See also in this respect Chapter xv, 'L'Oeuf' or pp. 232–6 in Chapter xxi, 'Le Poste de secours'.
7. See Chapter xiii, pp. 141–2.
8. Compare with this the outburst of Bertrand in an earlier chapter: ' "The future!", he suddenly exclaimed, with the voice of a prophet.' (p. 213) This passage also contains the famous and equally incongruous intoning of the name of Karl Liebknecht.
9. Among war novels much influenced by *Le Feu*, and to which the same arguments broadly apply, one might mention Marcel Martinet, *La Maison de l'abri* (Paris: Ollendorff, 1920) and *La Nuit* (Paris, 1921), and Raymond Lefebvre, *Le Sacrifice d'Abraham* (Paris: Flammarion, 1918).
10. This applies, for example, to the group of writers around Henry Poulaille's *Nouvel Age Littéraire* and the *Bulletin des écrivains prolétaires*.
11. See the work of such writers as André Thérive and Léon Lemmonnier, whose views were expressed in the *Manifeste du roman populiste* (1929).

CHAPTER 6

1. Dorgelès also wrote a three-act play, *La Corde au cou*, which remained unperformed. The most complete account of Dorgelès's early years is to be found in Albert Dubeux, *Roland Dorgelès* (Paris: Edition de la Nouvelle Revue

Critique, 1930). See too Maurice Rieuneau, *Guerre et Révolution dans le roman français de 1919 à 1939* (Paris: Klincksieck, 1974) pp. 29–51.

2. The one for which he is best known is his successful attempt to debunk contemporary fashions and tastes in art in 1910. A paintbrush was tied to the tail of the donkey belonging to Frédéric Gérand, the owner of the Lapin Agile. The resulting painting, 'Et le soleil se coucha sur L'Adriatique', was officially witnessed and hung at the Salon des Indépendants, where it met with considerable success!

3. 'Feuilles retrouvées' in *Bleu Horizon* (Paris: Albin Michel, 1949) p. 47.

4. For a good account of the European intellectuals' response to the pre-war situation see R. N. Stromberg, 'The Intellectuals and the Coming of War in 1914', *Journal of European Studies* 3, no. 2 (June 1973) 109–22.

5. See A. Dubeux, p. 26.

6. *Souvenirs sur 'Les Croix de Bois'* (Paris: A la cité des livres, 1929) p. 46. This text was republished in *Bleu Horizon* (pp. 9–37) in a slightly reworked form and included as part of the first section of this book entitled 'En Marge des *Croix de Bois*'.

7. Quoted in *Romans-Revues* (11 January 1920) p. 29.

8. *Souvenirs sur 'Les Croix de Bois'*, p. 50.

9. Ibid., p. 33.

10. *Une heure avec Frédéric Lefevre* (Paris: Nouvelle Revue Française, 1924) p. 124.

11. *Souvenirs sur 'Les Croix de Bois'*, p. 25.

12. Lefevre, p. 128.

13. See for example Georges Pacy, *L'Eclair* (20 April 1919); André Charpentier, *Le Crapouillet* (1 June 1919); Roger Allard, *Nouvelle Revue Française* (February 1920) and the unsigned reviews in *La Suisse* (18 May 1919) and in *The French Quarterly* (June 1920).

14. *Les Croix de Bois* was first published in 1919 by Albin Michel, Paris. The texts used in the preparation of this chapter are the *Livre de Poche* (1974) edition and the anonymous English translation published in 1920 by Heinemann. Page references to the latter are given in the text. I have occasionally amended the English renderings.

15. Dorgelès was a Catholic. After the war he felt that the loss of a religious spirit in France was in large part responsible for social and moral unrest. In addition to the title there are occasional allusions to religion in the text. The most interesting is the possibility that Demachy is intended to be a Christ figure who dies – crucified against a tree? (p. 409) – for mankind.

16. His name derives, of course, from *bouffe*, which means 'comic' and is a slang word for 'food'.

17. See René Pomeau, 'Guerre et roman dans l'entre deux guerres', *Revue des Sciences humaines* (January–March 1963) 77–95.

18. *Souvenirs sur 'Les Croix de Bois'*, p. 20.

19. Jean Norton Cru, *Témoins* (Paris: Les Etincelles, 1929).

20. See for example Alix Pasquier, *Bataille littéraire* (2 October 1919); Abel Hermant, *Le Figaro* (20 April 1919).

21. See in particular Chapters I, II, III, V, VII, VIII, XIII.

CHAPTER 7

1. Pierre-Eugène Drieu la Rochelle (1893–1945).

2. Gallimard, 1934. All page references are to the Livre de Poche edition, 1970. Quotations are taken from Douglas Gallagher's English translation, *The*

Comedy of Charleroi and other stories (Cambridge, 1973), unless otherwise specified. Translations from other works are my own.

3. Drieu la Rochelle, *Sur les écrivains* (1964) pp. 87–8.

4. Drieu la Rochelle, *L'Europe contre les patries* (1931) p. 149.

5. E.g. Drieu la Rochelle, 'Nouvel Empire par Fritz von Unruh', in *La Nouvelle Revue Française* CLXVII (November 1925) 627–30.

6. Drieu la Rochelle, *Genève ou Moscou* (1928).

7. Drieu la Rochelle, *L'Europe contre les patries*, pp. 141–51.

8. Drieu la Rochelle, 'La Comédie de Charleroi', in *Europe* (May 1933). 'Le Voyage des Dardanelles' first appeared in *La Nouvelle Revue Française* CCXL (September and October 1933).

9. See, for example, F. J. Grover, *Drieu la Rochelle and the fiction of testimony* (Berkeley and Los Angeles, 1958) p. 62. This is the only full-length study of Drieu in English. The same author's later book in French, *Drieu la Rochelle* (1962), is also essential reading.

10. Drieu mentions this in *Mesure de la France* (1922) p. 155.

11. In an open letter to Benjamin Crémieux in 1929 Drieu acknowledged the inauthenticity of the view he had given of the war in *Interrogations*. The letter is reprinted in *Sur les écrivains*, pp. 168–72.

12. Derogatory remarks about France in his contemporary *Drôle de Voyage* (1933) p. 257, confirm this view.

13. As developed, for example, by E. Van den Bremt, 'L'Unité intérieure de Drieu la Rochelle', *La Revue des Langues Vivantes* XXXIII, no. 3 (1967) 252–266.

14. In *Le Jeune Européen* (1927) pp. 21–2, Drieu had assimilated the American urban environment to the war several years before Céline's *Voyage au bout de la nuit* (1932). Comparisons of the war and urban society become more common in later war fiction. See, for example, Arnold Zweig's *Erziehung vor Verdun* (Amsterdam, 1935).

15. E.g. pp. 88, 115, 129, 140, 275, 309.

16. This myth, with its Nietzschean formulations, recalls Drieu's attitudes in *Interrogations*. It is significant that the narrator discards his *Zarathoustra* when he storms away, disillusioned, from the battlefield (p. 109).

17. An excellent analysis of this point is to be found in Pierre-Henri Simon's 'Drieu la Rochelle ou le Vertige du Tragique', in *Procès du Héros* (1950) pp. 107–69.

18. The problematical relationship of self and other in Drieu has not to date been studied in any depth. For useful hints see: J. Desnoyers, *Etude Médico-Psychologique sur Pierre Drieu la Rochelle* (thesis of the Faculty of Medecine of Paris, 1965); J. Plumyène and R. Lasierra, *Les Fascismes Français 1923–63* (1963) pp. 163–7; R. Girardet, 'Pour une introduction à l'histoire des nationalismes français' in *La Revue Française de Sciences Politiques* VIII (September 1958) 505–28; W. R. Tucker, 'Fascism and Individualism in the Political Thought of Pierre Drieu la Rochelle', in *Journal of Politics* 27 (February 1965) 153–77.

19. For example, Grover, *Fiction of Testimony*, p. 65.

20. This theme recurs frequently in First World War fiction. Examples include E. Florian-Parmentier, *L'Ouragan* (1921) and R. Dorgelès, *Le Réveil des morts* (1923).

21. This translation is my own.

22. The necessary relationship between the theme of decadence and the syntax a writer employs to convey it is discussed by Drieu in an article on Céline reprinted in *Sur les écrivains*, pp. 291–5.

23. This translation is my own.

24. This theme emerges with particular clarity in Drieu's later novel, *Gilles* (1942).

25. *Sur les écrivains*, p. 41.

26. Drieu la Rochelle, *Gilles* (Livre de Poche, 1967) preface, pp. 5 and 10.

27. Maurice Rieuneau, *Guerre et Révolution dans le roman français de 1919 à 1939* (1974) p. 214.

28. Rieuneau, ibid. p. 341. Rieuneau, however, does not himself include either the *Comédie* or *Le Sang Noir* in the same section of his analysis as the works of Céline and of Giono.

29. Representative of this mode are Henry de Montherlant, *Le Songe* (1922), Joseph Kessel, *L'Equipage* (1923) and Philippe Barrès, *La guerre à vingt ans* (1924).

30. A similar evolution takes place in Montherlant's attitudes. Two years after *Le Songe* he confessed, in a review of Ph. Barrès' *La guerre à vingt ans*, that the benefits of war no longer, in his view, outweighed the evils.

CHAPTER 8

1. Giono was born in Manosque in 1895 and died there in 1970. The first edition of *Le Grand Troupeau* was published by N.R.F. (Paris). The book has been translated as *To the Slaughterhouse* by N. Glass (London: Peter Owen, 1969). The Gallimard (Pléiade) edition of the *Oeuvres romanesques complètes* contains very valuable notes and commentaries; those on *Le Grand Troupeau* are by Lucien and Janine Miallet. General studies of Giono are: P. de Boisdeffre, *Giono* (Paris: Gallimard, 1965); C. Chonez, *Giono par lui-même* (Paris: Seuil, 1974); W. D. Redfern, *The Private World of Jean Giono* (Oxford: Blackwell, 1967).

2. *Oeuvres*, Vol. 1 (Paris: Gallimard, 1971) p. 1098. All textual references in this essay refer to this edition. The translations are my own.

3. 'It takes more virility to beget a child than to kill a man.' Giono, preface to L. Jacques, *Carnets de moleskine* (Paris: N.R.F., 1939) p. 23.

4. 'Aux Sources mêmes de l'espérance', in *L'Eau vive* (Paris: Gallimard, 1943) p. 126.

5. A draft, quoted in *Oeuvres*, p. 1091. In a late text, Giono argues that the Apocalypse is not the final annihilation of everything human, but rather a daily reminder of a universe in a state of perpetual flux. See 'Le Grand Théâtre', in *Le Déserteur et autres récits* (Paris: Gallimard, 1973).

6. See Odile de Pomerai's excellent study, *The Critics of Jean Giono* ((unpublished PhD. thesis, London University, 1964).

7. Preface to Jacques, *Carnets de moleskine*, pp. 28–9.

8. *Oeuvres*, p. 1102.

9. *Oeuvres*, p. 1092.

10. *Refus d'obéissance* (Paris: Gallimard, 1937) p. 15.

11. C. Lévi-Strauss, *Tristes Tropiques* (Paris: Plon, 1955) p. 40.

12. *Les Pages immortelles de Virgile* (Paris: Corrêa, 1947) p. 65.

CHAPTER 9

1. Preface to *Untel de l'armée française* (Amiens: E. Malfère, 1926). All references are to this edition. *Untel* was first published in book form by Payot,

Paris, 1918. All translations from Franconi and Wiechert in this essay are my own.

2. For the biography and army career see F. Divoire, Introduction to Gabriel-Tristan Franconi, *Poèmes* (Paris: La Renaissance du livre, 1921) and J. N. Cru, *Témoins* (Paris: Les Etincelles, 1929) pp. 604–6.

3. In the feuilleton of *l'Eveil*, October–November 1917.

4. E.g. 'Le retour', 'Le soldat perdu', 'En route', 'Exegèse de certaines phrases militaires' and 'Les nouveaux souvenirs de la maison des morts'. Cf. H. Talvart et J. Place, *Bibliographie des auteurs modernes de langage française*, Vol. VI (Paris, 1937) p. 215.

5. 'Ceux de l'arrière' 'La Dégradation' and 'l'Avion abattu'. This last chapter in some passages shows qualities one will later find in St Exupéry.

6. Notably the nights at the 'Riviera de Montparnasse' (that 'Côte d'Azur of the poor') the poignant wedding of Lulusse who has gone home, like John Bullock, minus one leg (pp. 193–6) and the feast at Camp B (pp. 225–31).

7. Even the two soldiers ceremoniously cast out of the Army (cf. 'La Dégradation') are no real exceptions.

8. Others are a general rising of the soldiers like dead people to demand a share in the feast of life (pp. 130, 250) which one also meets in Wiechert's short story 'Advent of the Dead' (*Sämtliche Werke* [see n. 29 below] VII, pp. 590–7), and a union of veterans and outcasts in a new Fifth Estate (pp. 123–5).

9. See F. Divoire's Introduction to Franconi's *Poèmes*, p. xxiv.

10. This also comes out in the satirical *Bisbur au Démocratic-Palace* (Paris: La Maison française d'art et d'édition, 1917) and, in quite a different way, in many poems. The poems generally have a quality corresponding to Georgian Poetry in England.

11. Williamson formally joined the B.U.F. in 1938, but was already in contact with Mosley's and similar circles earlier. Cf. C. Cross, *The Fascists in Britain* (London: Barrie & Rockliff, 1961) p. 189; A. Hamilton, *The Appeal of Fascism* (London: A. Blond, 1971) pp. 265–8; R. Benewick, *The Fascist Movement in Britain* (London: Allan Lane, 1969, rev. ed. 1972) p. 126. Cf. also the *Chronicle* novel *The Phoenix Generation* (1965). Henry Williamson did not reply to my request for an interview. My thanks are due however to Macdonalds, especially Mrs Fleming (Susan Hodgart), who generously gave me such information about Williamson and *The Patriot's Progress* as they had.

12. All fifteen volumes of the *Chronicle* were published by Macdonald, London. Philip Maddison is essentially a re-creation of his cousin Willie, the hero of the *Flax of Dream* sequence (1921–9); for *Tarka the Otter* (1937) see *It was the Nightingale* (1962), pp. 27 ff. and later. The 'autobiographical' *The Sun in the Sands* (writen 1934, published 1945) is taken over into *The Innocent Moon* (1961). *The Golden Falcon* (1933, rev. ed. 1947) inspired parts of *The Gale of The World* (1969), etc. Space forbids expanding this list and giving details.

13. *The Gale of The World*, p. 274. Williamson has been neglected by critics. The only serious study so far is J. Middleton Murry, 'The Novels of Henry Williamson' in *Katherine Mansfield and Other Literary Studies* (London: Constable, 1959) pp. 95–162. Murry of course had only the earlier parts of the *Chronicle* before him. His insights are all the more admirable.

14. He wrote: 'I didn't want to use one sentence of PP Prose', cf. 'Epigraph' to the edition: *The Patriot's Progress Being the Vicissitudes of Pte. John Bullock* related by Henry Williamson and drawn by William Kermode (London: Macdonald, 1968). All references are to this edition which is an exact reprint of the first, published by Geoffrey Bles, 1930. B. Bergonzi finds little merit in the *Chronicle* (*Heroes' Twilight*, pp. 213–19) and does not even mention *The*

Patriot's Progress. M. S. Greicus, in *Prose Writers of the First World War* (London: Longmans, 1973) pp. 21–2, shows some appreciation of the *Chronicle*, but calls the *Patriot's Progress* a political tirade 'of historical interest only'.

15. *How Dear is Life* (1954), *A Fox Under my Cloak* (1955), *The Golden Virgin* (1957), *Love and the Loveless* (1958), and *A Test to Destruction* (1960). To show the correspondences a separate study would be needed. Important links are provided by Williamson's *The Wet Flanders Plain* (London: Beaumont Press and Faber & Faber, 1929) and Captain D. H. Bell's *A Soldier's Diary of the Great War* (London: Faber & Gwyer, 1929) which Williamson as editor re-worked extensively.

16. *The Gale of the World*, p. 274.

17. For information about Kermode see the obituary in *The Times*, 6 February 1959, which Williamson also reprints in the 1968 edition.

18. This is what I. W. Girvan calls it in *A Bibliography and Critical Survey of the Works of Henry Williamson . . .* (Chipping Camden, Gloucs, 1931) p. 46.

19. Paris: Le Livre moderne illustré, J. Ferenczi & fils, 1938. Original edition, Amiens: E. Malfère, 1924. The woodcuts fit the story, but not the other way round. They remain ornament.

20. An extensive critical essay developing from a review of Edmund Blunden's *Undertones of War* for the *London Mercury* (January 1929), repr. in *The Linhay on the Downs* (London: Faber, 1934) pp. 224–62.

21. Cf. H. M. Tomlinson's remark: 'It is a sad mistake to suppose you may reproduce the sound of drum-fire by words resembling the rolling of drums' in the article 'War Books', *The Criterion* ix, no. 36 (April 1930) 412.

22. In the *Evening Standard*, 8 May 1930. The paper also serialised the book in 1930. It generally had a good press then, just as the 1968 reprint had. Williamson also reprints Bennett's review in the 1968 edition.

23. See my discussion of this aspect in a forthcoming article on Manning in the *Journal of Commonwealth Literature* (spring 1977).

24. Cf. Wilfred Owen, 'Exposure', second stanza: 'What are we doing here?'; *The Poems*, ed. E. Blunden (London: Chatto & Windus, 1963) p. 53.

25. First published in the *British Magazine* (June 1760), later as Letter cxix in *The Citizen of the World* (1762). Included by A. Friedman in *Collected Works*, Vol. ii (Oxford: Clarendon, 1966) pp. 458–65.

26. In his allusions to Bunyan, Williamson may have been influenced by the war novel he admired most: Wilfred Ewart's *Way of Revelation* (London: Putnam, 1921). Ewart quotes passages from the *Apokalypse* as mottoes for each part, the last being the New Jerusalem of *Apokalypse* xxi.

27. *The Innocent Moon* (1961) and *It Was the Nightingale* (1962).

28. There is no really good book on the Wiechert. One might look at the Festschrift *Bekenntnis zu Ernst Wiechert* (München: Desch, 1947); Ernst Ebeling, *Ernst Wiechert: Das Werk des Dichters* (1937, rev. ed. Wiesbaden: Limes, 1947); and an interesting attempt to chart some of the correspondences threading through his work: M. P. Jetter, *The 'Island Motif' in the Prose Works of Ernst Wiechert* (Vancouver: Continental Book Centre, 1957). For other studies see S. Kirshner, 'A Bibliography of Critical Writing about Ernst Wiechert', *Librarium* 7 (1964) 59–67.

29. Quotations from his autobiography, *Jahre und Zeiten* (1945–6) in *Sämtliche Werke in zehn Bänden* (München: Desch, 1957) Vol. ix, p. 482, cf. pp. 512, 538–9. All quotations refer to this edition, abbr. *SW*. Wiechert later tried to limit the damage done by the publication of this private 'purgation'. He refused to give a reading from *Totenwolf* to a Hitler Youth Camp and before his death restricted republication of his early work to the collected works edition.

30. At first thought of as friendly to the regime, he was only gradually

ostracised, particularly as a consequence of two public speeches which are available in *The Poet and His Time. Three Addresses by Ernst Wiechert*, trans. I. Taeuber (Chicago: Regnery & Co., 1948). An excellent study of his position in the Third Reich as reflected in criticism of his works is H. Chatellier, 'Ernst Wiechert im Urteil der deutschen Zeitschriftenpresse 1933–1945', *Recherches Germaniques* 3 (1973) 153–95. Things came to head in 1938 when he was sent to Buchenwald concentration camp but luckily released after a few months on condition that he keep quiet.

31. First printed München: Langen-Müller, 1931. I could only check the reprint in *SW*, Vol. III, pp. 303–538, against the 13.–16.000 issue, München, no date (presumably 1935). There are no variants. Unfortunately, there is no English translation. *Jedermann* is however available in French, trans. H. Thies as *La grande permission* (Paris: Livres de Poche, 1954, repr. 1967).

32. Especially from the training period, cf. *Jedermann*, pp. 326–67, and *Jahre und Zeiten*, *SW*, Vol. IX, pp. 461–6; also some other experiences.

33. Megai is one example of Wiechert's creation of sympathetic Jews (prefigured in the novel by Perlmutter ['Mother-of-Pearl'], a student acquaintance of Johannes' who is writing a ten-volume 'History of the Persecution of the Jewish People'); the most famous instance is Eli Kaback in the short story 'Die Gebärde' (1932), *SW*, Vol. VII, pp. 598, 612.

34. A motif spread widely through Wiechert's work, see for instance *SW*, Vol. IV, pp. 215, 561; Vol. VI, pp. 117–18; Vol. VII, pp. 131, 461.

35. Cf. Wilfred Owen's 'The Parable of the Old Men and the Young', *Poems*, p. 57. Bergonzi mentions other related English poems, see *Heroes' Twilight*, pp. 123–4.

36. Mrs Wirtulla and Klaus, esp. pp. 459–62, 520–1; The Countess and Percy, pp. 361, 511–13; the porter's wife and her dead son, pp. 513–14. The general homage to the mothers occurs on p. 375. See also Wiechert's war play *Der verlorene Sohn* (1933), *SW*, Vol. X, 35–113.

37. The action-packed Chapter v, framed by the Russian singing in Chapter IV (p. 390 ff.) and the mortuary scene in Chapter VI (pp. 431–2).

38. Cf. *Die Jerominkinder*, Part I (written 1940–1, published 1945, repr. in *SW*, Vol. V). Available in translation by R. Maxwell as *The Earth is Our Heritage* (London: Nevill, 1951).

39. *Der Totenwald* (written 1939, published 1945, repr. in *SW*, Vol. IX, pp. 197–329). Translated by U. Stechow (New York: V. Gollancz, 1947).

40. P. Sérant, *Le Romantisme Fasciste* (Paris: Fasquelle, 1959). G. L. Mosse also stresses the romantic derivation as an important element in fascism for Germany, cf. his *The Crisis of German Ideology* (New York: Grosset & Dunlap, 1964).

CHAPTER 10

1. This is the figure given by Jörg Drews in *Kindlers Literatur Lexikon*, ed. Wolfgang von Einsiedel *et al.* (Zürich: Kindler-Verlag, 1971) V, 4781–2; other works give different figures.

2. See the announcement by the Propyläen-Verlag, in Remarque's next novel *Der Weg zurück* (*The Road Back*) (Berlin: Propyläen-Verlag, 1931) p. 370; cf. Pavel Petr, 'Bemerkungen zu einigen deutschen Prosawerken über den ersten Weltkrieg', *Germanica Wratislaviensia* 7 (1962) 20.

3. Hans Habe *et al.*, *Erich Maria Remarque zum 70. Geburtstag am 22. Juni 1968* (no place: Kiepenheuer & Witsch/Verlag Kurt Desch, 1968) p. 38.

4. By Else Möbus, quoted in *Die Literatur* 33 (1930–1) 447.
5. E.g. 'Emil Marius Requark', *Vor Troja nichts Neues* (*All Quiet at the Gates of Troy*) (Berlin: Brunnen-Verlag/Karl Winckler, 1930).
6. Petr, op. cit., p. 30.
7. *Die Literatur* 33 (1930–1) 546.
8. *Die literarische Welt* 6, no. 50 (1930) 9; cf. Georges Sadoul, trans. Peter Morris, *Dictionary of Films* (Berkeley & Los Angeles: University of California Press, 1972) pp. 7–8.
9. *Die Literatur* 33 (1930–1) 485; cf. E. M. Remarque zum 70. Geburtstag, p. 38.
10. Petr, op. cit., p. 30.
11. Quoted in Anon., 'Zum Schaffen der Lebenden', *Die Literatur* 31 (1928–1929) 590–1.
12. See the three standard studies of his life and work: 'Mynona' (S. Friedlaender), *Hat Erich Maria Remarque wirklich gelebt?* (Berlin: Paul Steegemann Verlag, 1929), esp. pp. 251–8; Alfred Antkowiak, 'Erich Maria Remarque', in *Ludwig Renn; Erich Maria Remarque* (Berlin: Volk und Wissen, 1965) pp. 99–232, esp. pp. 101–2; and *E. M. Remarque zum 70. Geburtstag*, op. cit., esp. pp. 38–40.
13. First published in *Störtebeker*, 1924, no. 2, p. 37.
14. For a more detailed discussion, see Antkowiak, op. cit., pp. 102–3, 106–8.
15. Mynona, *Hat E. M. Rermarque wirklich gelebt?*, p. 255.
16. Richard Katz describes the crucial editorial conference in 'Ein Soldat der Wahrheit: Zum 60. Geburtstag Erich Maria Remarques am 22. Juni 1958', *Forum* 5 (1958) 226–7, see p. 226.
17. Berlin: Propyläen-Verlag, 1929, 288 pp. The German text is now available in paperback (Berlin: Ullstein Bücher, no. 56, 1956). For English readers, the original translation by A. W. Wheen (London: G. P. Putnam's Sons, March 1929) sold so many copies that it is readily available second-hand; there is also a recent paperback (St Albans: Mayflower, 1968). Quotations from *All Quiet*, in my own translation, are from the 1929 book edition; my copy is from the 501–525th thousand.
18. The two sensitive interpretations of *Im Westen* which have appeared in the last decade are both presented as comparisons with Anglo-Saxon works: with *A Farewell to Arms*, in Helmut Liedloff, 'Two War Novels: A critical comparison', *Rev. litt. comp.* 42 (1968) 390–406; and with *Her Privates We*, in Holger M. Klein, 'Dazwischen Niemandsland: *Im Westen nichts Neues und Her Privates We*', in *Grossbritannien und Deutschland . . . Festschrift für John W. P. Bourke*, ed. Ortwin Kuhn (München: Wilhelm Goldmann Verlag, 1974) pp. 487–512.
19. Anon., *Die Literatur* 32 (1929–30) 164.
20. Liedloff, op. cit., p. 391.
21. In 'Welches war das Lieblingsbuch Ihrer Knabenjahre? Eine Rundfrage', *Die literarische Welt* 5, no. 26 (1929) 3.
22. *Die Literatur* 31 (1928–9) 688, and 32 (1929–30) 99.
23. *Die Literatur* 32 (1929–30) 6.
24. '1 Million × Im Westen nichts Neues', *Hochland* 26, ii (1929) 217.
25. *Die literarische Welt* 5, no. 8 (1929) 5.
26. *Die Literatur* 31 (1928–9) 591.
27. Op. cit., p. 226.
28. 'Die Frontgeneration spricht', *Das Tagebuch* 10, no. 4 (26 January 1929) 155.
29. *Werther*, with Storm's *Immensee* and Keller's *Der grüne Heinrich*, is among the works that influenced Remarque at the age of fifteen or sixteen; and

he comments explicitly on the fact that it was they that first made him aware of literary form as opposed to subject-matter: see *Die literarische Welt* 5, no. 26 (1929) 3.

30. Liedloff suggests that the name Bäumer 'brings to mind both "Baum" [tree] and "Träumer" [dreamer], two terms which have considerable significance for Paul's character' (pp. 391–2); and he draws attention to other 'speaking names'. This technique may extend further: e.g. the name Leer [empty] for the womanising mathematician. At the same time, it is worth pointing out that Paul was Remarque's own second name, and Beumer the name of his paternal grandmother: see Mynona, op. cit., p. 252.

31. See Petr, op. cit., p. 32; Antkowiak, op. cit., pp. 113 ff.

CHAPTER 11

1. This essay is an extract from my book *Ernst Jünger: A Writer of Our Time* (Cambridge: Bowes & Bowes, 1953; New Haven: Yale UP, 1953), revised and adapted for inclusion in this collection. Later important studies of Jünger include: Gerhard Loose, *Ernst Jünger: Gestalt und Werk* (Frankfurt am Main: Klostermann, 1957); Gerhad Loose, *Ernst Jünger* (New York: Twayne, 1974); Karl O. Paetel, *Ernst Jünger in Selbstzeugnissen und Bilddokumenten* (Hamburg: Rowohlt, 1962); Hans-Peter Schwarz, *Der konservative Anarchist: Politik und Zeitkritik Ernst Jüngers* (Freiburg: Rombach, 1962).

2. *In Stahlgewittern*, 24th edition (Berlin: Mittler, 1942) p. 1. Currently available in the 26th edition (Stuttgart: Klett, 1961). The works of Jünger have been collected in *Werke*, 10 vols (Stuttgart: Klett, 1960–1965). *In Stahlgewittern* was translated into French (1930 and 1960), Italian, Spanish, Polish, Roumanian, Latvian; the English translation is by Basil Creighton, *The Storm of Steel* (New York: Doran; London: Chatto & Windus, 1929, repr. 1942). In my own quotations I have not used this or any other translation of Jünger's works.

3. Ernst Jünger (ed.), *Der Kampf um das Reich* (Essen: Deutsche Vertriebsstelle 'Rheim und Ruhr', 1929. 2nd ed., 1931) pp. 7–8. See also the Preface to *Der Kampf als inneres Erlebnis* (Berlin: Mittler, 1922; 2nd ed., 1938) pp. xi–xv.

4. *Der Kampf um das Reich*, p. 7. He was of course at that time too much of a nationalist to co-operate actively with Communism (cf. also his contribution to the anthology *Das Antlitz des Weltkrieges* (Berlin, 1930), esp. p. 108). For the passion that animated Communists like Rosa Luxemburg he had little sympathy.

5. See *In Stahlgewittern*, Chapter XVI (March 1918), 'Die grosse Schlacht', of which *Feuer und Blut* (Magdeburg: Stahlhelm Verlag, 1925; 3rd, shortened version, Berlin: Reclam, 1941) is an expanded account. For *Das Wäldchen 125* (Berlin: Mittler, 1925) which was translated by Creighton as *Copse 125* (London: Chatto & Windus, 1930), see *In Stahlgewittern*, Chapter XVII (June–July 1918) 'Englische Vorstösse'.

6. *Der Arbeiter: Herschaft und Gestalt* (Hamburg: Hanseatische Verlagsanstalt, 1932).

7. Thus in 1934 G. Günther included parts of Jünger's war diaries in 'Der Krieger: Aus der Zeit 1914–1918' in the volume *Das Reich im Werden* (Frankfurt am Main: Diesterweg, 1934). On the other hand Jünger refused to permit *In Stahlgewittern* to be serialised in *Der Völkische Beobachter*.

8. His name does *not* appear on the 1936 list of German writers who declared their loyalty to Hitler.

9. *Strahlungen* (Tübingen: Heliopolis Verlag, 1949) p. 343: entry Paris, 26 June 1943; cf. *Strahlungen*, p. 575. See also *Der Kampf als inneres Erlebnis* (2nd ed., 1938) pp. 33 and 94.

10. *In Stahlgewittern*, 3rd ed. (1921) p. 190. In the later versions (from the 14th ed., 1934 onwards), a further passage is interpolated.

11. *Feuer und Blut*, pp. 15–16.

12. *Strahlungen*, p. 12.

13. See *Der Arbeiter*, Preface, and also *Blätter und Steine* (Hamburg: Hanseatische Verlagsanstalt, 1934), p. 8 (stylistic exercises = practice in sharpshooting), p. 122 (metaphor = problem in artillery), p. 217 (essay = projectile with delayed action).

14. *Der Friede* (Hamburg: Hanseatische Verlagsanstalt, 1945; edition used: 'Die Argonauten [Holland], n.d. [c. 1948]) p. 32. This work was translated into English as *The Peace* by S. O. Hood (Hinsdale, Illinois: Regnery & Co., n.d. [1948]); so was *Auf den Marmorklippen*, Jünger's only book held together by a continuous story (*On the Marble Cliffs*, London: Lehmann, 1947; New York: Directions, 1948).

15. See in this connection J. P. Stern, *Hitler: the Führer and the People* (London: Fontana, 1975) p. 179.

16. Henry Reed: *A Map of Verona* (London, 1946); and *Von unten gesehen. Impressionen und Aufzeichnungen des Obergefreiten F.H.* (Stuttgart, 1950).

17. Frederic Manning, *Her Privates We* (London: Peter Davies, 1930, 2nd ed. 1964, repr. 1970) p. 274.

18. *Der Kampf als inneres Erlebnis*, p. 87.

19. *Der Kampf als inneres Erlebnis*, p. 12. See also *Gärten und Strassen* (Berlin: Mittler, 1942) p. 168; entry for 18 June, 1940. This type is elaborated in 'Oberfeuerwerker Sievers', in *Heliopolis* (Tübingen: Heliopolis Verlag, 1949) pp. 309 ff., but it goes back to the first edition of *In Stahlgewittern* (Hannover: printed for the author), Preface, p. iv.

20. *Der Friede*, p. 8.

21. *Murder in the Cathedral*, Thomas's final speech at the end of Part I.

22. 'The Wanderer', from *Anglo-Saxon Poetry*, translated by the late Gavin Bone (London: Oxford UP, 1941) p. 70.

23. This is a term which was not, I think, elsewhere applied to human beings until the Sicilian campaign of 1943; Jünger uses it already in *Der Arbeiter*, p. 171. See also *In Stahlgewittern*, 1942 ed., p. 217; introduced in the 1935 (16th) ed., p. 225, but absent in the earlier editions.

24. 'Nichts bleibt vom dem Unsäglichen, als es nicht zu sagen ...' (Karl Kraus in *Die Fackel* XXXVI, nos 890–905, July 1934, p. 24).

CHAPTER 12

1. 'Erinnerung an einen 1. August' in: *Essays*, vol. II, *Aufsätze zum Krieg und Frieden* (Berlin and Weimar: Aufbau Verlag, 1959) p. 8.

2. *Tagebücher* (Köln: Du Mont, 1957) p. 325.

3. This book was published in Leipzig in 1915; Zweig's review appeared in *Die Schaubühne* XI, no. 16 (April 1915) 163 f.

4. Cf. *Schaubühne* X, no. 50 (December 1914) 492–501.

5. Eva Kaufmann, *Arnold Zweigs Weg zum Roman* (Berlin Aufbau Verlag, 1967) p. 37.

6. Cf. Eva Kaufmann, op. cit., p. 78.

7. Layout and compass of this cycle can best be demonstrated as follows:

Title	Narrated time	Written in	Published
Die Zeit ist reif	August 1913– spring 1915	1929 and 1955/56	Berlin 1957
Junge Frau von 1914	spring 1915– July 1916	1928–30	Berlin 1931
Erziehung vor Verdun	July 1916– March 1917	1933–4	Amsterdam 1935
Der Streit um den Sergeanten Grischa	March 1917– November 1917	1926–7	Potsdam 1928
Feuerpause	November 1917– January 1918	1930 and 1952/53	Berlin 1954
Einsetzung eines Königs	February 1918– October 1918	1936–7	Amsterdam 1937
Das Eis bricht	–January 1919	Projected	———

8. Cf. Georg Lukács, *Schicksalswende* (Berlin: Aufbau Verlag, 1948) pp. 273 f.

9. Cf. *The Case of Sergeant Grischa*, trans. E. Sutton (New York: Viking Press, 1929) p. 8. All quotations from the novel in this essay refer to this edition.

10. Cf. *Weltbühne*, xv, no. 37 (September 1919).

11. Cf. *Essays*, vol. II, p. 29.

12. Cf. Emil Julius Gumbel, *Vier Jahr politischer Mord* (Berlin: Verlag der neuen Gesellschaft, 1922). [Gumbel himself became a victim of right-wing persecution later and went into exile in 1932.] Cf. here also H. and E. Hannover, *Politische Justiz 1918–1933* (Frankfurt: Fischer, 1966).

13. Friedrich Karl Kaul, *Kleiner Weimarer Pitaval* (Berlin: Verlag Das Neue Berlin, 1959) p. 96.

14. Hans-Albert Walter, *Deutsche Exilliteratur 1933–1950*, Vol. I: *Bedrohung und Verfolgung bis 1933* (Darmstadt and Neuwied: Luchterland, 1972) p. 35.

15. Cf. Walter, op. cit., especially pp. 33–89; 'Diffamierung, Behinderung und Verfolgung progressiver Intellektueller in der Weimarer Republik (1925–1932).'

16. Cf. Kaufmann, op. cit., p. 209.

17. Cf. Sigmund Freud/Arnold Zweig, *Briefwechsel*, ed. E. L. Freud (Frankfurt: Fischer, 1968).

18. As a Jew and socialist Arnold Zweig had to go into exile in 1932. From 1933 to 1945 he lived in Palestine. From 1948 to his death in 1965 he was a citizen of the German Democratic Republic. There numerous prizes and distinctions were conferred upon him.

The standard edition of Zweig's works is: *Ausgewählte Werke in Einzelausgaben* (Berlin: Aufbau Verlag, 1957–; fifteen volumes so far). Besides *Grischa*, some other works by Zweig are available in English translations: *Young Woman of 1914*, trans. E. Sutton (London: Secker, 1932); *De Vriendt Goes Home*, trans. E. Sutton (London: Warburg, 1938); *The Axe of Wandsbeck*, trans. E. Sutton (London: Hutchinson, 1948); *The Time is Ripe*, trans. Kenneth Banerji and Michael Wharton (London: Gibbs & Phillips, 1962).

The volume *Arnold Zweig zum siebzigsten Geburtstag*, ed. the Deutsche Akademie der Künste (Berlin, 1957) contains an extensive bibliography. The most immediately useful books on Zweig are perhaps Eberhard Hilscher, *Arnold Zweig* (Berlin: Volk and Wisen, 1968), and Eva Kaufmann's book. The special issue of the journal *Sinn und Form* (1952) devoted to Arnold Zweig is also worth looking at. So is H. A. Walter, 'Auf dem Wege zum Staatsroman: Arnold Zweig's

Grischa-Zyklus', *Frankfurter Hefte* 23 (1968). English readers might want to consult: Solomon Fisher, 'The War Novels of Arnold Zweig', *Sewanee Review* 49 (1941) 433–57 and Lothar Kahn, 'The Two Worlds of Arnold Zweig', *Chicago Jewish Forum* 19 (1960) 144–51.

CHAPTER 13

1. Josef Hora, *Hladový rok* (Prague, 1926).

2. Richard Weiner, *Lítice* (Prague, 1916; heavily censored).

3. Rudolf Medek, *Legionářská epopeja* (Prague, 1921–7; 5 vols).

4. For a more detailed biography of Hašek see Emanuel Frynta, *Hašek, The Creator of Schweik* (clumsily) translated by J. Layton and G. Theiner (Prague: Artia, 1965). This richly illustrated book contains useful information on auto-biographical elements in *Švejk*.

5. First complete collection published in *Dobrý voják Švejk v zajetí, Stati a humoresky z dob války* (Prague: Československý spisovatel, 1973).

6. After the October Revolution Hašek turns away from the idea of national revenge to one of social revenge.

7. Edition used: *Dobrý voják Švejk před válkou a jiné podivné historky* (Prague: SNKLHU, 1957). Henceforth referred to as the *Tales*.

8. For edition used see note 5. Henceforth referred to as *Švejk in Captivity*.

9. Edition used: *Osudy dobrého vojáka Švejka za světové války*, 4 vols in 3 (Prague: Československý spisovatel, 1967). Henceforth referred to as *Švejk*. As in other editions published since the Communist takeover the short message to Masaryk, insignificant as it is, except to demonstrate that Hašek like the rest still supported Masaryk, is omitted. English trans. Sir Cecil Parrott, *The Good Soldier Švejk and his Fortunes in the World War* (Harmondsworth: Penguin, 1973).

10. *Švejk in Captivity*, pp. 21 and 47.

11. *Švejk in Captivity*, p. 70.

12. For a pretty comprehensive bibliography of Hašek criticism see Radko Pytlík and Miroslav Laiske, *Bibliografie Jaroslava Haška, Soupis jeho díla a literatury o něm* (Prague: SPN, 1960). Laiske brings this bibliography up to date in *Česká literatura* 21 (1973) 164–78. Most established Czech critics did not pay much attention to *Švejk* until the German translation by Grete Reiner appeared (Prague: Synek, 1926). An account of both Czech and German criticism on *Švejk* is Pavel Petr, *Haseks 'Schwejk' in Deutschland* (Berlin: Rütten & Loening, 1963).

13. *Přehledné dějiny literatury české*, 4th ed. (Olmütz: Promberger, 1936–9) p. 1487.

14. Cf. 'The King of Bohemia', *TLS* 61 (1962) 665. There was in fact a Polish continuation of *Švejk*.

15. Cf. Zoltán Fábry, 'Na obranu Švejka', *Plamen* 8, no. 5 (1966) 127.

16. Article in *Q*, 1926, reprod. in *Stati o literatuře* (Prague: Svoboda, 1951) p. 94. See also Fučík's article in *Tvorba*, 1928, reprod. in *Stati*, pp. 121–2.

17. F. Táborský *O ruském divadle* (Prague: Radhošt', 1935) p. 50.

18. *Arbeitsjournal*, ed. Werner Hecht (Frankfurt: Suhrkamp, 1973) vol. 2, p. 569.

19. For Švejk's pedigree as a picaresque hero see Karel Krejčí, *Česká literatura a kulturní proudy evropské* (Prague: Československý spisovatel, 1975) pp. 379–86; J. P. Stern, 'War and the Comic Muse: *The Good Soldier Schweik* and *Catch-22*', *Comparative Literature* xx (1968) 193–216, and Radko Pytík

'Švejk jako literární typ', *Česká literatura* 21 (1973) 131–52. The last is the best article written on *Švejk* in recent years.

20. Švejk is imaginable without this anchor-point; much recommends a comparison between him and the Vicar of Wakefield.

21. Cf. Jaroslava Pašiaková's review-article on a Hungarian book on Hašek, 'Haškův svět', *Česká literatura* 20 (1972) 357–9.

22. Cf. Ludmila Nováková, 'K otázce nespisovných prvků v jazyce Haškova Švejka', *Slavica Pragesia* VIII (1966) 373–9.

23. *Barbara oder die Frömmigkeit* (Berlin, Vienna, Leipzig: Zsolnay, 1929) pp. 358–64.

24 Cf. Stern, 'War and the Comic Muse'.

25. On Kraus see particularly Paul Schick, *Karl Kraus in Selbstzeugnissen und Bilddokumenten* (Hamburg: Rowohlt, 1965); Hans Weigel, *Karl Kraus oder die Macht der Ohnmacht* (Wien, etc.: Molden, 1968; repr. Munich: dtv, 1972); Harry Zohn, *Karl Kraus* (New York: Twayne, 1971); Mary Snell, 'Karl Kraus' *Die Letzten Tage der Menscheit:* An Analysis', *Forum for Modern Language Studies* 4 (1968) 234–47. For other studies see below and consult: Otto Kerry, *Karl-Kraus-Bibliographie* (Munich: Kösel, 1970).

26. The standard edition is *Werke*, ed. Heinrich Fischer, Vol. V (1927, repr. Munich: Kösel, 1957). Edition used: *Die letzten Tage der Menschheit*, 2 vols (Munich: dtv, 1964). Henceforth referred to as *The Last Days*. No English translation exists.

27. 'Karl Kraus: The Last Days of Mankind' in *The Disinherited Mind* (Cambridge: Bowes & Bowes, 1952; 2nd ed. Harmondsworth: Penguin, 1961) p. 217.

28. See Hans Mayer, 'Karl Kraus und die Nachwelt', *Sinn und Form* 9 (1957), repr. in: *Ansichten zur Literatur der Zeit* (Hamburg: Rowohlt, 1962) pp. 71–84.

29. Cf. Mayer, p. 81.

30. In one scene the Nagger enters only to repeat the word (emotion?) 'Sorry', *The Last Days*, I, pp. 62–3.

31. *The Last Days*, II, p. 110. Cf. *Švejk*, vol. 3, p. 80.

32. *Švejk*, vol. 3, p. 104; *The Last Days*, II, p. 234.

CHAPTER 14

1. Corrado Alvaro, *Vent'anni* (Milan: Treves, 1930). G. A. Borgese, *Rubè* (Milan: Mondadori, 1928). C. E. Gadda, *Giornale di guerra e di prigionia* (Florence: Sansoni, 1955). Giovanni Comisso, *Giorni di guerra* (Milan: Mondadori, 1931). Emilio Lussu, *Un anno sull'altipiano* (Paris: Edizioni italiane di coltura, 1938). Paolo Monelli, *Le scarpe al sole* (Milan: Treves, 1921). Attilio Frescura, *Diario di un imboscato* (Vicenza, 1919). Antonio Baldini, *Nostro purgatorio* (Milan: Treves, 1918).

2. See F. T. Marinetti: *Guerra sola igiene del mondo* (1915, but most of it already in *Le futurisme*, Paris, 1911), *Democrazia futurista* (1919), *Al di là del comunismo* (1920), *Futurismo e fascismo* (1924), *Marinetti e il futurismo* (1929), all reprinted in the anthology *Teoria e invenzione futurista*, ed. Luciano De Maria (Milan, 1968).

3. See Adrian Lyttleton, *The Seizure of Power* (London, 1973) chap. 14, and *Italian Fascisms* (London, 1973); Shirley Vinall, *Italian Avant-garde Attitudes to French Culture*, unpublished Ph.D. thesis (Reading, 1975) Chapters 6 and 8; Mario Isnenghi, *Il mito della grande guerra* (Bari, 1970); Roberto Tessari, *Il mito della macchina* (Milan, 1973) Chapters 1–4.

4. F. T. Marinetti, *L'alcova d'acciaio – romanzo vissuto* (Milan: Vitagliano, 1921; 2nd ed. Milan: Moncadori, 1927). All references are to 1921 edition. The title means 'The Steel Alcove – a novel lived'; the word *alcova* in Italian carries very strongly the connotation of bedroom and place for making love.

5. *La battaille de Tripoli* (Milan, 1912).

6. Norman Gladden, *Acros. the Piave* (London: HMSO, 1971).

7. *La battaille de Tripoli*, p. 20, cf. *Alcova*, pp. 123–4.

8. *Marinetti e il futurismo*, in *Teoria*, pp. 522–5.

9. Richard A. Webster, *L'imperialismo industriale italiano 1908–1915* (Turin, 1974) p. 271.

10. Piero Melograni, *Storia politica della grande guerra* (Bari, 1969) pp. 549–553.

11. Enzo Forcella and Alberto Monticone, *Plotone d'esecuzione. I processi della prima guerra mondiale* (Bari, 1968).

12. *Come si seducono le donne* (Florence, 1917); pp. 171–5 in 3rd ed. (Milan, 1920).

13. Melograni, *Storia politica*, p. 553.

14. *Manifesto tecnico della letteratura futurista*, in *Teoria*, p. 44.

15. *Distruzione della sintassi*, in *Teoria*, p. 61.

16. 'La guerra elettrica' in *Guerra sola igiene del mondo*, in *Teoria*, pp. 273–8.

17. 'Contro l'amore e il parlamentarismo', in *Guerra*, in *Teoria*, pp. 250–1.

18. Translated from the Italian version of the manifesto: *Fondazione e Manifesto del Futurismo*, in *Teoria*, p. 10.

CHAPTER 15

1. Herbert Read, *The Contrary Experience* (London, 1963) p. 64.

2. Edmund Blunden, *Undertones of War* (Oxford, 1928) p. viii.

3. Robert Graves, *Goodbye To All That*, rev. ed. (Harmondsworth: Penguin, 1960) p. 7. All further references will be to this edition of the work and will be noted in the text itself.

4. Robert Graves, *Goodbye To All That* (London, 1929) pp. 13 and 440.

5. David Jones, *In Parenthesis* (London, 1937) p. xv. All further references will be to this edition of the work and will be noted in the text itself. (The Somme offensive appears to be the specific occasion of his narrative.)

6. Paul Fussell, *The Great War and Modern Memory* (Oxford, 1975).

7. Robert Graves, *Occupation: Writer* (Portway, Bath, 1951) p. ix.

8. Herbert Read, *Naked Warriors* (London, 1919).

9. Blunden, *Undertones of War*, p. 256.

10. Karl Miller, 'Hello To All That', *New York Review of Books* XXII (16 October 1975) 28.

11. Wyndham Lewis's detached and sharply sardonic *Blasting and Bombardiering* (London, 1937) is perhaps another exception. As autobiography, it is still private but operates in a brash and self-confident manner with close attention to dramatic events that is different in tone from the gentleness and enquiring self-analysis which enclose and make private the works, for example, of Sassoon, Blunden, and Jones.

12. Bernard Bergonzi, *Heroes' Twilight* (London, 1965) p. 155.

13 Robert Graves, *But It Still Goes On* (London, 1930) p. 51.

14. For further reading see David Blamires, *David Jones: Artist and Writer* (Manchester, 1971); Jeremy Hooker, *David Jones, An Exploratory Study of The*

Writings (London, 1975); and Kathleen Raine, *David Jones, Solitary Perfectionist* (Ipswich, 1974).

15. See Jones's essay 'Past and Present' in *Epoch and Artist* (London, 1959).

16. The poem is an episodic account of a battle in which 300 men are killed fighting the Angles. According to varying interpretations, there are either three survivors or there is one survivor. In either case, the soldier Aneirin who writes the poem is a survivor as was the poet Jones in an attack on the German lines during the Somme offensive.

17. Jones, *Epoch and Artist*, pp. 57–8.

18. Anthony Cronan (ed.), *Penguin Book of Welsh Verse* (Harmondsworth: Penguin, 1967) p. 24.

19. Compare the sacrifice of Melchisedech whereby oblation followed the slaughter of the kings by Abraham (Genesis xiv, 18; Hebrews vii, 2) to the sequence of the Last Supper and Crucifixion in the New Testament.

20. St Matthew xxvi, 42.

CHAPTER 16

1. *Her Privates We* (a bowdlerised version of *The Middle Parts of Fortune*, which had been issued to subscribers in 1929) was published in 1930, and five impressions were called for that year. The novel was reprinted in 1935, 1937, 1943 (introduction by Peter Davies), 1964 (introduction by Edmund Blunden), and 1970. Messrs Peter Davies estimate total hardback sales at around 50,000. A Pan Books edition came out in 1967. My quotations are from the 1964 edition.

2. See, e.g. *Times Literary Supplement*, 16 January 1930; *The Times*, 17 January 1930; *Spectator*, 25 January 1930. The review in the *Army Quarterly* XX (1930) 177–8, reveals professional soldiers' reactions to the book.

3. Douglas Jerrold, *The Lie about the War* (London: Faber, 1930), for instance.

4. Francis Wolle, 'Novels of two World Wars', *Western Humanities Review* v (1951) 279–96.

5. L. T. Hergenhahn, 'Frederic Manning, a neglected Australian writer', *Quadrant* VI, 4 (1962) 5–18, and 'Novelist at War: Frederic Manning's *Her Privates We*', *Quadrant* LXVI (1970) 19–29.

6. *The History of the King's Shropshire Light Infantry in the Great War*, ed. Major W. de B. Wood (London: Medici Society, 1925).

7. Information from the Curator of the K.S.L.I. Museum; Mrs R. A. Hards of the Imperial War Museum has helped over piecing together Manning's career in the army.

8. Siegfried Sassoon, *Siegfried's Journey* (London: Faber, 1945) p. 69.

9. Eric Partridge, 'The War continues', *The Window*, I, 2 (1930) 62–85.

CHAPTER 17

1. *Death of a Hero* (1929; first unabridged edition, London: World Distributors, 1965). All textual references are to the latter edition.

2. D. Daiches (ed.), *The Penguin Companion to Literature I* (Harmondsworth: Penguin Books, 1971) p. 17, claims that Aldington was born in Hampshire; A. Kershaw and F. J. Temple (eds), *Richard Aldington: An Intimate Portrait* (Carbondale and Edwardsville: Southern Illinois UP, 1965) p. vii, that he was born in Kent. Kershaw and Temple also state Aldington died near Sury-en-Vaux,

France, whereas D. F. prefaces Aldington's autobiography *Life for Life's Sake: A Book of Reminiscences* (1941; London: Cassell, 1968) p. 7, with the absurd statement that Aldington died in the United States having remained there since the war.

3. Quoted in Kershaw and Temple, *Richard Aldington*, p. 78.

4. I.e. one whose novels tend to be autobiographical, or at least potently re-creative of personal experience. Orwell, Lowry and Amis are similar in this respect.

5. *Death of a Hero*, p. 23. Aldington's characterisation is at times reminiscent of the 'humours' of Jonsonian drama.

6. I.e. 'a joke'.

7. Walter Allen, *Tradition and Dream* (Harmondsworth: Penguin Books, 1965) p. 162.

8. Quoted on the cover of *Death of a Hero*.

9. Ibid.

10. M. S. Greicus, *Prose Writers of World War I* (London: Longmans, 1973) p. 16.

11. Greicus, p. 15.

CHAPTER 18

1. On the way fiction and other literature 'prophesied' the war, see I. F. Clarke, *Voices Prophesying War, 1763–1984* (London: Oxford UP, 1966) and Bernard Bergonzi, 'Before 1914: Writers and the Threat of War', *Critical Quarterly* 6 (summer 1964) 126–34.

2. The best study of the impact of modern eschatalogy, ideas of death, violence and the body, on modernist form is Frederick J. Hoffman, *The Mortal No: Death and the Modern Imagination* (Princeton UP, 1964), which has some admirable analyses of the international effect of war on style.

3. *The Good Soldier: A Tale of Passion* (London: John Lane, 1915). Variously reprinted, including a paperback (New York: Vintage Books, 1955).

4. For Ford's life (1873–1939) see Arthur Mizener, *The Saddest Story: A Biography of Ford Madox Ford* (London: The Bodley Head, 1971).

5. *When Blood is Their Argument: An Analysis of Prussian Culture* (New York and London: Hodder & Stoughton, 1915); *Between St. Dennis and St. George: A Sketch of Three Civilisations* (New York and London: Hodder & Stoughton, 1915). The latter especially had gigantic sales at the time.

6. See *It Was The Nightingale* (London: Heinemann, 1934), Part II, Chapter 2, pp. 172–207.

7. For a fuller discussion of Ford's co-ordination of modernism and historical realism see my 'Virginia Woolf and Ford Madox Ford: Two Styles of Modernity' in *Possibilities: Essays on the State of the Novel* (London and New York: Oxford UP, 1973) pp. 121–39.

8. Edition used: *The Bodley Head Ford Madox Ford*, Vol. III, *Some Do Not*; and IV, *No More Parades* and *A Man Could Stand Up* (both London, 1963). *The Last Post* (New York: The Literary Guild of America; London: Duckworth, 1928) is not included in this edition.

9. W. H. Auden reviewed *Parade's End* in *Mid-Century* 22 (February 1961) 3–10.

10. *A Man Could Stand Up*, pp. 462–3.

11. Central discussions of *Parade's End* are J. Delbaere-Garant, 'Who Shall Inherit England?: A Comparison between *Howards End, Parade's End* and

Unconditional Surrender', English Studies L (February 1969) 101–5; J. M. Heldman's, 'The Last Victorian Novel: Technique and Theme in *Parade's End'*, *Twentieth Century Literature* XVIII (October 1972) 271–84; Rita Kashner, 'Tietjens' Education: Ford Madox Ford's Tetralogy', *Critical Quarterly* VIII (summer 1966) 150–63; and Alan Kennedy, 'Tietjens' Travels: *Parade's End* as Comedy', *Twentieth Century Literature* XVI (April 1970) 85–95. Also see Ambrose Gordon, Jr., *The Invisible Tent: The War Novels of Ford Madox Ford* (Austin, Tex., 1964) and Robert J. Green, *The Novels of Ford Madox Ford* (Ph.D. thesis, University of Warwick, 1975).

12. *It Was The Nightingale*, p. 49.

13. *Some Do Not*, p. 11. For different appreciations of this passage see Paul L. Wiley, *Novelist of Three Worlds: Ford Madox Ford* (Syracuse UP, 1962) pp. 224–5; and Bernard Bergonzi, *Heroes' Twilight* (London: Constable, 1965) pp. 196–7.

14. *Some Do Not*, p. 181.

15. See the letter to Eric Pinker, written 17 August 1930. *The Letters of Ford Madox Ford*, ed. Richard M. Ludwig (Princeton UP, 1965) pp. 196–7.

16. See Jeffrey Walsh's essay on Cummings in this volume, pp. 32–42 and Malcolm Cowley, *Exile's Return*, rev. ed. (London: 1961), which explores this as social history.

17. The quotations are taken from Townsend Ludington (ed.), *The Fourteenth Chronicle: Letters and Diaries of John Dos Passos* (Boston: Gambit, 1973), 'A Hotel Childhood', last portions, pp. 71 ff., and 'One Man's Initiation', pp. 77–198.

18. First published by Allen & Unwin (London, 1920); repr. Ithaca, New York: Cornell UP, 1969.

19. See Stanley Cooperman's essay in this volume, pp. 23–31.

20. Edition used: *USA* (New York: The Modern Library, n.d. [1937 and later]. References are to this edition. There is also a paperback (Harmondsworth: Penguin Books, 1966).

21. *The Big Money*, pp. 461–6.

22. *Nineteen Nineteen*, p. 198.

23. Jean-Paul Sartre, 'John Dos Passos and *1919'*, in *Literary and Philosophical Essays* (London, 1955). Other key discusions are Marshall McLuhan, 'John Dos Passos: Technique Versus Sensibility', in H. C. Gardiner (ed.), *Fifty Years of the American Novel: A Christian Reappraisal* (New York, 1968), John William Ward, 'Lindbergh, Dos Passos and History', *Carleton Miscellany* VI (summer 1965), and Brian Lee, 'History and John Dos Passos, in M. Bradbury and D. Palmer (eds), *The American Novel and the Nineteen Twenties* (London, 1971).

Bibliography

This is a list of general and mostly recent studies. For earlier works and for studies on individual authors see the notes to each contribution in this volume.

ALDRIDGE, JOHN W. *After the Lost Generation: A Critical Study of the Writers of Two Wars* (London: Vision Press, 1957, repr. 1959).

BARNETT, CORELLI 'A Military Historian's View of the Literature of the Great War', *Essays by Divers Hands* xxxvi (1970) 1–18.

BERGONZI, BERNARD 'Before 1914: Writers and the Threat of War', *Critical Quarterly* 6 (1964) 126–34.

—— *Heroes' Twilight: A Study of the Literature of the Great War* (London: Constable, 1965).

CLARKE, IAN FREDERICK *Voices Prophesying War, 1763–1984* (London: Oxford University Press, 1966).

COOPERMAN, STANLEY *World War I and the American Novel* (Baltimore: The Johns Hopkins Press, 1967).

CRU, JEAN NORTON *Témoins: essai d'analyse et de critique des souvenirs de combattants édités en français de 1915 à 1928* (Paris: Les Etincelles, 1929).

CYSARZ, HERBERT *Zur Geistesgeschichte des Weltkriegs: Die dichterischen Wandlungen des deutschen Kriegsbilds 1910–1930* (Halle/Saale: Niemeyer, 1931).

DÉDÉYAN, CHARLES *Une Guerre dans le mal des hommes* (Paris: Editions Buchet/Chastel, 1971).

DUCASSE, ANDRÉ, JACQUES MEYER, GABRIEL PERREUX *Vie et mort des français 1914–1918: Simple histoire de la grande guerre* (Paris: Hachette, 1959), esp. 'Appendice: La Guerre et les écrivains'.

EVANS, B. IFOR *English Literature between the Wars* (London: Methuen, 1948), esp. Chapter XI, 'War and the Writer'.

FALLS, CYRIL *War Books: A Critical Guide* (London: Peter Davies, 1930).

FIELD, FRANK *Three French Writers and the Great War: Barbusse, Drieu la Rochelle, Bernanos: Studies in the Rise of Communism and Fascism* (Cambridge: Cambridge University Press, 1975).

FUSSELL, PAUL *The Great War and Modern Memory* (New York and London: Oxford University Press, 1975).

GEISSLER, ROLF *Dekadenz und Heroismus: Zeitroman und völkisch-nationalsozialistische Literaturkritik* (Stuttgart: Deutsche Verlags-anstalt, 1964), esp. pp. 76–103.

GIBSON, ROBERT 'The First World War and the Literary Consciousness', in John Cruickshank (ed)., *French Literature and its Background*, Vol. 6, *The Twentieth Century* (London: Oxford University Press, 1970) pp. 55–72.

GOBIN, PIERRE B. 'Le Héros et le soldat', *Culture* 21 (1960) 266–79.

GREICUS, M. S. *Prose Writers of World War I* ('Writers and their Work', no. 231; London: Longmans for the British Council, 1973).

GRUBER, HELMUT '*Neue Sachlichkeit* and the World War', *German Life & Letters* 20 (1966) 138–49.

HOFFMAN, FREDERICK J. *The Twenties*, 2nd ed. (New York: Collier Books, 1962), esp. Chapter II, 'The War and the Post-War Temper'.

—— *The Mortal No: Death and the Modern Imagination* (Princeton, New Jersey: Princeton University Press, 1964).

ISAY, RAYMOND 'La Guerre de 1914–1918 et le mouvement intellectuel et littéraire', *Revue des Deux Mondes*, June 1965, 390–403.

ISNENGHI, MARIO *Il Mito della grande guerra da Marinetti a Malaparte* (Bari: Laterza, 1970).

MILLER, WAYNE CHARLES *An Armed America: A History of the American Military Novel* (New York: New York University Press, 1970).

MORGAN, CHARLES *Reflections in a Mirror*, second series (London: Macmillan, 1946) pp. 195–212.

PANICHAS, GEORGE A. (ed.) *Promise of Greatness: The War of 1914–1918* (London: Cassell, 1968) esp. 'Literature of War', pp. 477–555.

PARTRIDGE, ERIC 'The War Comes into its Own', *The Window* 1, no. 1 (January 1930) 72–104.

—— 'The War Continues', *The Window* 1, no. 2 (April 1930) 62–85.

PFEILER, WILLIAM K. *War and the German Mind: The Testimony of Men of Fiction who fought at the Front* (New York: Columbia University Press, 1941).

POMEAU, RENÉ 'Guerre et roman dans l'entre-deux-guerres', *Revue des Sciences Humaines*, Fasc. 109 (1963) 77–95.

READ, HERBERT 'The Failure of War Books', in *A Coat of Many Colours* (rev. ed., London: Routledge & Kegan Paul, 1957) pp. 72–6.

RIEUNEAU, MAURICE *Guerre et révolution dans le roman français de 1919 à 1939* (Paris: Klincksieck, 1974).

SCHRÖTER, KLAUS 'Chauvinism and its Tradition: German Writers at the Outbreak of the First World War', *Germanic Review* 43 (1968) 120–35.

Sontheimer, Kurt *Antidemokratisches Denken in der Weimarer Republik: Die politischen Ideen des deutschen Nationalismus zwischen 1918 und 1933*, 2nd ed. (Munich: Nymphenburger Verlagsanstalt, 1964).

Spindler, Russell S. *The Military Novel* (Wisconsin: U.S. Armed Forces Institute, 1964).

Stromberg, R. N. 'The Intellectuals and the Coming of War in 1914', *Journal of European Studies* 3, no. 2 (June 1973) 109–22.

Swinnerton, Frank *The Georgian Literary Scene: A Panorama*, rev. ed. (London: Dent, 1950), esp. Chapter 12, 'The War-Time Afflatus'.

Thérive, André 'Littérature de guerre ou de révolution', *Revue des Deux Mondes*, April 1959, 468–78.

Tison-Braun, Micheline *La Crise de l'humanisme. Le conflit de la société dans la littérature française moderne*, Vol. ii, 1914–1939 (Paris: Nizet, 1967).

Tomlinson, H. M. 'War Books', *Criterion* 9, no. 36 (April 1930) 402–419.

Walcutt, Charles C. 'Fear Motifs in the Literature between the Wars', *South Atlantic Quarterly* 46 (1947) 227–38.

Ward, A. C. *The Nineteen-Twenties: Literature and Ideas in the Post-War Decade* (London: Methuen, 1930), esp. Chapter vii, 'Unhappy Warriors'.

Williamson, Henry 'Reality in War Literature' in *The Linhay on the Downs* (London: Faber & Faber, 1934) pp. 224–62.

Winter, Sophus Keith *The Realistic War Novel* (University of Washington Chapbooks, no. 35; Seattle: University of Washington Bookstore, 1930).

Wolle, Francis 'Novels of Two World Wars', *Western Humanities Review* 5 (1951) 279–90.

Index

Numbers in bold indicate major discussions of works; numbers in parentheses indicate entries referred to but not actually named.